Life Poetry of an A

Poems of Spirit and Transformation

Benita Rainer

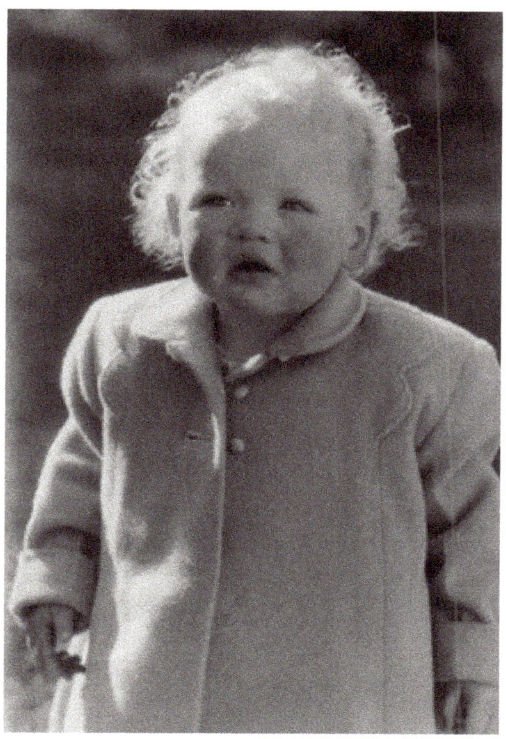

Zodiac imagery by Jeremy Blake

Artwork by Benita Rainer

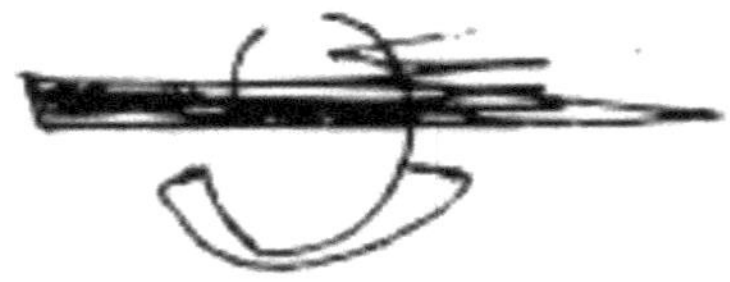

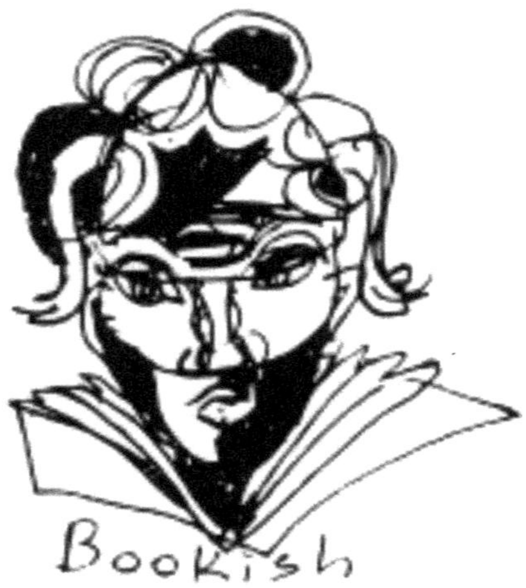

First published 2021

ISBN 978-0-646-82559-5

Inquiries should be addressed to:

gaiascharts@hotmail.com

or

Benita Rainer

P.O. Box 186

Katoomba 2780 NSW Australia

When a newborn baby is permanently separated from its mother, nodes in the brain to do with attachment and the ability to form natural relationships do not develop as they should.

This causes lifelong difficulties for that infant, which may manifest as : depression, anxiety, loneliness, difficulty in forming the bonds of relationship, or suicidal ideation.
An innate difficulty with all connectedness is born; an existential angst and corresponding difficulty in seeing the meaning in life.

You have lost all sense of who you are, where you come from, where you belong.
Perhaps It is the same as losing part of your soul.

At an enquiry into the effects of adoption on newborns, I heard a midwife state words to the effect that on the day the mother went home without them, and even if they had not cried before, and even if they had never been allowed to see their mother, the cry of the separated infant would start, first in fearful distress, then going to rage, and then, finally, the whimper of apathy.

And then to the silence of grief and forced acceptance. The midwives would say to each other "The mother must be going home," and rock the baby gently in a special chair reserved for comforting them.

* * *

I was adopted by lovely, loving parents.

So I have been strong enough to never stop crying.

Benita Rainer

30th. August 2020

Housekeeping Note:

I would like to add that, for best fit, and following in Shakespeare's great tradition,

I have reserved the right to invent some of my own words.

Table of Contents - Through my Life Line

From a fellow adoptee...

"The main reason that many aspects of higher brain function remain dormant (on average for the first 12 months), is to ensure that effective and appropriate emotional and environmental interpretation, integration and response pathways, develop in the child before adding in the complexity of the higher brain and all its nuances.
When this is altered, as is the case with pre-verbal and in-utero trauma experience, the cerebral cortex engages before it has fully developed. This engagement means a reallocation of normal function to support the overwhelmed threat response parts of the brain.

This leads to overly strong predispositions to seeing the world and the relationships within it as a threat rather than a blessing. This, even when worked on either by self awareness or therapy, still results in seeing all interaction and relationships, romantic or otherwise, in a completely different way to those who did not experience trauma in the early stages of life.

Much like combat veterans, those who have experienced significant early childhood trauma feel instinctively separate from the world around them. Some require an over stimulation to feel part of, and some are easily overwhelmed.
Some also, such as myself, see relationships and friendships in a depth that most find threatening, or as is often the case, feel a profound loss that ... becomes a lessened experience, never reaching its potential.

Many also experience predispositions to over- respond to emotional interactions and this often results in a nature to withdraw rather than engage ...

- Erik Standing Bear

For further research, Erik recommends the following authors on the subject of trauma:

- Bowlby's theory of attachment
- Prof Porges' polyvagal theory
- Dr P. Levine and Prof. Dr. Bessel van der Kolk's work on altered limbic states resulting from developmental trauma.

In addition, there is a growing body of research into in-utero and pre-verbal trauma response states.

Poem for The Kennedys

Speeding bullet, path fore-mapped,
All of time could not hold it back.
Of common make, of destiny great,
This piece of metal,
A vessel of fate.

When in the earth,
In your mother ore still,
Did destiny guide
The emancipate drill?
Was the name yet writ
That soon would find,
The brain of its sake,
In the heart of his mind?

* * *

1968

Untitled

Life sings, surges, flows?
But no, I know it does not;
But bleeds, bleeds, bleeds,
And drops away
Tear by Tear.
O for the bright fangs of eternity.

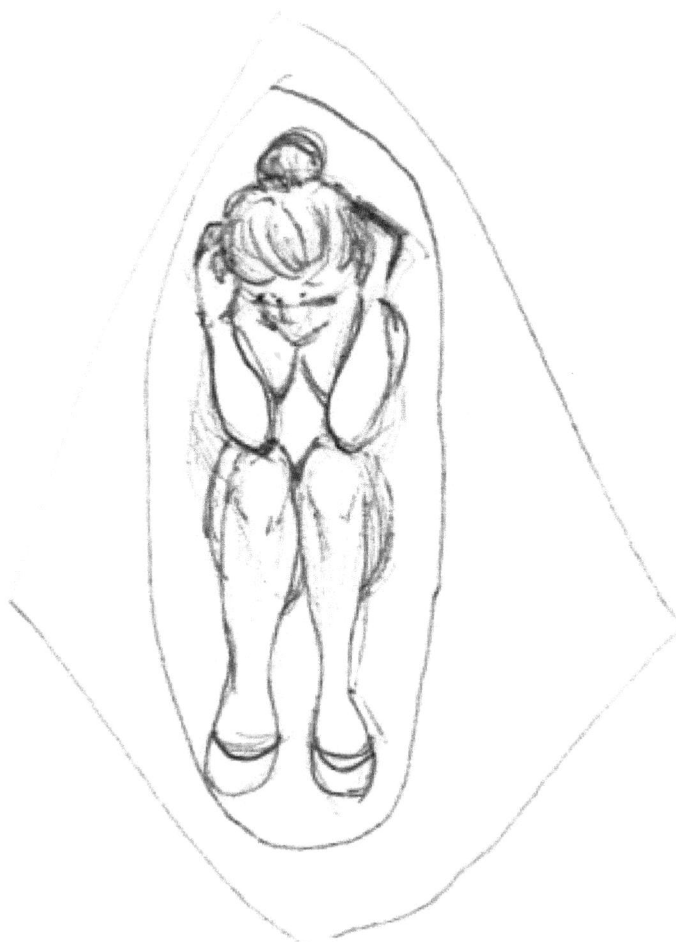

* * *

1970

Song of Stephen

If you go away, as I know you want to,
For you wish to stir the flow of the world again,
To leave the warm rose folds of the womb
We created...or entered,
Then do not tread so loud to break
The shell of ash that will be
When you go.

For one day more I want to think of you,
And always to keep you.
For you have made a mould.

***

March 1970

In Homage to Bad Romanticism

Gold is the fall of your hair
On your brow,
Or past the far-flung blue-drift
Of your eyes
When they leave me to return
To the wind-swept sun-mellowed
Snow-thaw of Cossack plains in Springtime.
And grey as the ice-burdened
Suspense of winter skies
Are your thoughts then;
The time when I cannot be,
When I wander as a waiting shadow
Of the you that will be
When you return.

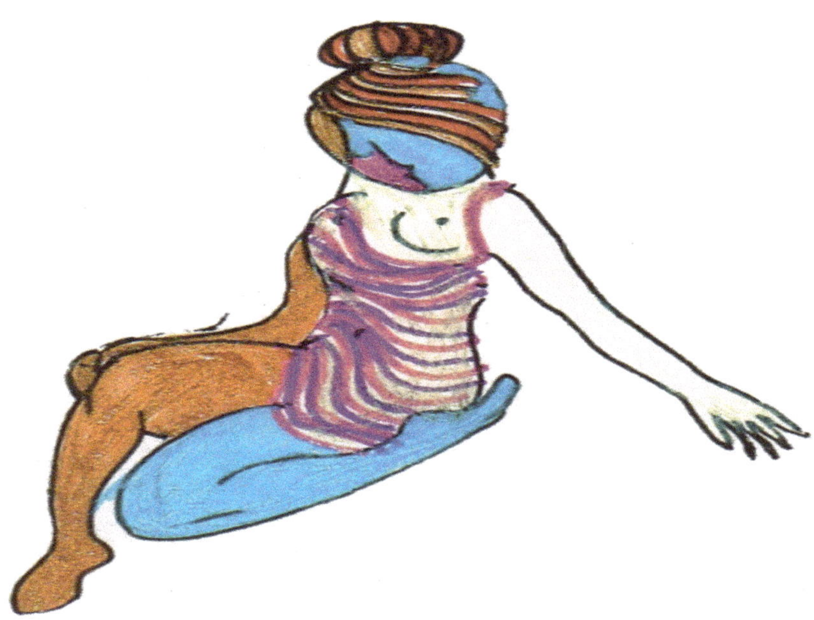

* * *

Mid 1970

A Prosical Thought
-Reflections on Gail's Friendship-

The taste of a good friendship
When it is dying,
Is the saddest thing
Left to experience.

New faces, new things to do,
To fill in and make more varied
My life
Pale most frighteningly,
When I feel a life-pulse
Gradually flicker and fade.

For, in my mind,
A friendship that formed as I
Formed,
...Seemingly long ago,
Becomes deeper than just
Part of my life.
...It is one of my largest,
And last,
Ties to myself;
And with its death
I might die a little.

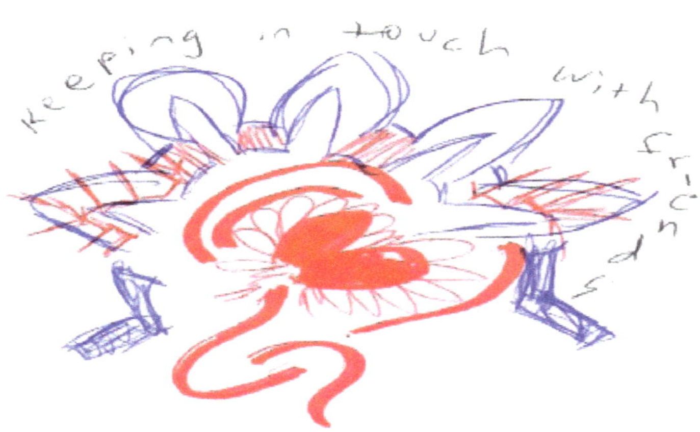

***

September 1970

Train Ride Down the Coast

Crowded by a cube analysis
Jumble of cups, I sit and think
At a mid-day rising time,
Of parents and comforts
To which I'm going home tonight,
And I am confused
With my young life.

So I sit and brood
In a night-time carriage rattle
Down my lifeline,
And stare out of year-smudged
Grey train windows
At a misty blue sea swell.

I sit and look, and think of me,
But my thoughts roll under
With those nature-powered engines,
Which thrash the sunlight,
Moonlight, insight of the stars
Into their very being.

The glory of them
Has drawn the worship of mankind.
But how heedlessly!
As the leaf would pay
Green homage to a sap that wells to fill
Bud, fruit, branch, tip and it
Does mankind bow and twist and search
To find, or test, or wonder at
The life force that ***must***
Flow purposefully.

But the one's the part of the other;
All a part of the One.
A vast whirlpool
Of no end, beginning or peak;
Each drop an equilibrium
For the other.
And the dying drop-
Whatever it may be…
Replenished anew
And never lost.

* * *

Saturday 26th. December 1970

Automaticism

Sing all hopes in splendid harmony.
Come into this pinecone of me.
It will flow feeling to your door.
...You will germinate.

* * *

Early 1971

Caravanserai
-South Coast in Flood Time-

The caravans lie there
Still with despair.
The caravans turn away,
A closed face on a grey day.
And the raging, triumphal
Kaki of the plundering sea,
Thrashing and crashing
And soaring away,
Throws its tons of detergent seafoam
Like crocheted mats of densest lace
Slinking onto beaches of granite rocks
And dead sea gulls.

The outer world so pale,
I catch a green hill
Peak to its plateau.
Arching like the neck of a despondent swan,
It snakes its beak, kamikaze-gay,
Into its own breast.
The sea's life-blood clots
Into eternal globular suds
Upon the knife-edge
Of the harbour-break.
Being so restless,
Infinitely young,
The yellow sands of age
Have no place here.

The grey clouds perform
Their testy merger
Into the boundaries,
(Beyond limits) of the rough horizon.
Speckled with white flecks,
To announce its coming victory,
The sea surges relentlessly,
Landwards bound.

On the land,
The water-sogged corn crops
Blend with the Vandyke soil.
The backs of the grazing cows
Accept their monolithic status
And briefly disappear
Into their misty cloud-claimed domain.
Swamp reeds, purple-tipped,
Become water lilies without flowers.
Sad lotuses! They sink into
The depression of the battered hills,
For here, all is resistance.

My eyes move upon an inland sea
Of disappearing virtue.
It bespeaks no rainbow,
And, nearer to me now,
Trees rise, thickly together,
Out of dry land.
High on a rise,
A white horse stands alone,
An equestrian sentry
To a brilliant farmhouse
Of bright, green-painted walls
And a white-topped roof.
Its unpainted outsheds
Offer a backdrop to flimsy starlings.

This train will go on,
Past the crimson poinsettias,
Through the amazing forest,
Beside the swollen river,
Below and beyond the hedged mansion.
The distant hills are swathed in mist now,
And the sea is left
Far behind.

Bloated mud
Makes a hard track
For weary cows
Trudging back for milking.
Some late-summer calves
Freeze, away from their mothers' flanks.
Hay lies rotten in the fields,
Or tumbling out of red iron barns.

From out of the sky's snow-drifts,
The sun's rays emerge slowly, with hesitation.
All at once the inner sea has returned,
And lonesome, half submerged firs
Rise like Christmas trees
From a tinsel-covered floor.
Laconic birds
Flap their wings
Over unfamiliar territory.
Their land offers
No guiding marks to them,
And any clump of trees
Must offer a new home.
Wheel tracks stand out.
Parallel silver snake trails over the meadows;
Not a soul can be seen,
It is time for tea.

Still the white gulls hover,
Their valiant aerobatics
Harsher now, and out of control;
Somehow more desperate
Than their land-eased brothers.

Farmyard fowls
Peck disconsolately,
For the grass is sour.

* * *

1971

Fern Flames

Ashes on blue fire,
Dark blocking bright;
Trying to light my...
Conditional night.

Why stub a frond flame
Reaching the sun?
Rest deep in cool loam,
Be not the one.

My day it is midnight,
Heat's not for such.
My sun's a pale echo;
My light is your touch.

* * *

August 1971

Reflection

Why is just
Being alone
So very bad?

Sitting quiet,
...deathly still,
One learns
Of one's great weakness,
Being as we are
Always face-to-face
With death.

Scientists say,
Given probability,
That it is more likely
That we should all die,
Rather than live.

Nature itself
Seems to conspire
To weaken us,
We who are already frail.

Quiet, then is no balm, but a bane
To my unquiet soul.
I would live wild,
Being free and passionate.
I would live
Lustfully, dissipatedly,
Hungrily,
Excessively;
To be perverse to
My ear's stillness.

But does this grant
Rest to my heart
In silent hours?

No. For sharp and shrill
To my ear
Is the shadow disturbed
From the pit of time
If I do not grant it
Peaceful flow.

From savage actions
And many wasted hours
I do not lay my
Pure-white ghost.

It flits in shadow
To my side, in times
Of losing depths;
To never let me be
...Unaware.

It will wax full
Under a silent moon;
A ready, unwanted
Reminder of its
Always-felt presence.

It would compel me
To be subdued
If I let it.

It would compel me
To a different fate
Than that which
I struggle to fall
Pell-mell in front of;
So as to be smoothly crushed
In one blissfully senseless blow.

* * *

18th. September 1971

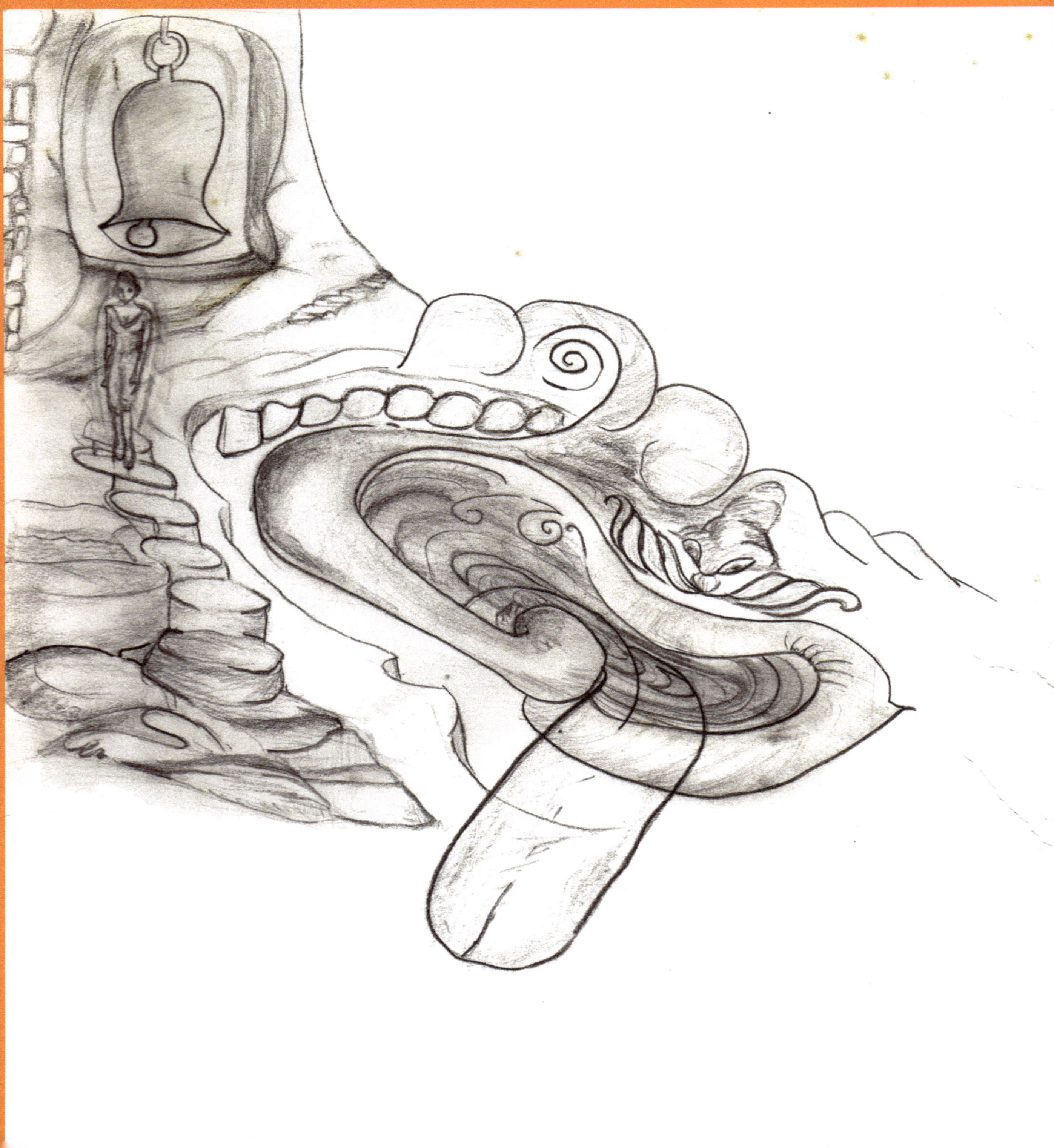

Number 8

Pushing and pulling
Over a meatless bone
I go
All the time.

When I turn my head
I sniff a fuller heart
Blowing in the wind.

Maybe G.O.D.
Will fertilise my mind.

Shhh!...I hear a backwards rustle
In the grass.

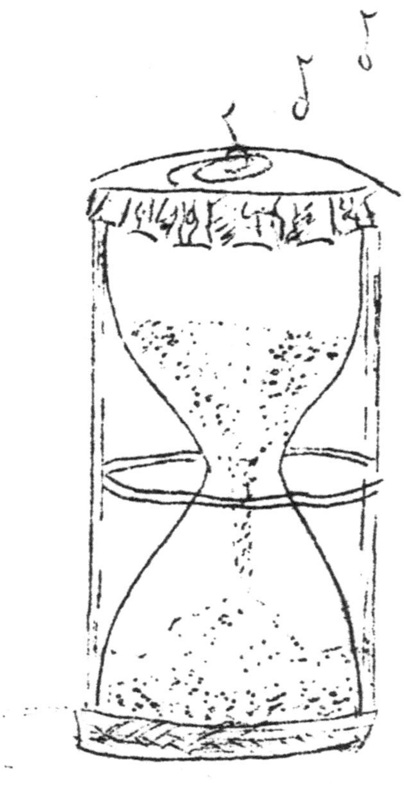

* * *

7th. October 1971

Time Fragments
-Fragment made in Jest-

Fairy floss drips pastel-pink,
The stick drips not at all;
But fixes in Eternity's eye,
Which never, never, blinks.

* * *

10th. March 1972

This, the one that was very wrong

Can I have filled my lust for life,
Perhaps worn myself out with it;
Or maybe it is just the feeling
That has gone,
And I remain,
Dead and unwanting.

Is life for lust?
Lust for coin, roof, car,
Countries unknown, talent fulfilled,
Love?
If so, then the one who has lost
Is the one who has all this…
Or has had.
He can only then
Take his status
Among the satiated dead.

I am satiated,
But I have none of this…
I am just dead.

* * *

September 1972

Nemo Land

Boredom seeps thickly
Through the quiet hills
Of Nemo land,
Where thick green air
Suffocates the stirring leaves,
And dares a star
To twinkle through
Its death-weight comforter.

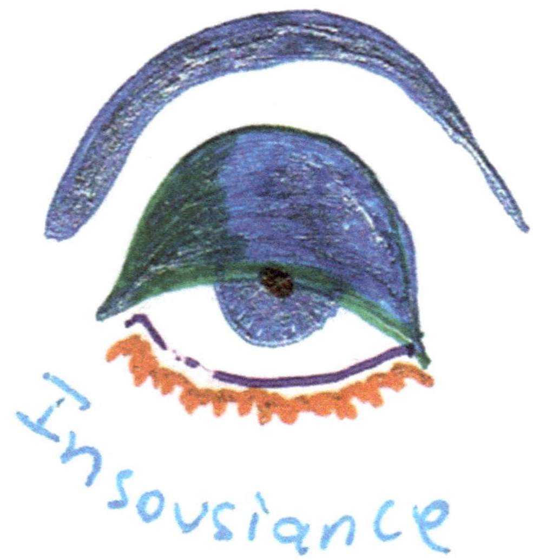

Purpose creeps silently
To an open crypt,
To join imagination...
Sitting in front
Of a blank tombstone,
The chisel in his hand
Has long since
Trickled away.

Lying dimly, stretched out
In the stuporous wastes,
Confusion waits to talk to you,
Ready with a cracked kaleidoscope
To taunt you.
"Oh, see the pretty colours,
Watch them crumble before you.
They were really
Only faded flowers you had brought
...To discard.
Or perhaps a flicker of light
Reflected through
The thick medium around you;
To illuminate a neurone
Dangling in the corner of your mind,
And, before you pounce,
Ready to vanish
Once
...Again."

* * *

2nd. September 1972

Paul
-Two Poems-

I

Time runs closer now for you.
I wonder if
You see me shining
Burnished gold
In front of your
Setting sun?

Or has the light
Caught my blaze
And flattened it
To a cut-out
From the fabric
Of your fantasies?

II

Sunshade man,
Mandrake-Max;
Sad-vicious gnome
Gnawing yourself
Dry on
Masturbated mind-entrails.

* * *

* * *

Early September 1972

Abortion

Doubts I have and plenty, too.
What's the best to say to him?
How to soften,
Question, probe,
Choose the depth
In which to launch
The vital facts.

Ask for fear?
Ask for sympathy,
Help, or mutual made
Decision.
Why should it be
Me alone
That faces this night,
When before it
Was two figures
Joining restlessly together,
However antipathetically,
...To extinguish the dark
For just a while.

I do not know if it is right
To kill a life only half mine.
From whence comes the "right?"
For that matter,
Poetry – the language of the soul,
Is not the word or medium
In which to decide this!

* * *

* * *

After 14th. November 1972

When the World's Coils

When the world's coils
Snake knots in your heart,
Stop your tongue,
Drive our two hands apart,
What secrets, then, can you and I share?
Why simply to tell each other
That we care.

That's the mark of deepest trust,
When it hurts to say so
Speak it we must.
Little more can anyone do
Than to feel, and say,
"How I love you."

****

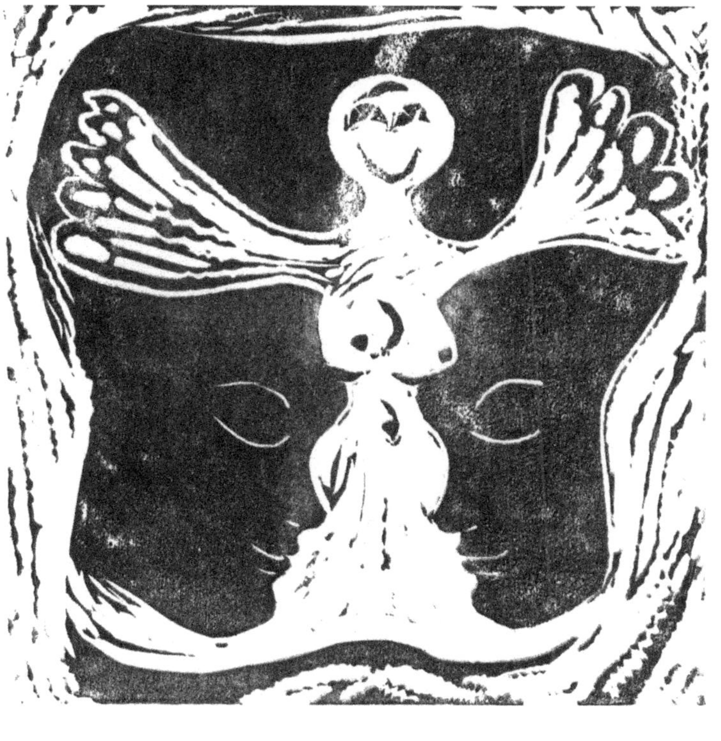

****

1973

To One Most Highly Loved and Respected

When a child is born
Parents rejoice at the wonder of its
Coming into being.
This joy is never lost,
Tempered, at most,
By the necessities of
Putting the new life
Upon a course new cut;
Especially made,
That it alone can take.
The bumps along its way
Are smoothed by love's flow;
First by parents,
Then by lovers and friends,
And, in general, by
The best of life's gifts.
When I have a birthday
I think of what has been done,
To make my path the easier.
Now, that you, my father,
Who mean so much to me,
Must think your life's course
Through again,
(For birthdays, like the
Pointers on a clock,
Are God's way of making us
Most aware,)
I hope that you will see
A peaceful flow
Behind, and that you will guide it
Through all the coming years.
For life is like a whirlpool,
Of no real beginning,
End, or peak;
Especially if
The passing years,
Like droplets in the depths of time,
Are never lost;
But replenished,
In Wisdom's knowledge,
And nourished in its fruition.

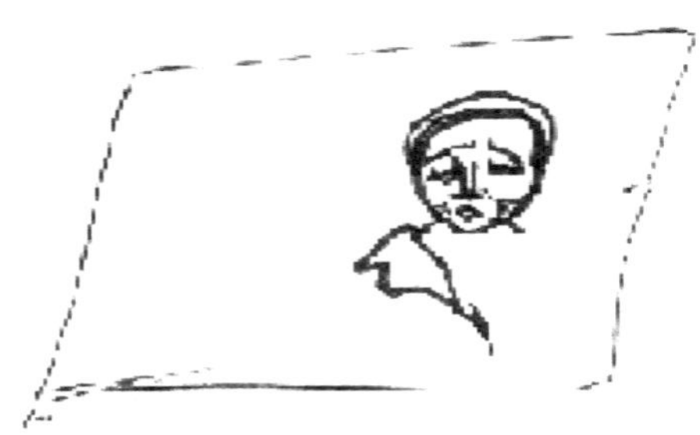

* * *

20th. July 1973 (Dad's birthday)

Feeling
- For my Parents -

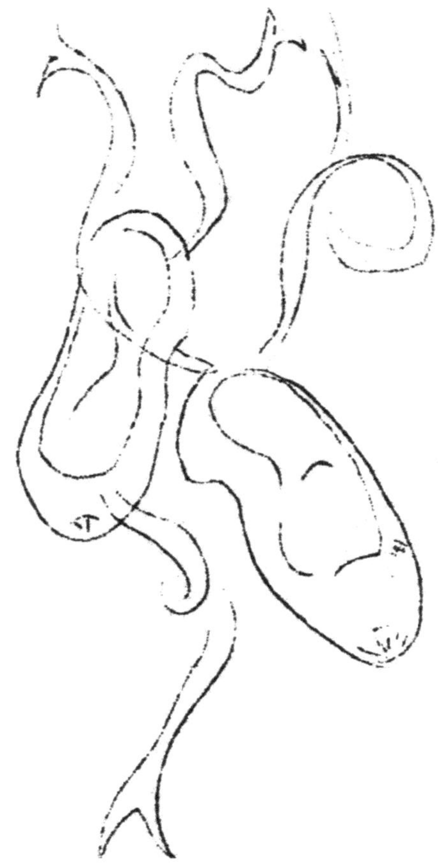

If you wonder, sometimes, how I feel for you
I'll tell you.
My love is often clumsy,
Slow to act, like a dancer who loves the beat,
But, having two left feet,
Is slow to glide along as 'custom' needs...
Over-keen at unwelcome times,
Judgement lacking, but always looking
To see how it can help, or assert itself
Just to let you know...it's there.

But my love for both of you
Is always there. It hurts when I am away
And stifles when I'm near.
Its presence, day by day, year by year,
Is really as eloquently constant as silence;
Just as sweet, and just as dear.

* * *

In this World

In this world, wasted, now by disunited powers
Unbalanced within themselves,
We have raped the Earth,
Plundered the seed
Before we could give birth to it
Within ourselves.

* * *

1973

Geometry

We have invented Geometry for our own use.
In nature there is a formless harmony alone.

The half-curve of a seagull's wings sharpening to corners,
As it suddenly dips for its meal,
The ovals of rose petals that open to a near circle;
Much richer for the greater details of confusion
That make it ripe for the young child to pluck.

The hexagons of a spider's web,
The circle of the moon;
Which, we are told, is not perfect either.

Or a group of people banded together, knee to knee;
The compass point lying somewhere between all.
We are imitating the womb shape of closest communion.

It is all the more comforting
For its lack of definition.

The triangles, cones, double helix
Of computer art
Can sing the glories
Of two-dimensional scientific precisions,
Which waver in continual flux
Across the drawing board
Of man's truth.

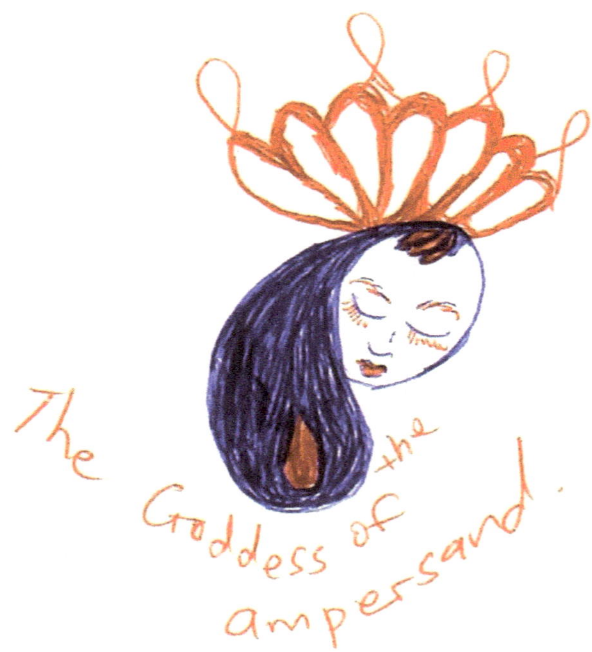

* * *

1973

Poets' Dialogue, Thursday Poems -My dialogue with a literary lover-

I

Him to Me

Lady, this little poem of mine
Hopes you'll find it in your mind
To forgive its author feckless
Since he finds that he's been reckless
In promising to dine on Sat.,
For he had forgotten that
The dogs must run that very night;
Please forgive-he's not too bright!

All the same, he hopes on Sunday
To see you at Macbeth, and one day
To make up for his awful slip
In a dining partnership
Somewhere better than the Union,
With nicer cates than steak 'n onion,
In less than a fortnight's time,
Otherwise, it were great crime.

II

Me to Him

Dear Sir,
...I, your page did find,
Abrim with most unkindly rhyme,
On this and that,
But mostly at,
That on this Sat.,
I shan't grow fat,
From dining at,
Your restaurant.

But... to take a quote,
From a kingly Scottish throat,
..."Good digestion stays
On appetite..."

Thus he spake,
Though rather late,
For Banqo's ghost
Had ta'en his plate!

But back to state;
Fri's the date,
And that's the fate,
So on your presence
I will wait.

III

Him to Me
Dawn at The Gap

No rosy fingers spread their light
When we loved in the car last night;
Beams of quite another name
Into our metal arbour came.
Unzipped, undid, I quickly spent,
Into your nether tenement,
While buses came and stopped and went.
Their drivers looked and looked again
At us in our glory, and our pain.

Then re-attired we climbed to view
A rising of a different hue.
Grey-gold set off some ships at sea;
I looked at you, you looked at me.

West, mirror-windows showed the sun,
His daily course had just begun;
Gold-grey the harbour seemed to glow;
I loved you, and yet not quite so.
We, who'd just come, turned now to go.

Returning to your empty flat
We talked of this and surmised that;
Looked left, right, forward, back, above,
To hide, hint, cover, expose love.

IV

Me to Him

My cold, cold fingers
Warmed, dear,
When to your comforts
I drew near.
They blushed rosy,
Rosy red,
Then to your garments
Quickly sped.

Love's doves did coo,
The mopokes too,
As me and you
Love's juices shed.

Aurora's light
Saw ne'er a sight,
For frigid night
Had faded...quite!

Quote is from Shakespeare's 'Macbeth'

* * *

October 1973

Self and Otherness

Your body – wall like
Looms as a barrier
Between myself
And the light.
The paradox is
That the light seems
To stream through
Your dematerialisation
And not from the darkest gloom
Illuminated by
Your pale outline.
From within
The powder blue confines
Of your torso
I sense a child's head
High in the sky
Beyond my balcony's railing.
You are inside my room,
But the child flies beyond it…
The cup she is offered contains
The white star flowers grown
In her own garden.
I wonder……
Why I have to get through you
To get to her.

* * *

1974

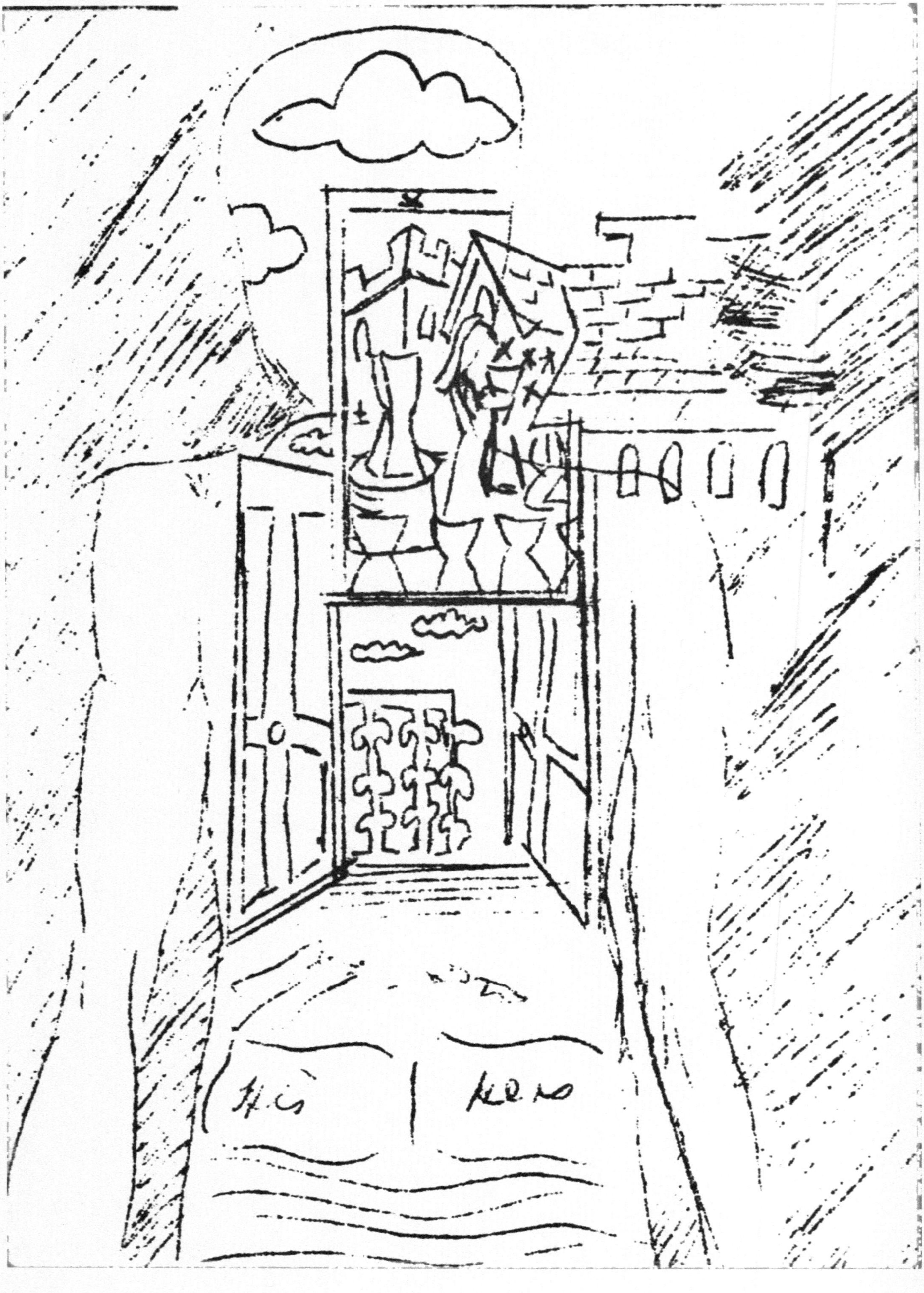

Song for an Unborn Child

Child of the sun, child of the morn,
Child of the morning dew.
Given to me on a silver cloud,
Fresh from the dawn's
Sweet view.

If I could see with your pearly eyes
What riches would lie in store!
Seeking after the light of day
Emerald, jasper, and cool slate grey,
(Onyx would take all your joy away.)
Opal will darken your deeper pools
(So store it away, with your dearest jewels.)

Place 'em all in an ivied tower,
They'll pipe sweet dreams
In your nursery bower;
Bring you glory, riches, power,
(Love is naught for a child of this hour.)

Climbing up on the slithery vine
The lotus and lily both entwine,
The sweetest carols fade on the tide,
The waters wash,
The sands subside.
The panther rolls his eye divine,
Enjoy the fruit, abjure the wine!

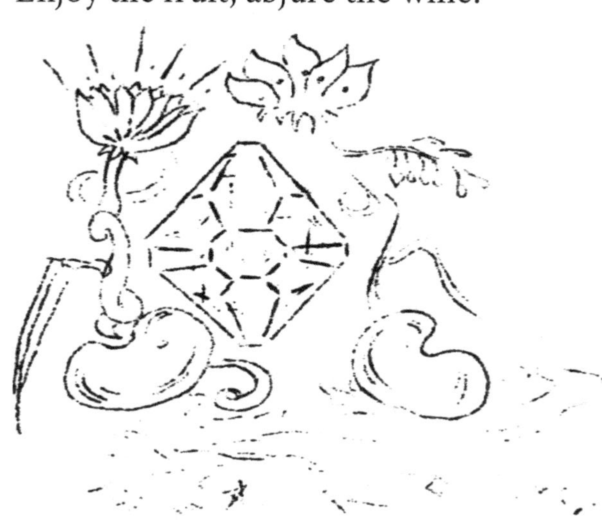

* * *

24th. August 1975

Sandman in Bernstein
-A Symphony in Two Parts-

I

If I said "Stay!"
You'd surely
Fly
Quicker than
A light beam
Past my eye.

If I asked
You to stay
You'd surely
Go

Quicker
Than a raindrop
On a
Fresh
Fall
Of
Snow.

So
Do not stay,
And,
Do not go!

But
Skim like a hare
On
My
Polished floor.

It's not as smooth
As some, I know,
But it skates!

Like
I
C
E.

Or leave me in Peace.
For no angel dares disturb
The folds
That play
Upon my brow.

II

Bernstein in Limbo Land
Symphony for a Night Owl

Filching fibres
On a scattered page,
My feathers fly
On a bed of rage.
My
Two
Hands
Stretch
Out

Barely daring
To try,
And cross,
This holiest of firmaments.

A Riddle
I asked a man to stay a while,
He answered, with a smile,
"Oh, that indeed I'd do, my love,
If it were you that asked, not I!"

* * *

27th. September 1976

The Druggy's Dream

There was movement, in the station,
For the word had got around
That a cigarette machine
Had broken down.
And in a secret corner
In a right-hand upper spot,
A marijuana cigarette was found.

And one was there, a veteran,
From the plains of Gunnedah,
Who had weathered many trips
'Neath that hazy, summer sky.
He'd travelled near, he'd travelled far,
He'd seen the sights of Marble Bar!

At Nimbin once, (as veterans tell,)
He'd dropped three tickets
Down a well.
He was as cool
As pure-white smack;
The world would freeze
When he turned back!
His hearts were huge,
His scars were many,
He'd do most anything
To beat the levy.
But there was much he couldn't recall,
(The smell of rosebuds
On a polished floor.)
His name was Tom,
(As I recall,)
He was a fat cat, too,
Of that I'm sure.
'Twas even said
(I do not lie)
He knew one thing
To make big men cry.
A secret farmland
Far from town,
Where grass grew tall,
Not a pig to be found!
The gold-tops there
Were as big as plates;
A feed a day,
Never mind the snakes!

Tom took one look,
He took one peep,
He threw his caution
O'er the brink.
He lit a match,
He took a seat
And he smoked that joint
Right down to the quick.
Now it's possible some tales are false,
It's possible that some are true;
But this was the day,
Down Central way,
When my friend Tom...
Disappeared from view!

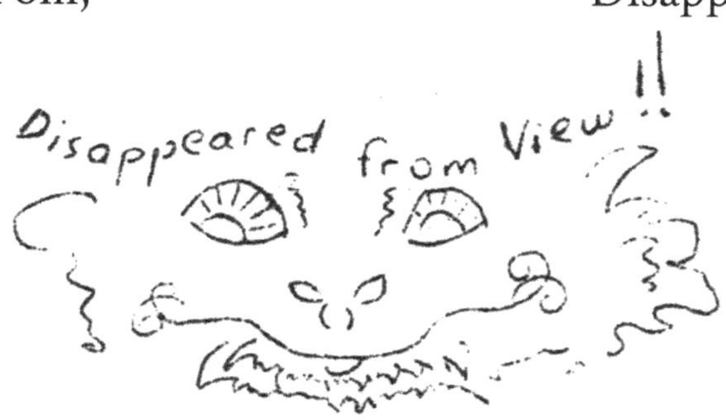

* * *

1st. March 1977

For Gail, on the Occasion of Transition from Jean-Louis to Others

You say you do not find your place,
Striving, in the human race,
Being paramount.

But give to joys of love
And needs,
The hidden assets,
Warmth and ease
That should be ground down
Bowed low
To your will?
No.
Should rather be
Full-blown grown
And shown.
Make again the Isles of Spice
For man's fancy
To grasp
And enrich
His other appetites.

* * *

October 1977

The Earth Creature

The Earth creature waits,
Dumbly encoiled against the dark.

Lovelessly, each man flails
Towards it;
Not knowing, nor recognising
That to which he strives.

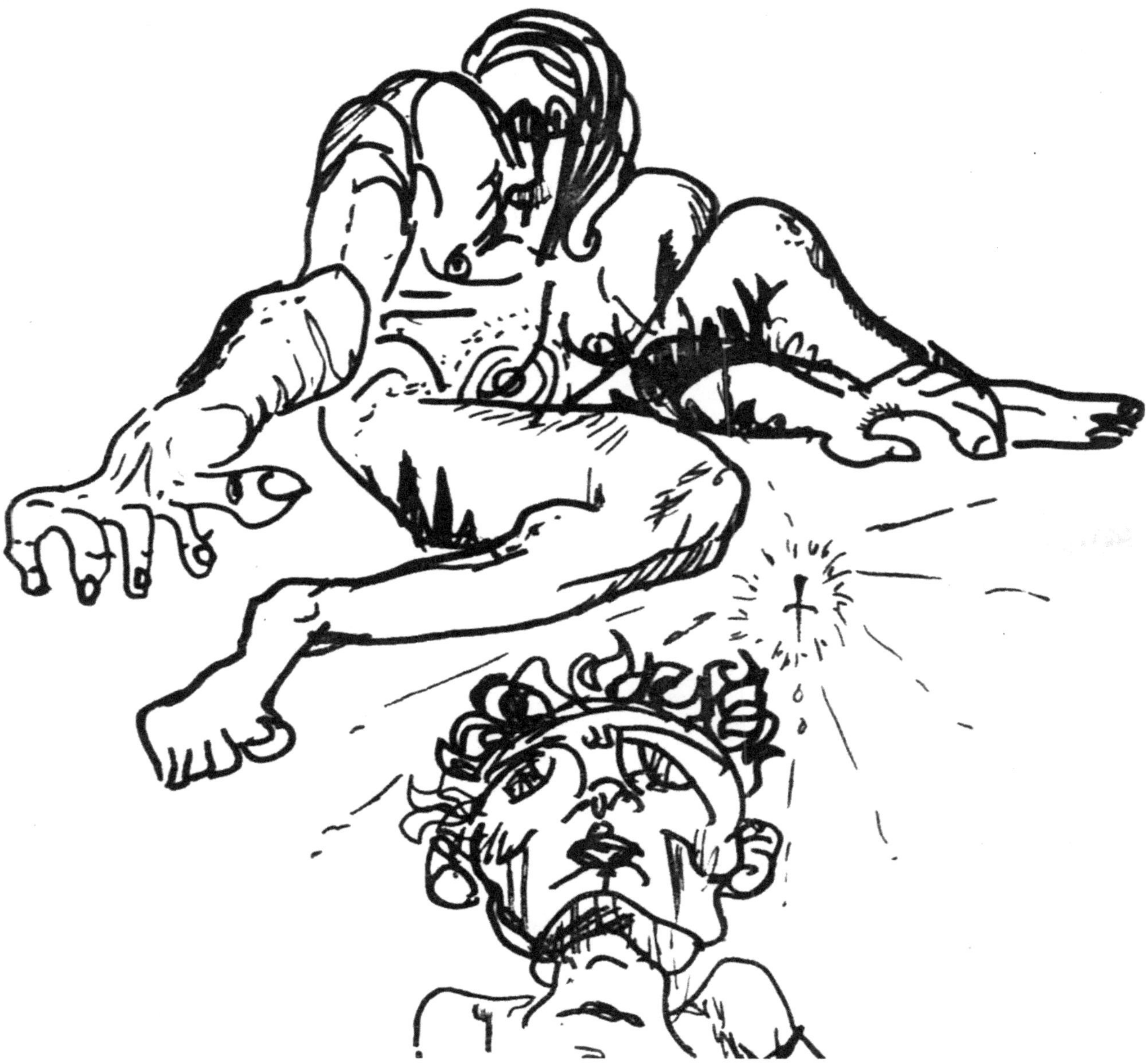

* * *

December 1977

From my book:

Today I dropped my father's glass;
It was the last of its own kind.

* * *

18th. March 1978

Individualist

I am an individualist,
And though my heart may break,
Within that mound
Strength is found;
But I never cease to ache.

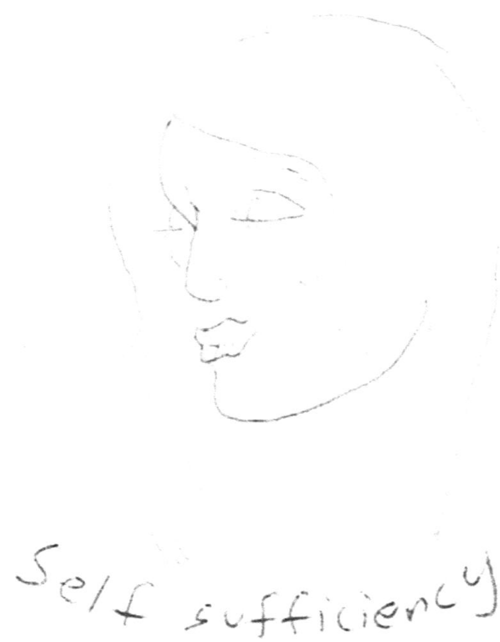

* * *

2nd. June 1978

The Song for Virgo

When a Virgo's not engaged in his employment, (his employment)
Or maturing his many balanced plans, (balanced plans)
His capacity for diligent enjoyment, ('gent enjoyment)
Is just as great as any honest man's!

When ascribing to a critical imperative, (imperative)
His judgement is as sharp as sharp can be;
He can calculate the sine wave coefficients; (coefficients)
He can make them align to a tee!

Their feelings they with difficulty smother,
When precision is the name of the game,
Ah take one consideration with another, (with another)
A Virgo's lot is too entirely sane!

When Venus' rays confront a Virgo's prism, (Virgo's prism)
When Ceres sends an urge for sowing seeds, (sowing seeds)
His mercurial syncopating rhythm,
Pays punctilious devotion to your needs! (to your needs)

But for all that we may parody perfection, (perfection)
For all that we are likely to say,
The Virgo is the worker of this world, (of this world)
He urges us to seek a purer way! (purer way)

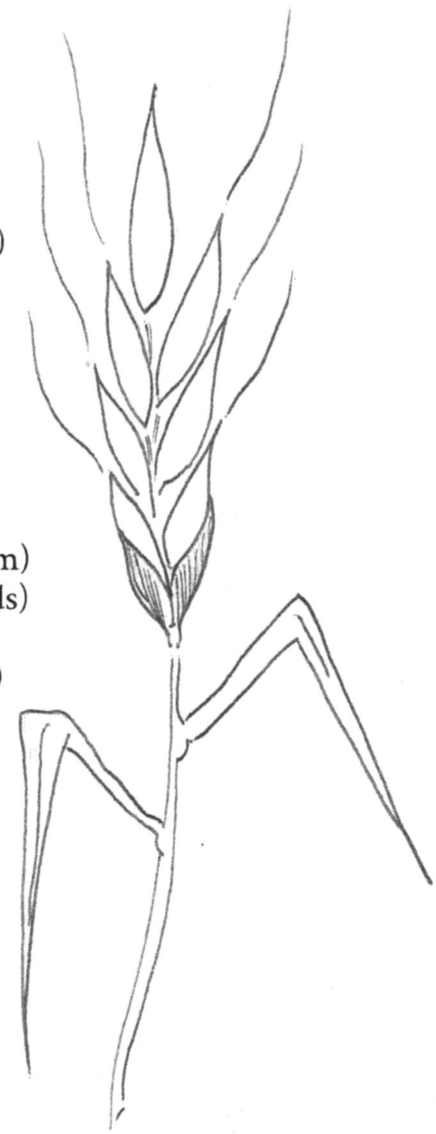

* * *

(With acknowledgement to Gilbert & Sullivan's 'The Sergeant's Song')
Written for a Zodiac Party at The All Nations Club
& with apologies for the mathematical nonsense.

* * *

1979

Three Poems for Cathy

I

Flash Jack

He sat on your bed,
Recumbent...
Triumphant...
Aware of the joy of the act.
Of another pair's
Darts of electricity.
The spark from his eye
Was the exact measure
Of their velocity.
And I felt, as he said it,
The child
Of his jointure
With you.

II

Scorpio Jo

The injury
Of a motorbike
Exploding into
Autumn air
Provides me
With a tone
To speak with you
Of how
Jo took me to my bed
And said,
"Let me show you my room."
I, with an innocent eye,
Surveyed our androgynous room
And said,
"What big books you read!"
Like
A little Miss Riding Hood
Of the cloistered pathway
I trod willingly, but warily.

***

III

Venus and Mars/Pluto Retrograde
Together (To Cathy and Jack)

The world encircles, scribes our
Eddies, flows
Fantasy sends past
To Present to Future
Many strange dark fragments
For our attention.

Upon which do we choose to ride?
Which will feel
The steel-edged toe
Of our pointed boot
Whizzing off
Into the nullity;
The shattered, silver-fly orbit,
The feeding grounds
Of inner-sphere mind?
The inscription
Of worlds and wheels
In alliances;
All outside your human wheel
hemispheres,
Gyrate slowly
As twin satellites of Pluto
Circumscribing, enclosing,
Instructing Cerberus himself
On the darkness surrounding all things in
Hades and his zone;
Brilliantly lit
By your celestial voyagings.

Cerebrations expanding
Beyond Ceres...
What
Do
You two
See...
...Together?.

* * *

24th. March 1979

To Barbara -
Damned Sighting

A grey day,
Of flat, tiled-roofed
Bungalows resisting
All change, all variety.
All those things
For which I crave...
And yet
Fear to pursue.

Accepting...
Children, decency, a home,
Adoption of standards
Imposed by others,
Stubbornly embedded in
That part of my soul which is acquired or?....
I do not know.
Me, a 27 year old female school teacher.
Alone, because,
Not wanting to connect.
The alternatives?... But today
I cannot think.... the children
Have tired me greatly...
Inspiration is lacking.

I know, only, that I am
Not classifiable.
That, not caring greatly for many things...
I have ceased to care.
What will happen to me?
(An irrelevant, yet persistent question that
Begs present urgent conflicts
That should not be
So devalued or ignored
For the real potential
Power of change lurking there.)

No other person cares about that point
No matter how affectionate they can be.

That's no point.
I care for no-one in any great measure;
No, not only/even/always
Myself
...That interesting vessel.

Energy is sadly lacking for most exploits.
Men pale, fade, vanish in interest and
Life-force motivation.
Education, too, becomes a risky affair
Of interests.
And...
No money free
To holiday into
Another
Reality.

The need for a sudden
Break, change, risk,
Plunges
Life into madness.
Chaotically and randomly...
Not? Cells flow,
Interlinking both
Darwinian evolution
And institutional description.
Do they, by such sound company,
Render themselves any less mechanical procedures
For change?

I should not stand this any longer.
I cannot hear their voices chatter
Like self-possessed monkeys...
Hammering their lives into shape,
Without I hear the inner grief
Of being left behind
To maybe... observe,
And, hence,
Go under.

Overseas…
Another ebb, another flow…
Another
Lack of progress within;
Of order without.
Another series of places I don't belong.
Through being innately unfitted
To make belonging happen;
Or merely lacking
The necessary energy…
Fate, perhaps.

Back home…
Psychedelia of inner investigation;
An art course,
Centredness, structured
Job and freedom of friendships.

Freeing myself
To run wildly
Where I please
No matter where it leads
Me to choose, quite free,
To take me
Structurally.

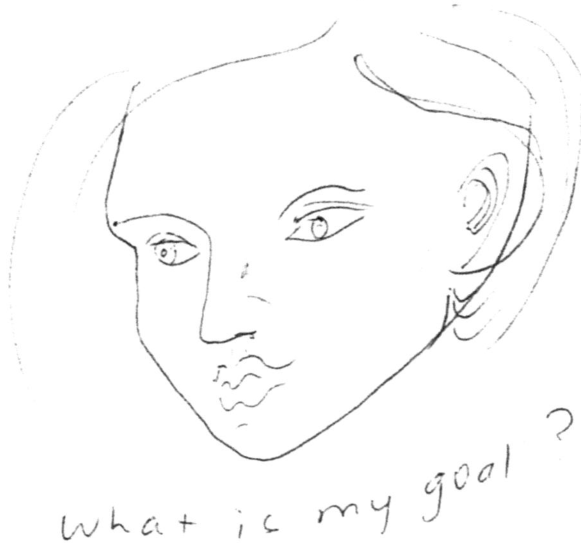

* * *

27th. April 1979

Directions to Myself

I

Free your mind through travel
Free your soul through Beauty...
And leave your heart
To open, at your own pace.
Is this not your life?

II

Mounting my own poetry beautifully
I create a beautiful environment
Fluidly, freely, opening
And feeling myself move
Towards living a self-integrated life;
Opening up the doors to myself,
Beyond mismanagement, beyond ego...
I am you, and I am;
Can you be me et tous....tous (all.)

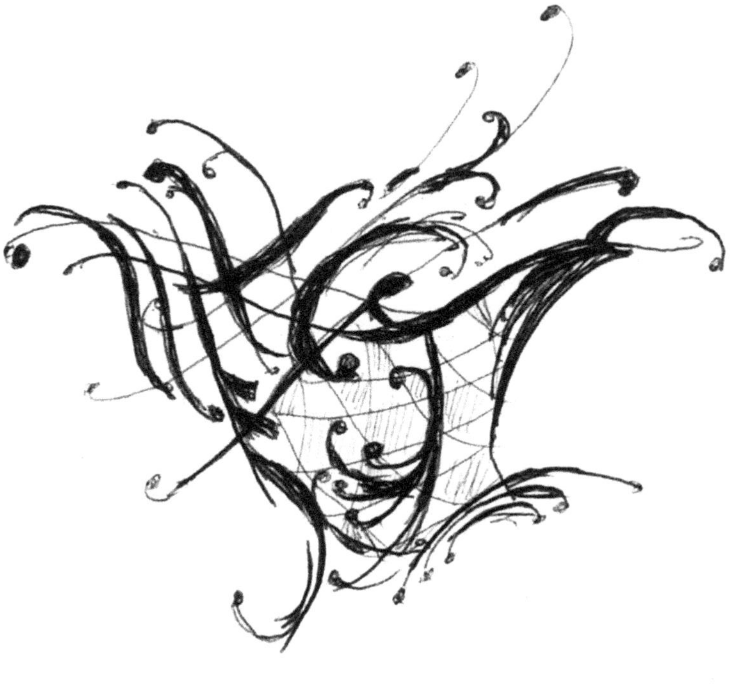

* * *

10th. August 1979

We are The Earth's Children

We are the Earth's children, but, in our greed for more,
We have torn deep into her womb. Patient mother,
How deep is your scar?
And what self-heal will do
For You, who,
For all man's purposes,
Have nurtured the seeds
And now must bear the mark
Of your ill-placed trust?

Death should laugh
At such feeble mockery
As his own playthings
Seizing the avenging pick.

Strike, hammers, drill, rods...
Furrow back the soil of your own destruction.
For as a mother would tenderly part the
Blankets shrouding the face of her new-born child,
Only to cover the body more securely,
Shall Gaia allow man to build the walls
Of his own destruction.

The wheels of change roll on.
Epochs pass into printed shadows on man's books
That have the power to distort memory itself.
So, we dream, imagining that we 'know';
Know?
Our knowledge becomes more practical;
Our entrenchments into the solidarity
Of the past and present
Scrape the sky
And spike into the heart of the Earth.
But between these
Two...
What a vast impediment
Is a wearied soul.

* * *

3rd. October 1979

Contra-Diction

There's a neat clinical box
For everything.
(Emotion, please note.)
Expectations of others…
Dues payable,
Mutual self-righteousness!

Above all, please note!
Three's a crowd!

But, what a fairground is this,
Fingers,
When sometimes,
I realise that
I just cannot
Seem to count!

* * *

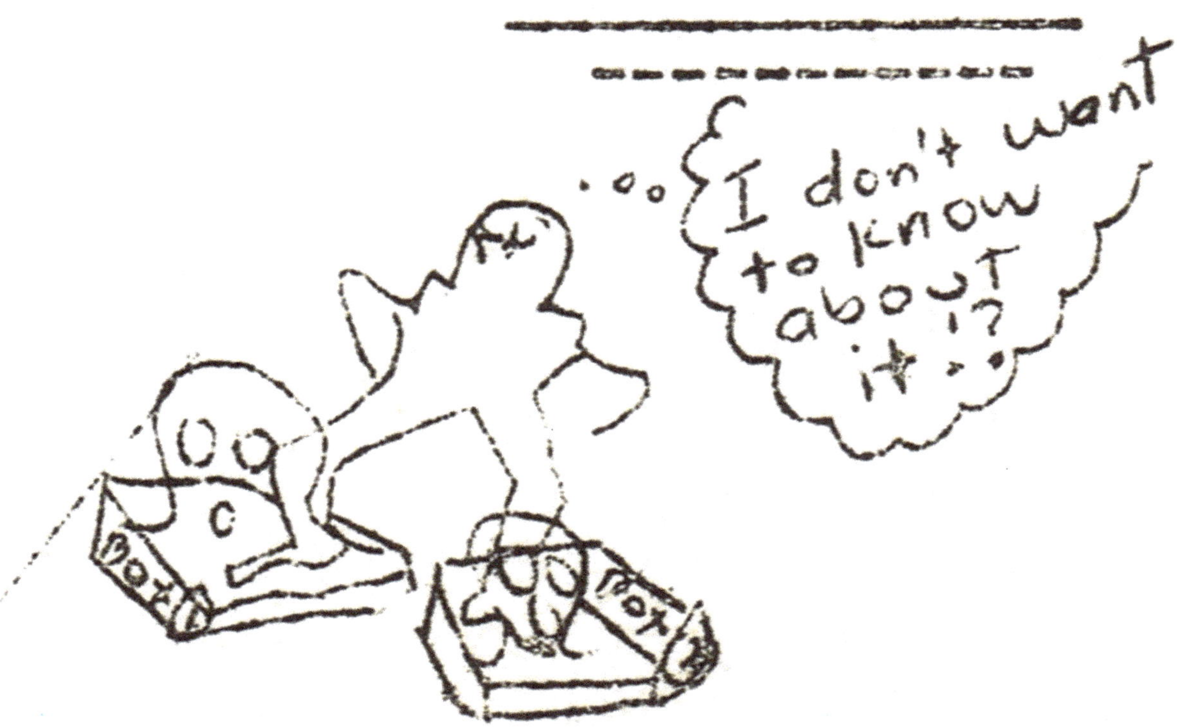

* * *

3rd. October 1979

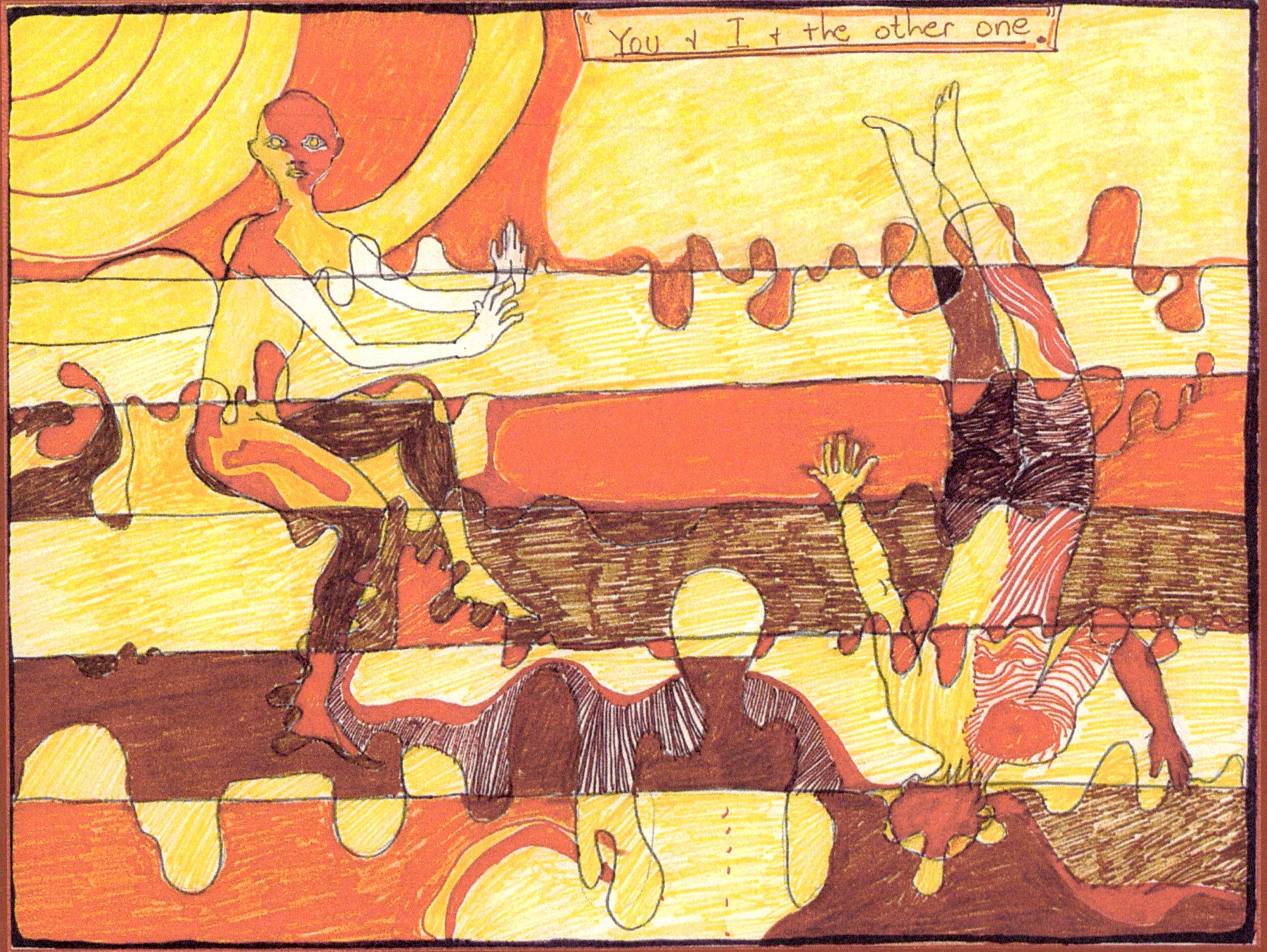
"You + I + the other one."

Two October Poems

I

October Train

This is a day of scope.
The sky bares its barrow breast;
Its curls and wisps
Are bands to define
Depth and variety.
The experiences of my day
Reach before me;
Rivulets in clouds, illuminated
riverbeds
To follow along the course way,
But moving inversely...
Scanning the fertile widths around.

White edge of the coming heat...
Sear these impressions through my
Sight not staying, but expanding
Around my retina.
I am in a flood of light;
Radiation...
The spectrum of possibilities
Above me.
As above, so below...
What a show!

Thoughts can interflow
Like waves.....

Shining experience,
Comforting blue-spread
No end,
Emphasises the white
Display
...Of my day's glyphs,
The part in the whole.

The whole...proud of
Its decorations,
Is, nevertheless,
Noncommittal.

The general sends out his finest
Soldiers to the outposts
To act as a beacon to his might.
The sum of their parts
Must reflect only a part of his strength;
There's a greater impact in mystery!

And yet
I believe it.

Life, and its experiences,
Is a broad map,
Presenting its boundaries only
Once they are crossed.

* * *

October 1979

Two October Poems

II

Day Two

This is a day whose essence
Encloses and concentrates,
Narrowing its span
To a few important issues.

A blanket cover-all
Of definition.
A hot-house humidity
With a dispelling breeze.

The impression of vapour
Lies above your head;
A light thickness
That urges you
To refinement.
A sweet, Venusian
Compulsion to order,
That, fountain-like,
Yet not so,
Urges you to concentrate
In order to
Rise above.

This might be so,
But is no less a method
Than many others,
If conducted purposefully
And with confidence.

* * *

October 1979

Sparrow Love

I

Why do birds fly away
When I walk by,
Hushing along on tippy toe
And they eating their bread?

I'm going to my breakfast,
They to theirs.
I don't want to disturb them,
Just watch them feed.

They prefer to flit up to their
vegetable stakes
Fighting it out...
King of the castle.

Leaving the real object of their need
Lying, unused, on the ground.

Jesus said..."Here is my body,"
(Referring to bread)... "Break it
In remembrance of me."

But they preferred the body.

St. Francis came to me and said
"I want to talk to you
Of lilies and of bread.

Consider the lilies of the field;
They reap not,
Nor do they sow;
And yet Solomon
In all his glory,
Is not arrayed like one of those."

II

"So what?" I said.
"They don't have to
Work for a living."

"They do, they do!" Cried he.
"They seek down roots to tap the soil
For the water and nutrients
Coming to them.
They accept the sunlight
That gives them the energy
To grow towards their needs."

"True," said I.
"They might die.
They have to grow
Or die."

"Now you're talking!" He said.

"But I need this, 'n this 'n this and this
And everything I see I might
Possibly want."

"There's a lot of it," he replied.
"If you were a lily you might do a
Colour- show freak-out;
Overcharge the circuits,
Die of over- nutrition...
Cancer of the root,
Petal tumour.
You'd never be satisfied until
You'd drained the field of
All of its nutrients,
And become

* * *

III

The biggest and brightest
Lily around."

"Yes," sez I,
(Thinking to catch him out
At his own game,)
"But think of how well I'd shine!"

St. Francis paused,
Pulled out a spray can
Called 'Lily-of-the field Glow:
To be used to encourage
Native specimens to grow
When over-cultivation has
Denuded soil of
All its nutrients;
Encourages an artificial glow
In the blackest of times.'

IV

"You'd need this, then."

So saying, he gave me the spray can
Quite freely. (I think he'd picked
It up at a sale,)
And walked over to some other birds
...Bread
In
Hand.

* * *

28th. December 1979

On Hobart Waters I See

Light shimmer frenetic
On Hobart waters.
Black.
Mt. Wellington's neck
Swivelled up through rain-mist,
Is a brooding, twisting,
Rejecting mass.
Wrest
Point Casino,
A Spanish doubloon;
Propped, artificially shining,
The new smugglers' lure;
While Hobart's mountain
Communes with the older Gods.

* * *

1979

John S.

I

As two travellers would...
Meeting at a water-place,
Exchange news and
Cordial greetings...
Friendly solaces at sundown,
So do you and I bask together
In our mutual need for comfort.

Fearing myself to be a stealer,
Guilty robber of vulnerability
From you.

Protecting myself
From your fear
That you are doing
Exactly that to me.

Surely fear
(Mutually shared)
Can cancel itself out
If it's brave enough?

* * *

9th. January 1980

II

How am I vulnerable?
Let me count the ways.

You could hurt me by
Calling me a whore,
A "Harlow with a T."
And yet,
I'd rather be hurt
Than free.
Would much rather agree;
Act her out, than me.

You already know that.

Did you also know
That, if you're looking for
Layers...depths in people...
You end with nothing
Once all of them are peeled?

Harlow might go away
To see if you return.

The trouble with the human race
Is that it prefers dreams...illusions;
Erected fancy barricades
To hide...shut out...real people.
We're all quite average, really,
Except when we go about
Stoking the fires.
What colour flames do you prefer?

You see, I'm so desperate, really,
Truly .... So sad.
To think I've reached my maturity;
That...this is it...the fruit's quite ripe.
And, after all,
What have I got to show for it?

I don't want masculine pity.
It would only degrade me further;
More's the pity.

I suppose you think
That, once you have categorised
You can discard me.
I keep fooling you, though.
A new façade keeps jumping on up;
But... John.... I do get tired of this.

I wonder why the words
"You've met your match"
Sound so ominous to my ears?

Help me to strike a light.
It gets awfully dark.

* * *

9th. January 1980

To Sylvio
My "Bacchus of the Overturned Cup"

Sight of the night life
Merging to light
Life like a blast
Of liquor's might.
Smiling freely,
Living easy,
Free-wheeling.

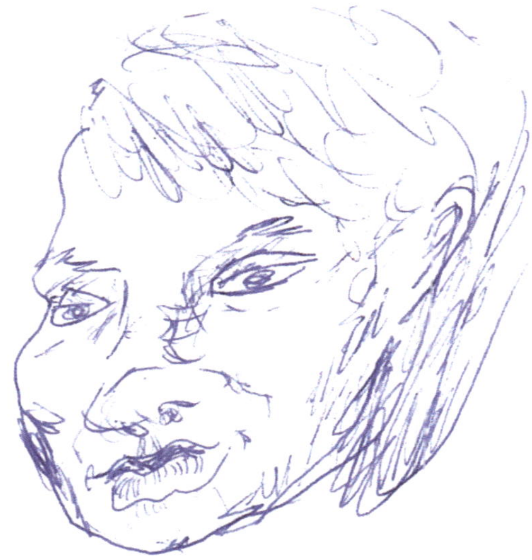

Endlessly yearning,
Endlessly teasing
Sea breeze meeting me.

It's a suit, it's a pair,
It's a meet, it's a street.
It's a match!
Flash! Of white,
Teeth of night;
Steel trap, don't leave!

Life flows endlessly,
When it's not called anything;
Paged off the page,
Out of sight, man!
And.. all of these
Other words, sounds, clowns,
Meeting freely...
Easily...
It's a fit
It's a skit,
It's a two-way flit.

* * *

17th. January 1980

Unity

Unity comes in twos and threes,
Subtle or sharp harmonies;
Tunes can play in rondos,
Syncopated rhythm,
Allegro prestissimo
Or in sharp upbeat.
We're all beatniks
In the end.

* * *

17th. January 1980

Sheets

I take the sheets out of storage,
Because it is my practice to be practical.

They are whitened crisp like parchment.
Crackling like goatskin scrolls
Along their ridges
Yellowed in long strips,
(The Gaza desert,
Plodding over sand-dunes,
Scrambling over piles of rocks.)

They have strips of
Old-patterned, embroidered lace edges.
Quality sheets, alright.
Irish linen
That my sister-in-law gave
To Dad, years ago.

They remained unused.
Pristine. Too much
For an old man
Whose wife was in
A nursing home
And he, so abandoned,
Preferred candy-striped
Woolworth's.

* * *

25th. January 1980

Why?

When my lover and I love
I never want him to leave me,
As, still and soft, or hard and fast
I'm there with him,
The two together.
Lazy summer, sweet sweat-drenched sheets;
Sun locked out, limbs sprawled in childish
Carelessness of propriety.
Two together….at last!
Oh, and how I dread the rise up
From unconscious mutual acceptance of our state,
As fantasy shapes retreat to electric flash of thought.
Sudden twitch of limbs…electric reality mind pulse…
Reality instructor at it again.
Stiff self-consciousness intrudes into our mutual swoon.

Why does self-consciousness
Mean separateness?
What's the alternative?
There's hope in the moment beyond expectations.
We have its suspense.
Memories are not real,
They're fluid distortions;
Rainbow flashes in an alki's metho flask.
They dehydrate your brain,
String out your soul
And make you die
In the midst of plenty.
Ride the moment-
See where it'll get you.
The self falls away…
The seeing is in the seeing,
The doing is in the doing.
Learn about the value of time
Being in each living moment.
…It's a jewel.

* * *

31st. January 1980

Poem to Bill

From unstated presence comes
The desire to see.
Open steadiness of gaze,
Dilated pupils, show the
Intensity of the need.
Reaching truth
Silently.
Soft words of inspiration
From the fruits of experience
Restore calm to confused perceptions.

* * *

26th. February 1980

(Mexico – Plaza de los Tres Culturas) Song of the Shaking Earth

Each stone a person's head
Notching one up for civilization.
Children of the country's heart
Formed of pumice and fire-smoked stone
First by nature, then conquistadores.
Who, strangely bereft, must steal for their
Own monument…
Stone by stone, wrestling with the dead.
Didn't they know
That all souls will look the same
When self-liberated?

* * *

8th. March 1980

Poem Written in the Museum of Art and Industry

"Jupiter" rolled on
Tracks of The Santa Cruz Railroad Co.
I am amazed at human ingenuity
Persisting, stubborn hope.
(All amount to destiny!)

I, tired, over-weighted, over-heated,
Lost, lonely, almost desperate...
Life unworthy, with no purpose
Except: to observe, admire, amaze at
Man's spirit.
I do not feel a part of it.
A small percentage only
Of this race drags the rest of us along
On wheels of iron determination...true grit.

Jupiter joyfully giving
His name to The Santa Cruz Railroad Co.
Driving through the swamps of human resistance,
Torpor, nullity,
Streaming, smoking, whistling;
Blasting Pan into the shadows,
Raping Nature.
Strong representative of unwilling Man
Over-taking Mercury; doing his
Job quicker and better.

* * *

28th. March 1980

New-York New-York Thoughts

There are cliffs/canyons/shelves here
Over which the dead have jumped
Or do I mistake?
At their base/shaft/floor
Walk many of them.
Alive.....seemingly.
How can the dead...having jumped,
Live on, unless I am wrong.
Values are not as I perceived them.
The....

I stagger back...lurch, really.
Flushing the cistern,
The weakness in my thighs
Betrays love....newly made;
Strength out of weakness
Like too much in life.

* * *

4th. April 1980

Plane

In knife-edged sharp
Of dragon teeth two
Red flashes of fire shadow
I see it…neatly wound
Firefly winking; snout-like.
Man's electric light… an
Understandably reliable, constant glow
On the tip of the plane's wing
Vertex point to the sky.

The sky is lightening
A heart-stopping blue chill beneath
God's eyelid opening on the
Sky –sea junction
As we….
Take our fire to Thee.

Columbia pictures burst like a flash;
Liberty from the blue of glowing clouds…
600 takes a second.
Within, the hostess asks me…" Could
You lower your blind please."
Complying,
I leave all that man shuts out,
To ignore his structured, feeble, substitute
With Peter Ustinov's short story
Of mystic cause and effect,
Involving two Swiss watches,
One industrialist,
One Italian maid,
A beautiful boy's sloth
And a communal feud.
Both scenarios, (God's and Peter's)
Return me
To the
Sun.

* * *

13th. April 1980

At the Colosseum

Little flowers, mauve, yellow-tongued,
Leaping sensuously towards the light and life
Proceeding around them,
Rooted in red-baked clay-earth
Mortar of the bricks of
The Colosseum.

You give me means
To make sense of these ruins.
You are a scale to magnificence;
Serenely content to be part of this whole.
Stepped blossoms opening
One by one on the tiered bricks.
You remind me that once these bare walls
Were filled with living things;
Beings screamed for blood.

The innocence of the flower strikes me more gently
Than the static testimonial of the iron cross,
But they are both preferable sights.
Happily, gently swaying in the breeze,
Your spark of life, contrasted to this dead monument,
Reminds me
Of the temporary nature of all pain.

* * *

16th. May 1980

By the Church of St. Agnese, Piazza Navone, Rome

When I first travelled
I thought that
Reality would be different,
Overseas.
Now that I sleep, in Rome,
I dream that
Youths take me to the countryside
To make tender love.
Differences exist
Only in life.
So, only my dreams are "reality."

* * *

17th. May 1980

Amsterdam – Van Gogh Museum

Oh, I love you Van Gogh!
Strike, in me,
Might, in me…
Sighing tree…
Rise, bird, swiftly.

You inspire in me...
That's what it is…
Light headedness,
Light heartedness,
Whole heartedness.

* * *

31st. May 1980

Going Home

People are at their best like this,
Filing in happy expectation
Down an aircraft's corridor;
Excited to be going home.
Planning with each other,
Perhaps strangers,
In that air of quiet relief
Known to all who travel,
That we are going home!

* * *

8th. June 1980

If I were to Die Today

If I were to die today, oh where could I lie?
On what sweet chariot vehicle
Could I fly to Thee?
And as the night sky fades,
And dawn's rooster cries,
I feel my life-pulse
Beat apace,
And feel
The
Emptiness.

* * *

1st. July 1980

Blue Sea

Blue sea
You always
Surprise me.

Lapis Lazuli
Lapping lazily,
South Coast sea.

Flame trees,
Laced webbed,
Fronting the lee
Of the sea.

I have my father's
Love of you,
South Coast blue.
Crystal made sun
Undimmed by industry,
You hum with rugged definition,
Knife like revelation
Of nature.

Lapis Lazuli,
South Coast sea,
Your brilliance will always
Surprise, delight
And invite me.

* * *

19th. July 1980

Other Times and Other Ways

I've known of other times
Many happy paradigms
Energetic androgynes!
Playing in the dandelions.

* * *

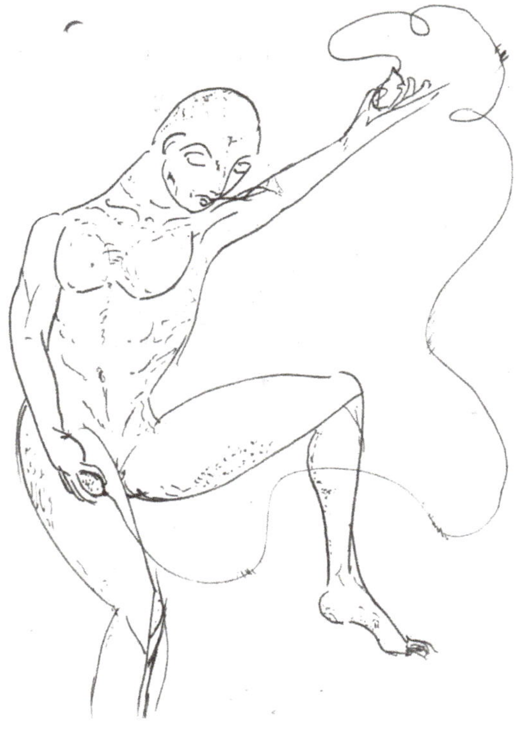

Note :

(I've known other times,
By the way…
The men and women of the future
Will be androgynous.
I believe in arranging situations…
Accordingly.)

* * *

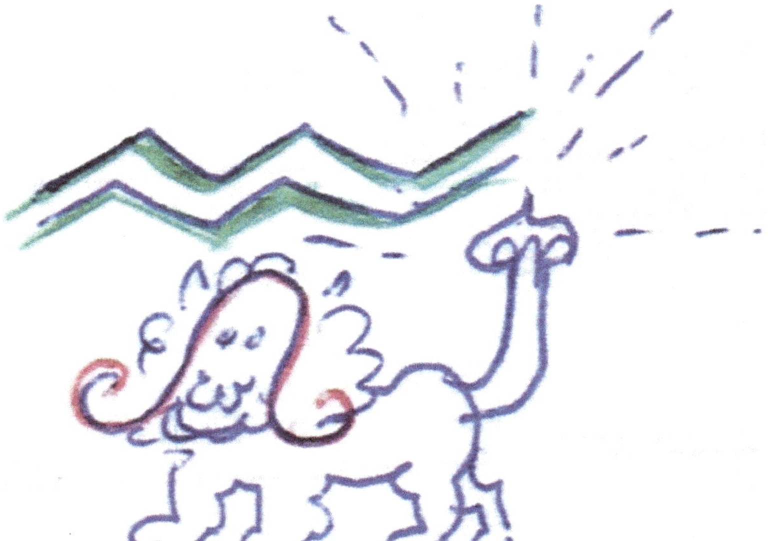

26th. August 1980

The Eskimo Woman's Revolt

The Eskimo woman
Will not stand the same fate as
Her mother, in the cold anymore.
The Eskimo woman's grey-white hair
Mirrors her mother's.

She rises on the crest of the snow.
There are a million different names for cruelty...
Wasteland isolation.

The frost covers the fingers
Of her abandoned dead.
Is it herself who lived there,
Dead on the frozen plain?

Her mother's hands,
Gnarled as walrus hide
Themselves smoked in the fires
Of a hundred seasons.

She will not stand
The fate of her ancestors.

The women of the frozen north
Sit, now, in the consciousness
Of the south land.
Women of Australia
Unite.

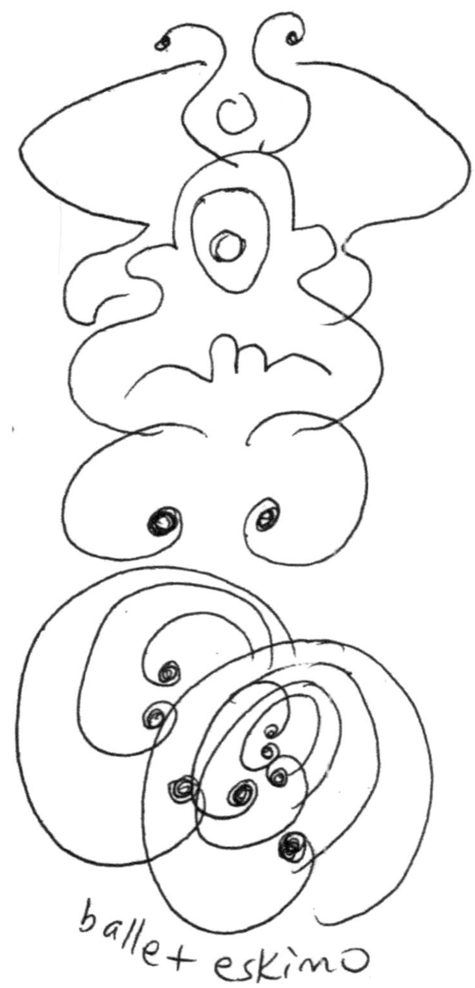

* * *

(Written upon viewing a woman in the Teachers Federation Club, after a discussion regarding women's rights, with Doris, Anne, and their radical friends who were standing for office.)

November 1980

Fern Flames Two

I once spread my legs
(Dolls scissor cutout)
To match the cardboard
Plane that was
My emotional substance.

Now I do not like making love to strangers;
A shadowy fabric
Of their fantasies.

They lay close,
Thinking of old loves.
I saw it in the glaze
Of their eyes
And in the confusion
Of their souls
As they looked past
My presence.

I do not want
To make love to strangers;
For although I was fresh, every time, to them,
They were not that honest to me.

I want to inflate
Emotional richness
Into my 2-dimensional plane.
Want to fill out, get to know,
I mean really know
Someone……. everyone.

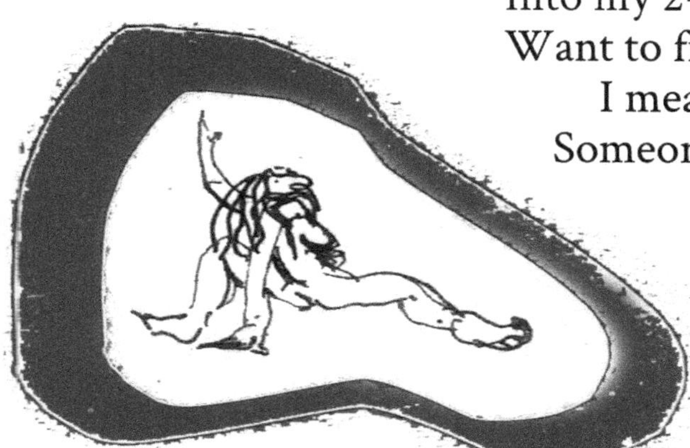

***

6th. September 1980

On Doing an M.A.

In the time of the play reading
She drew her legs together,
Placed the book across them, for balance.
And with the paper that spoke of plays to come,
To see, and
Unfinished readings,
(Prop to her emergent objectivity,)

Wrote of world arrangements.

* * *

* * *

16th. October 1980

For a Black Man at The Poets Conference

The black man spoke his rage,
Hammering it against, no, above
Our heads. His brow-rash
Blazed reds at me
And mesmerised, I looked on.
When off, just off the stage,
There was the moment to catch
As his face – just for a moment-
Crumbled sadness and rolled tiredness
Despair after rage...
So, I believed him.
So, I perceive him.

* * *

* * *

December 1980

Colin

He threw his hands up
Not so much
In the renunciation of care,
But, as a strong blast of wind
Would pick up a paper,
And blow it away.
The act of picking it up
Incorporates sighting
And holding.
The paper was well moved on.

He rowed away,
Merging silver on silver,
Skin tones, sea tones,
One.

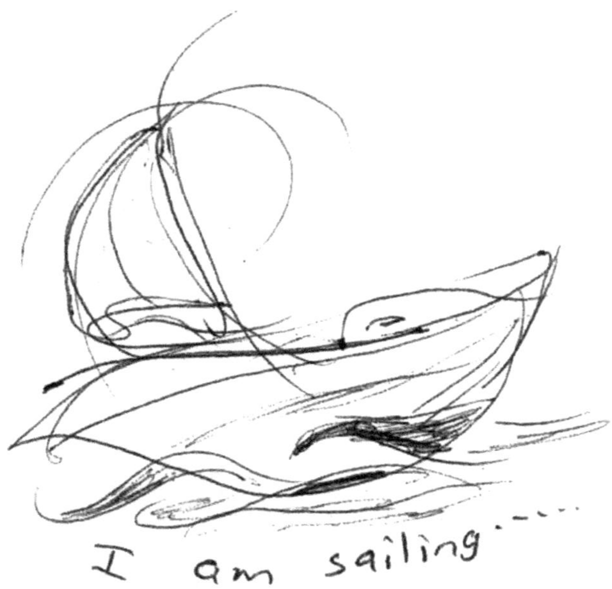

(Poem written for an ocean-going crafted sailor without an engine, and who was temporarily lost for words at a bourgeois dinner, over my lack of understanding of his lifestyle.)

* * *

2nd. January 1981

The Talker

He'll take your palm
Soul side up,
Examine your lines
And offer you words.

But as not from the heart,
He's got nothing to offer.
Yes, he's got feeling,
It's there,
But sensitivity's blocked,
So he's got nothing to say.

Nothing? You say, and why is that?
Tho' his words ring true
He's got nothing for you,
And just some urgency
Of the bodily kind.

Where there's no heart
There's no sight.

When there's not a way to be made
Then it's better left unsaid.

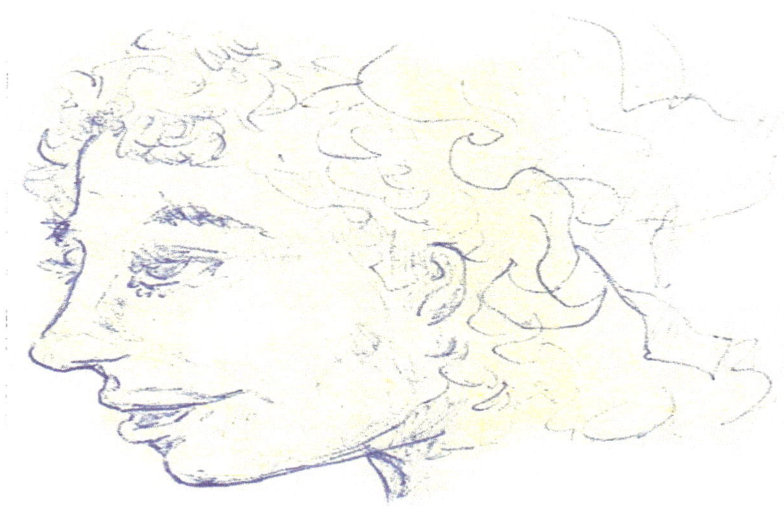

* * *

2nd. January 1981

These and Those

There are people who seem alone amongst their friends,
Huddled, in a crowd.
There are people who are alone,
Huddled in a crowd.
They are living their illusion of separateness
To their fill.
They are full
Of friendship;
They are full of
Separateness.
They can choose one,
Ignoring the other.
They are tunnel-visioned
And narrow-funnelled.

They are full of choice
And they rejoice to their fill of separateness.
Feeling of fullness and mulled separateness
They come together and go apart.
Endless rhythms, partial resolutions,
Growing their precious individualism,
Their "take-it-or-leave –its."

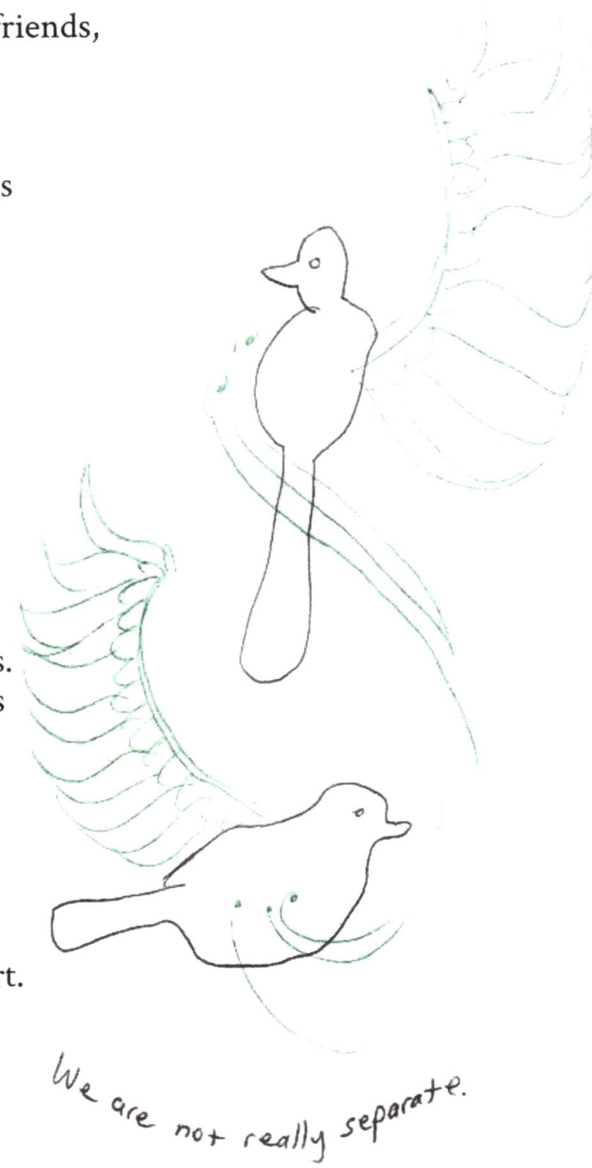

Wind rustles leaves on trees,
Pushing them together, vibrating them apart.
Attracted to individual twigs that lead to
Common branches,
Their vital fluids
Stem from the one trunk.
I wonder if we can bear
To acknowledge it?
We need our illusion of separateness.
Each leaf needs air and unshadowed light
To live and grow in.

* * *

18th. January 1981

This 'n That

What's that written on the tree?
Those wriggly shapes of glee?
Self-satisfied to their full
With eyes that shine back at me?

If you like hieroglyphics
They'll look like that,
Or Tibetan mandalas
If that's where you're at.
They're Jewish scrolls
Or biblical tales,
Eleusinian mysteries
Or tarot card readings;
In Cabbalistic routes,
The declaration of Independence.
The inquisitors' creed,
The Protestant work ethic,
Existentialism.
The lawyers' items
And the civil code.

They're anything you need
To keep you clutching your key;
Holding on to that tree
Gives spiritual life, you see.

It's trite and it's tight
As can be.
It's rules as rulers clutch,
Rulers in their hands
To measure with.

Themselves they go by,
They sigh and sigh and sigh.
So very few are true;
But, they knowing
And, you knowing,
How can we bare them?

It's come to this,
That you and I
Must agree
Which goods to sacrifice,
Which own things are greed,
And which are for to breathe.

If breathing is of air,
And we all need it,
Then we can agree,
We can share it.

(Written During Poet's Conference, Sydney Festival, 1981)

* * *

18th. January 1981

Longford Folk Festival:
In the Shadow of the Dammed Wilderness

Thousands of people here today
Show us the world to be.
It's easy to switch off,
Harder to live right
Where is our energy?

Favour a river, or jobs for the workers?
Go ask the water seers,
They'll tell you it's stupid to
Feel for the country;
Think of the economy!

But consider a world not far away,
Man-scarred, corporately raped;
Short-term solutions, mutilated usage,
Unemployment, again, as your fate.

Think! Sun power, Wind, not water, dead forest,
Small businesses, self-generated power;
New trees in the soil, a reason to toil,
Tassie, alternative state!

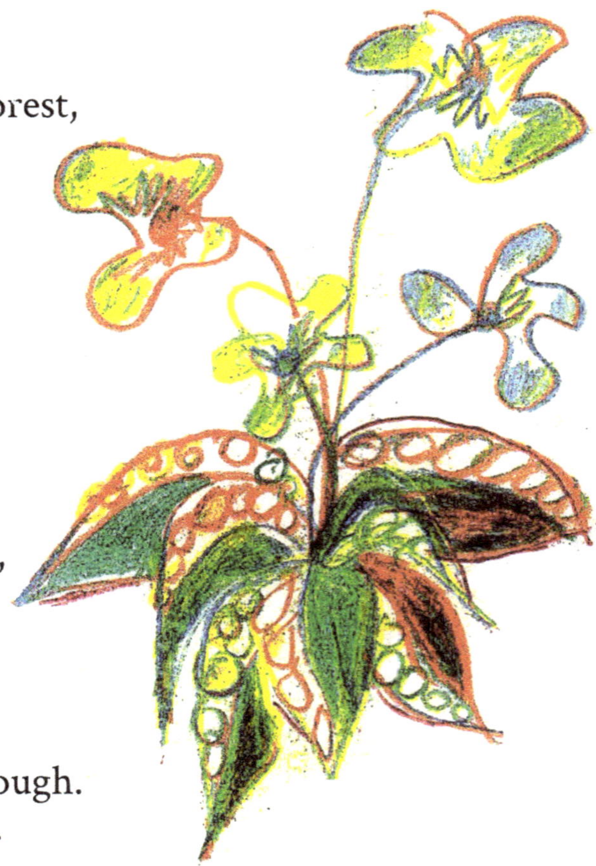

Of the companies you finance
The energy's too great.
They use it, abuse it, and ship it away;
Oh, what will you do when it's gone?
Build a dam, if that's your yen,
And watch jobs for hundreds fade to ten,
A dependent economy, fallen again.

The point is, develop alternatives now!
For the future will not be given to you.
Three wildernesses left, the whole world through.
Just leave it, don't spoil it, it can't renew.

* * *

The animals and plants have a right to just be
God's unique features for the children to see.
All have that chance when young and strong;
It's enough just to know that it's there.

Forty-two dams mean enough energy to share
For all who are willing, for all who care.
If you keep the rate going
This globe we live on
Will not be worth having.

Our spirits need quiet,
Freedom, space, mountain air;
Our minds can reach up,
Our souls expand there.

* * *

January 1981

Anti Urban

Tightly banded,
Uniform sprawl,
The soul's decay,
Society's fall.

* * *

January 1981

A Sheep's a Sheep for a' That

(This poem was written with heavy reliance on, and hopefully humorous reference to,
Robbie Burns poems "A Man's a Man for all That" and
"The Death and Dyin' Words o' Poor Mailie-My ain Per Ewe- An Unco Mournful Tale")

As blasted gales of foreign wrath
Ol' Scotland's shores have long assailed,
I am in mind a tale to tell
I've swoorn an aith, I'll not be doitin' (doddering)
I'll blaud it weel, I'll dinner blether (screed) (well) (not gossip)
For 'tis of a subject poor and lowly
As oft is nearest to my heart.

Old Nannie was the best o' ewes
She bleateth never out o' tune
When lambies young skipped all thy lane
As they gang oft agley (often go astray)
Twas Nannie, gude for al' the bairns
Who as their mither gaer al' for scoutin'
No for any more o' courtin'
For many a summers hae she.

One braw day in the month o' June,
As sweet birdies fell al' to croonin',
And as the sheep roamed o'er the muir (moor)
Dyke back, a quean and her swain were (behind a hedge) (a saucy girl)
Al' for loutin'.

* * *

It feel to pass, as fate would hae' it,
That Nannie's troubled eye had noted
A dearth of lambies 'pon the muir.
O'er where they'd roamed she'd ne'er a cluie
But one moorlan' tipp hae' seen the scout. (moorland ram)
And so she fell to searchin'
'Neath every bush and stone up-turnin',
Until she spied a flash o' white
Sparkin' thru' the under-grawth
Yon whaire the river trickled slow
'Twixt grassy braes al' to and fro'.

Our saucy swain and rustic quaen
Down to the petticoats full 'n rustlin'
Had gathered heat an al' to lovin'
Were pressin' fo' to couplin'.
The buxom wench, her heart palp'tating
Of her father was deliberating,
As he, a fearsome squire, ha' said,
Ne'er to give before 'twas wed;
And, fearsome were his blackened rages.
So she stooped to stop what 'twas engagin'
In their mutual rustic bed.

* * *

Our lovesick swain was fain to stap,
But, fidgin'-fain to hear't, (tingling with delight)
He thought a slee thought and aired it, (sly)
O Hoe to sklent the lyart pow. (cheat the grey head)
"Oh Nellie girl," (he spak full weel,)
"Com' spie out yonder ewe
Among the nettles stuck 'n bleatin'
Al' warstled on the brae; (floundered)
Jus' ye lie here graceful a mo'
And I shall tae' off mi tam o' shanter, (plaid, beret)
And aeso mi' coat o' cloot (wool)
To put on tha' ol' ewe,
An' she sha' be the target
For your guidman's shower o' sparks, (father's)
For fu' weel I knae he'll come a meddlin'
Wi' his shotgun fu' o' darts."

'Sae spakin' out, he threw of al' his gear,
Whilst Nellie's sobs had trickled to a tear,
He dress'd ol' Nannie in each of his plaids
And meekly she stood, for low of heart was laid
Al' tangled up in thorns sharp and drear.

And back they fell to ridin' time (copulation of animals)
With many a tickle and many a laugh
A' lying on the heather (manners)
And thinkin' havins never
Of Nannie in her pain and suff'rin',
The anguished pangs, of a stifled mither.

* * *

'Twas 'round high noon in the Douglas hame, (home)
And tea had been a'stewin
For mickle past an hour.
Ol' squire Douglas, from his plowin',
Heard the cows a-lowin'
And knew it time for lunchin'.

So seekin' out his daughter,
He heard the sounds of laughter,
Not on homeward paths,
But comin' from the waters!

A stupid man he ne'er ha' been,
His forebears had seen many a peer
Of English stock pierced full weel
An' griddled thru' the heart.

An' sae, as does a douse man (prudent)
He knew tha' ill had befa' his girl.
In bushes dark he tracked the lark
Until his feet had crossed the path
Towards the lovers' tristin' place.

Ol' Douglas' eyes were naught sae sharp
As when he'd been a lad,
And when he saw the briars move,
And when he heard the lovers laugh,
And seein' brightly coloured plaid
He next espied the fateful pom
'Pon the tam o'shanter laid
'Twixt poore ol' Nannie's ears.

* * *

He knew not what foul act was done,
He moan'd and groan'd four moments long,
He caretna' who or what was smarted, (cared not)
Just that his rage to let full outed
Like paitricks scraichin' on the rout. (partridges screaming)

Forthwth he lifted up his gun,
And sighted down the barrel long
the bright red tuffs o' wool.
He pressed the trigger, and minded never
As Nannie's blood flew out.

Is there a man- a coward slave
(We call him that, nae less,)
Who for the sufferin' of an ewe
Couldna' spare a tear?
O sae, if then for mi tale
A deal of fluids shed
For one poor ewe
Who never knew
What sorry fate befell
Her lamblings sweet, on rocky crags
And dismal glens, to birds o'prey
And other fell things
That sorry shepherds tell.

What though on hamely fare they dine,
Eat spiky green an' a' that,
Gie fools their wine and lowly ways,
A ewe's a ewe for al' that.

* * *

For a' that an' a' that.
Humanity's guile and lo' deceit,
The honest sheep, tho' e'er sae meek,
Is worth the lot, for a' that.

Ye see yon birkie, ca'd a lord,
Wha struts, and stares, an' a' that;
Tho' hundreds worship at his word,
He's but a coof fo a' that. (fool)
For a' that, an' a' that,
The ewe o' independent mind,
She looks and laughs at a' that.

Then let us prae that come it may,
(As come it will for a' that,)
That Sense and Worth, o'er a' the earth,
May bear the gree, an' a' that.
For a' that, and a' that,
That ewe to Man, the world o'er, shall brothers
be for a' that.

* * *

25th. January 1981

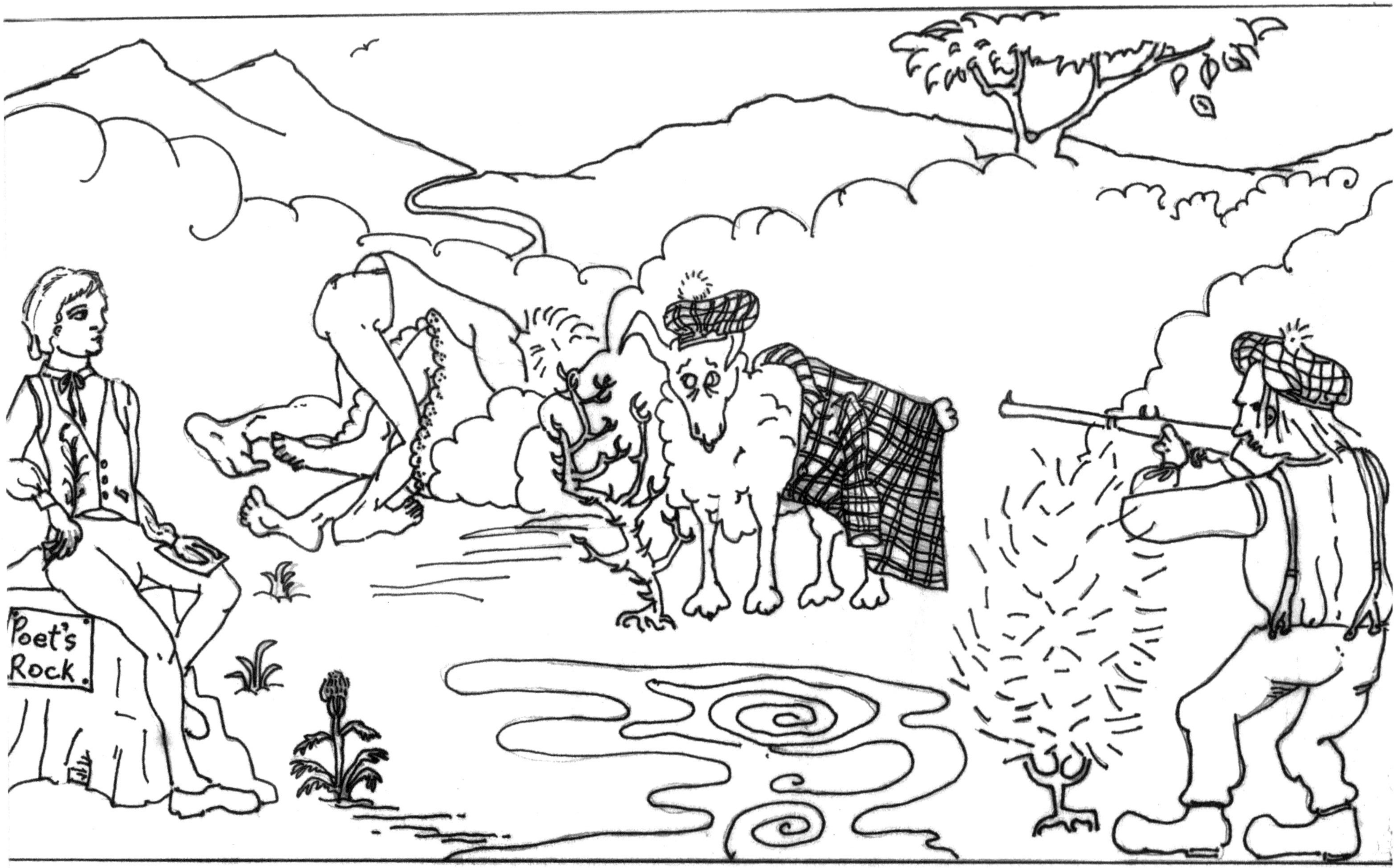
Poet's Rock.

What I Did Today

Today….
I liberated a rose
From her transparent box.
And noticed
Her bow her head low.

I could not bear to look her in the face,
Her beauty so noble,
Whilst quiescent,
She had expanded in tight perfection
To fill up her three-walled space.

Brilliant petals,
Cooled from the heat
And all time….
For days she had stood ageless
And the virility of wild leaves,
Just some marked….
Supported her unblemished state

I thought it time to experiment with her;
Shook her out,
Put her in a green vase,
Couldn't free her from the vial,
Sprinkled her with sugared water,
Saw her raised head wither,
From its own weight,
And sensed how I participate
In slaughter.

Her petals blew out.
Little blackened creases
Became visible.
A subtle, diffused, loss of colour
Was almost immediate
And, although for some seconds
Her symmetry of perfect cone
Trembled, it expanded blowzily,
And she has taken on a coarse, cheery,
Openness. It has taken over.

* * *

Is it wrong to put so much
Onto a flower?

My rose has settled down, now,
And her beauty is ordinary.
I can cope better with her.
Beauty should be transitory,
And hence,
Only peripheral to life.

The relentless screaming of old age
Is the only enhancer
Of fresh, untrammeled purity.
Purity dormant, unknowing,
Makes you want to cry
For its innocence.

It betrays by its removal from life.
By giving up
We'll gain it again;
With this time,
All the marks, blemishes, effusions
Of experience.

Becoming the revealer
Of living, life, variety.
For nothing in a sheltered, translucent
Covering
Truly lives.

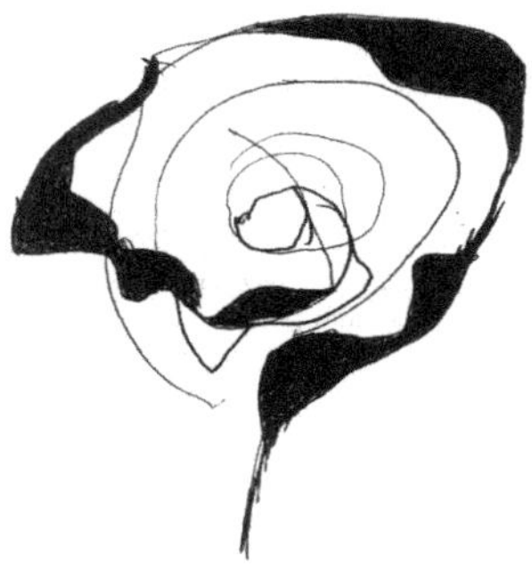

* * *

1st. February 1981

The Eye of Hammurabi

You present day kings
In high rise thrones thrust skywards
And extend over oceans.

Your wants are as always.
These things haven't changed.
Power, wealth, status, women...
And the aggressive thrust
To protect your accumulations
Is the root of your delight
In these.

What of the others
Who don't have these things?
Most women, and all of the poor
People of this Earth.
Does a crisis come upon your masculinity
When others strive
To topple your throne?

When might is right,
When damage is to
Be metered out
In proportion to
The threat which applies,
Then women, and all of the poor,
Find themselves gazing into the eagle eyes
Of the new Hammurabis
As they wield
Their two-dimensional power
Over this Earth.

Their weapons are
The economics of
Multi-National corporations.
(Wealth makes wealth.)
This excludes women
From higher management positions,
And seeks to make the poor richer
Only to exploit them
So much the better.

A Hansel and Gretel situation.
We are fattened only so fat...
When economic crisis threatens
Retrenchment and unemployment
Are the name of the game.

You latter day kings will compromise
Not one whit.
Not your expense accounts,
Entertainment funds,
Overseas trips.
And, you growl as
The workers strike for a 35-hour week.

Inherited wealth and social position
Ensure the princedoms
For your male children.
Inherited poverty
Ensures the new
Form of the wage slavery
For countless millions of others.

Hammurabi promulgated a new law.
You have ensured us
Relative lack of material want;
But the increased wealth of the few
Makes only so much more apparent
The injustices... still the injustices
Of the imbalance.

Hammurabi, ... the one
Who came after you;
The one with pity for humanity,
The one who spoke
Of the eye of the needle
(You know him, now),
What would you say to him?

We need to see the eye of the dove;
Of arms stretching
Around the world,
Making all people one.

* * *

4th. March 1981

Sex to the Power of Two

The celebration of sex,
Our last instinct.
Plastic porno ice-cubes.
You could fill them with pink dye
And, sucking,
Your hormones would re-experience
The stimulus for sexual excitation.
We once sucked our mother's breasts.
Early feelings of comfort perhaps come into
This secondary excitation.

Once is never enough
In sex and all else.
The need to re-experience
All instincts
No longer possible,
We have placed a heavy demand
On sex. (No matter we are not satisfied.)
Love, yes, friendship, yes, comfort, yes.
Where there lies a problem
Is in the bonding.

When sex has entangled itself
To every warm and comforting human expression,
Confusion can arise.
Sex is a singularly powerful force
For welding people together,
But it is a simple thing, too.
It cannot be overvalued in its own right,
But, like anything,
It has its place.
This has nothing to do with morals,
But natural expression,
Energy levels,
Instinct.

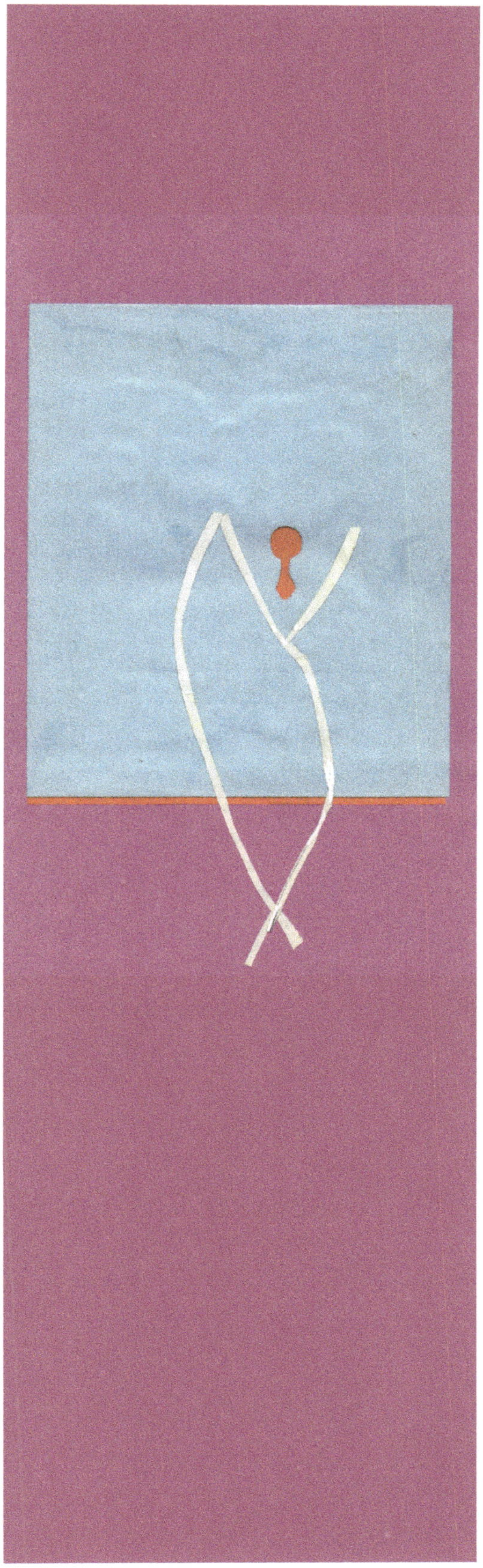

* * *

A warm feeling, a desire for contact,
Sexual feelings.
"Let's go to bed, shall we?"
A warm time together. Perhaps loving words.
Perhaps time spent together.
Then the acceleration (before knowledge, experience,)
Of doubts, criticisms, need for freedom.
After all, the sensation has been satisfied.
This need, for sensation, becomes heightened
The more you use it; use governing need.

You can make 'love' to many people
Whom you would not make friends of.
They are sensation partners.
What I'm trying to say
Is that we have combined many 'needs' (instincts)
Under the heading of sensation.
No wonder warmth turns
To withdrawal of need.

Take out money, buying.
Replace it with the sighting
Of genuine need and its immediate gratification.
I am hungry, I take food.
I am lonely, I talk to:
A stranger, a workmate, an acquaintance,
A friend, a relative, a lover.

Expanding degrees of intimacy.
Make your own list.
If, though, I am lonely, and I take a lover,
Making love to strangers is
Mistaken need,
Confused instincts.

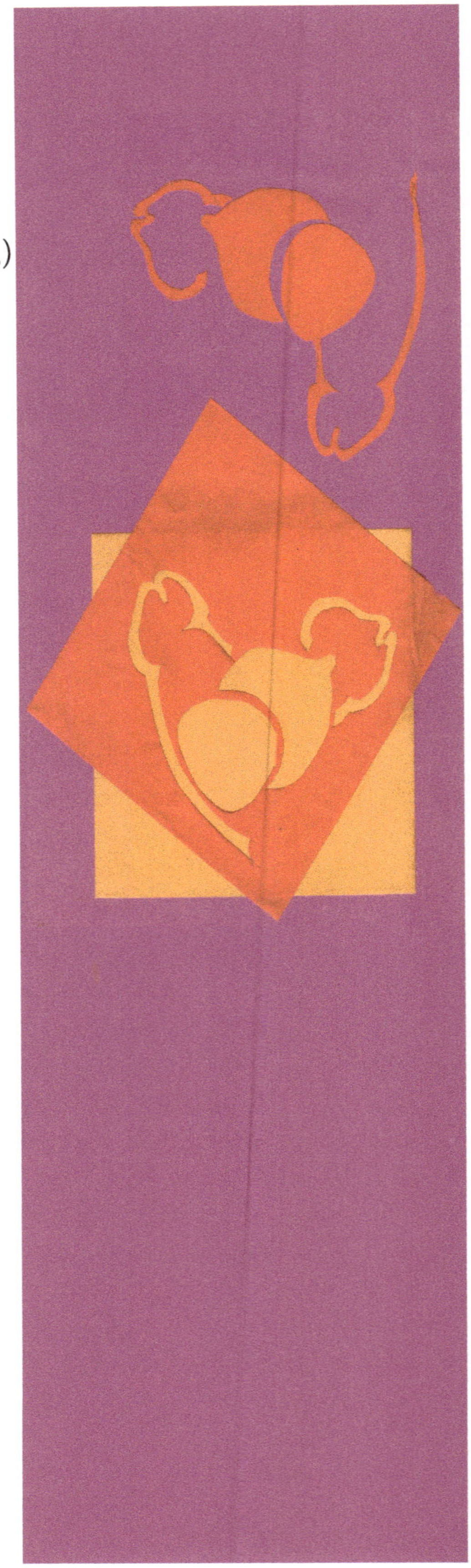

* * *

Used to the intermediary stage of currency
We feel we can make anything into something else.
Not so sex.
It is an implicit bonding tool.
We cannot bond to strangers.
How can we, before the stranger
Has become friend, or relative?

In this culture, men have been taught
To shut off their emotional links
To their instinctual drives.
Aggro. Macho. "You've got to make it with a chick"
At 14.
The initial experience being not as promised,
He has to face the issue of respect.
Of the woman. Of himself.

It's very hard to compare the male and female egos.
We've been taught different expressions.
The male as the separate, powerful individual
Who has to strive to be successful.
Relationships as secondary.
The woman as the person who gains
What else she may want
After she has gained a successful relationship.

Do we always mature past our adolescent dream beliefs?
Do we ever?
And, if we see a continuum, how do we cope
Faced with, at one polarity, the idealised mythologies
About positively realised love, complete bonding;
And, at the other end, the instinctual drive,
Towards sensation.
Or, is there no conflict when the correct use of time
Has walked us along the continuum?

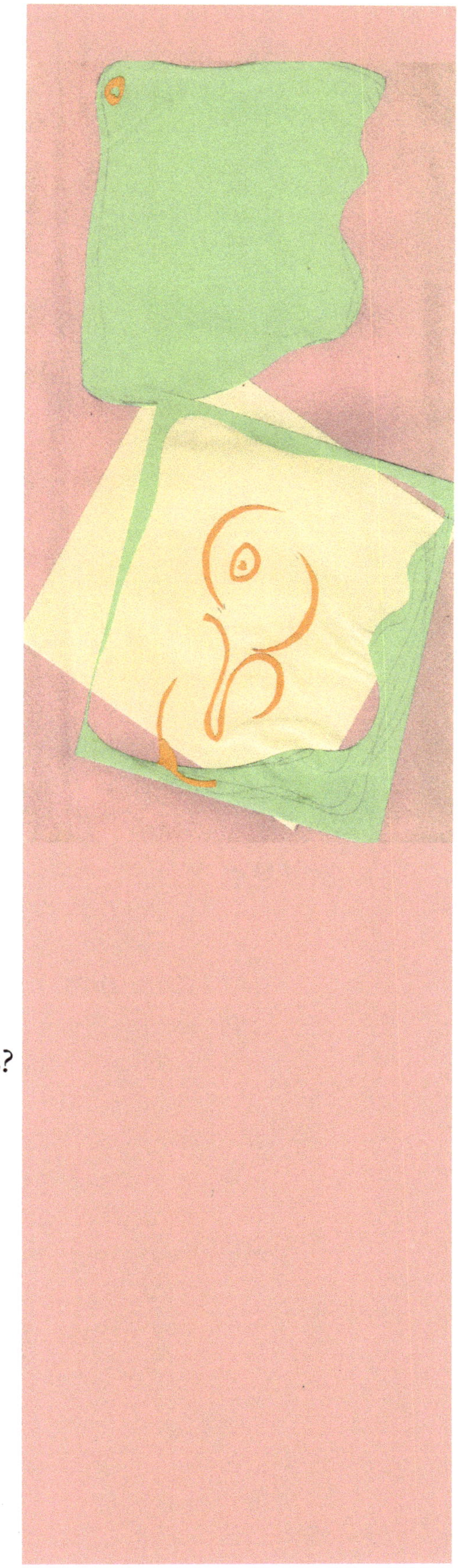

* * *

Yin and yang. Correct balance.
But, understanding must play its part.
Constant awareness of
The whole in its parts.

Isn't understanding the fruit of experience?
Isn't experience the fruit of time?

As creatures of habit our levels of experience
Grow slowly.
Man doesn't mature in a day
Except in fictional medias.
And, if we reject experience, live for the day,
Aren't we living for sensation? On the level
Of sensation?

Perhaps we might not die
If we learn how to truly live today.
Then, if living truly, does it matter
If we do die?
This has nothing to do with martyrdom.
What is death, when we know that by living
We have accelerated the pace of hurting others
Who must die, like us.

Common humanity is the realisation
That we all come from the same place,
Mostly have two legs,
And will die.
Within the continuum from birth to death
Why should we carry on the pain
Inflicted on us by others
To the power of all the generations
Who have ever lived?
What about those
Who are yet to live?

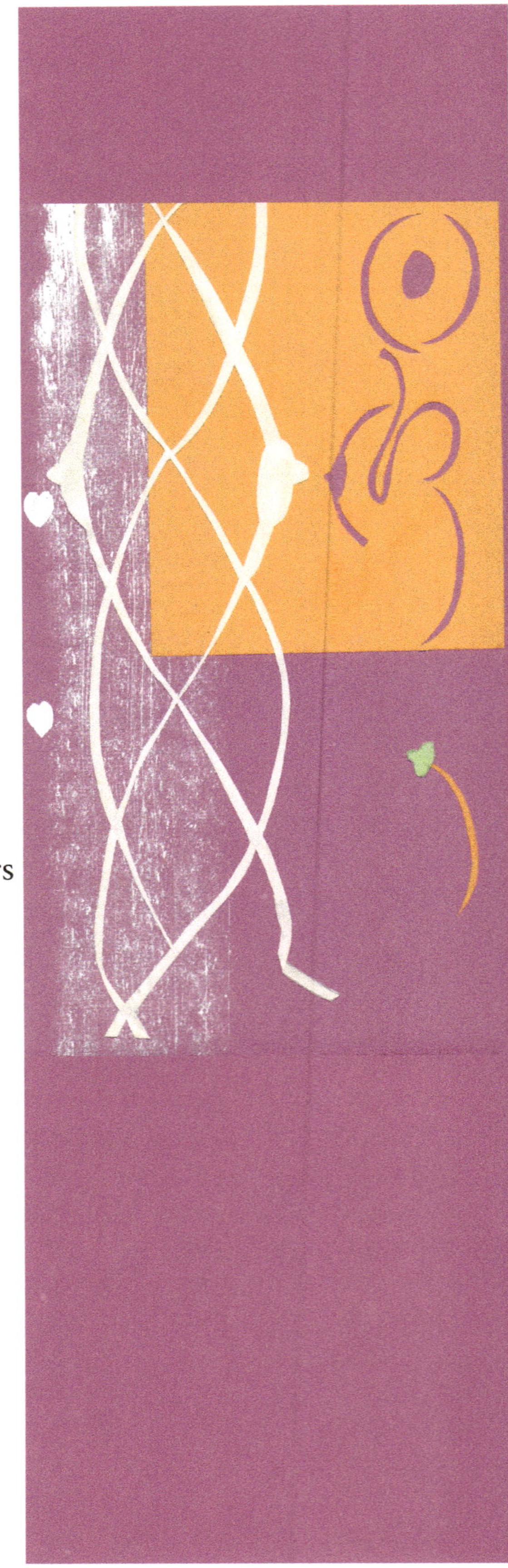

* * *

If we do not live properly,
We wish to hurt others.
Sensing that others are more complete
We try to grab from them
What we do not have.
Experience, truth, growth, understanding,
Change that.

I cannot draw
From the well-springs of life
When I have no cup,
When I have drunk too much,
When I have no others
To help me lift my cup
So that we may all
Be nourished together.

* * *

10th. April 1981

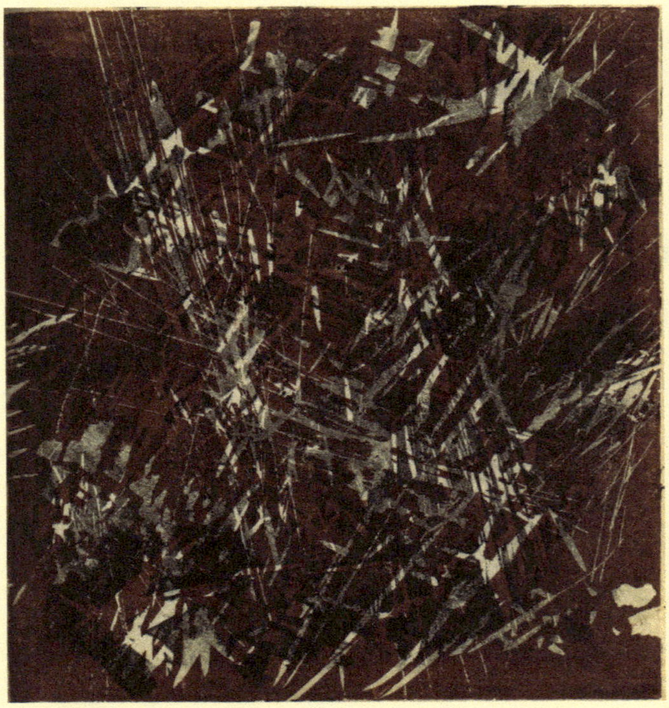
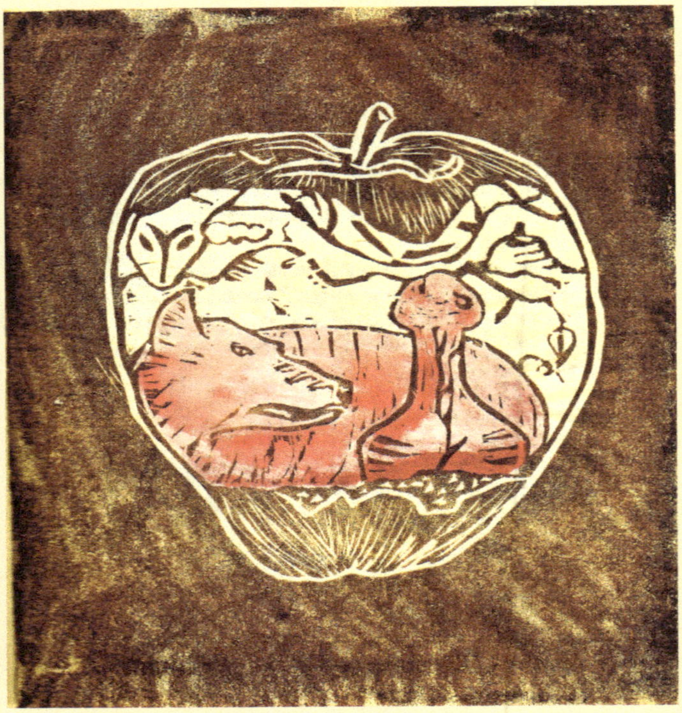
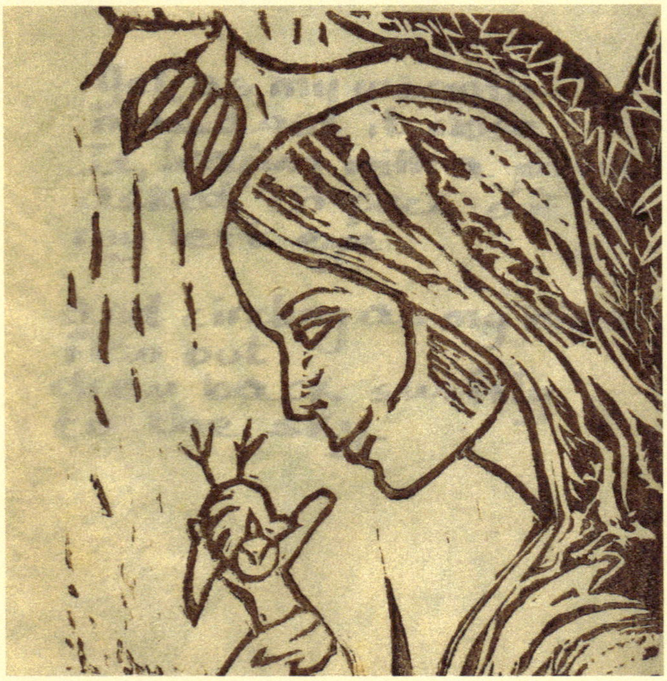
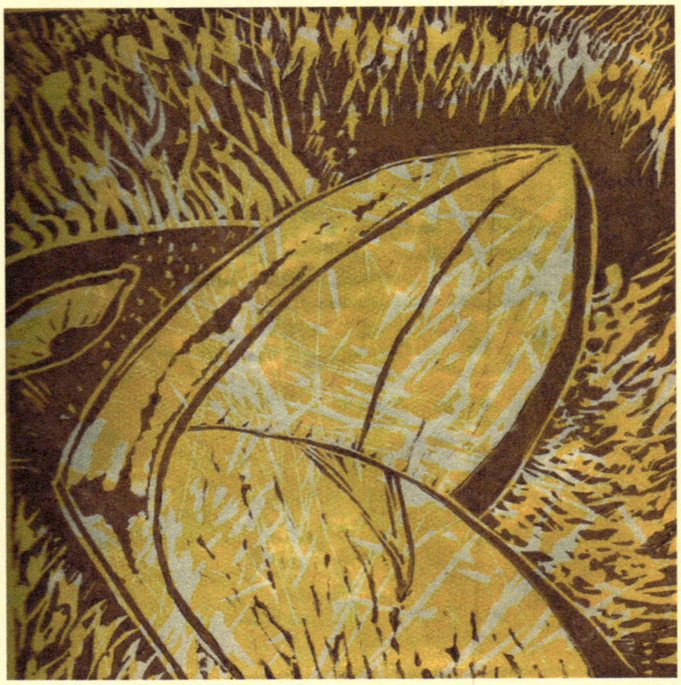
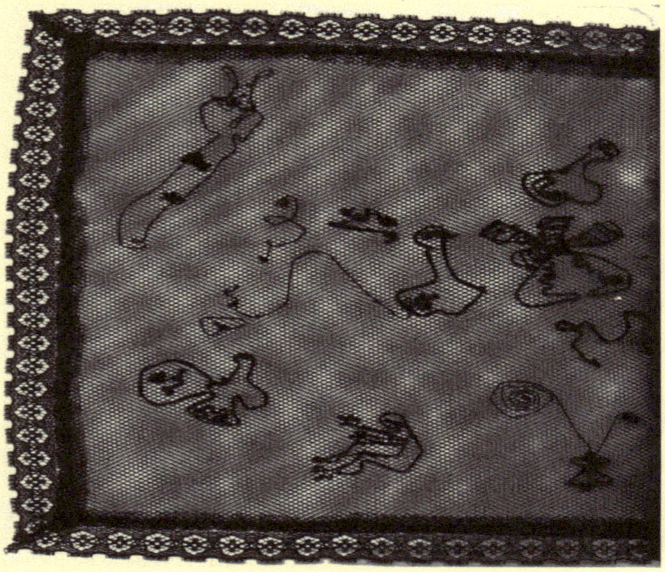
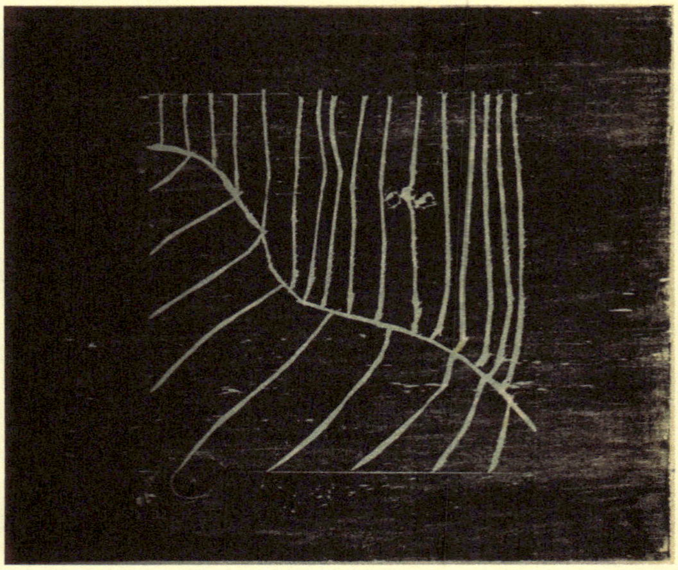

Lovers Prospect'us

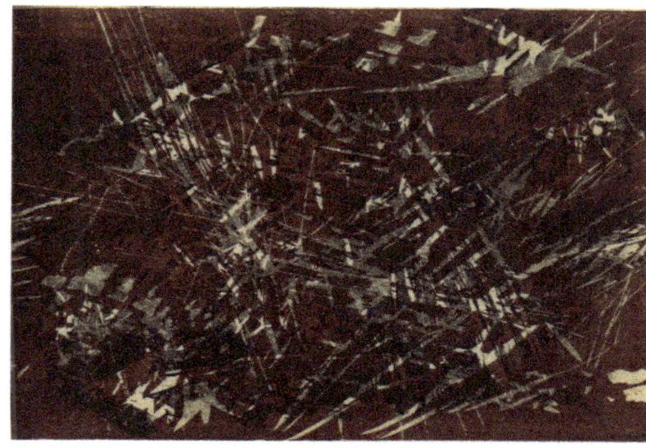

It would be easier for me
To tell you, as I climb the tree,
That of the golden apples,
All are gone.
I sent them home
For pigs to feed on.

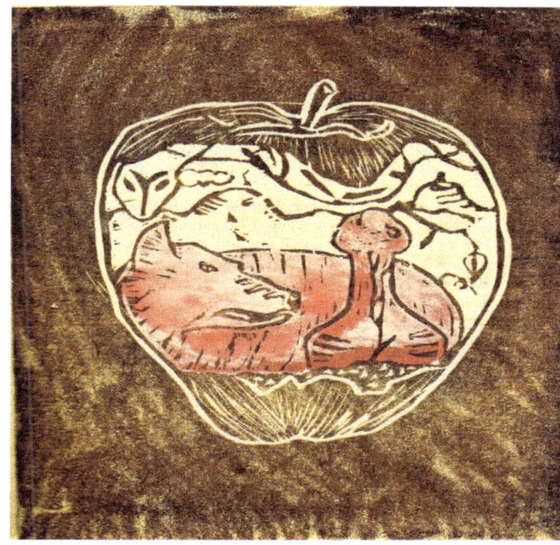

It would be easier, you see,
If I could only tell the birds
That they at least need not fear me.
One day I sent my sharpest stone
Soaring amongst some flying gulls;
To my surprise one bird fell down,
And nestled numbly
In my hand.

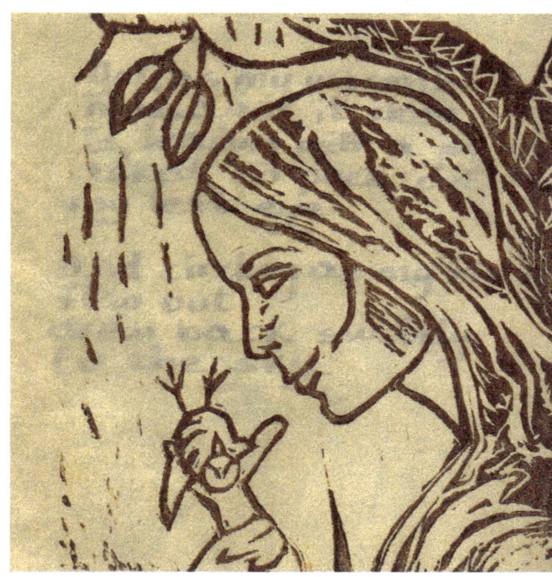

It seemed to me so small and still
That it should surely fade and die...
Yet, as my warmth massaged it close,
It, leaping with a joyful cry,
Asked to peck out my left eye,
And, circling as my blood flew out,
Drew back swiftly to the sky.

It would be easier for me
To paint the hills a sunset hue;
To draw a mourning veil across my door
And tell the world
It can't come through.

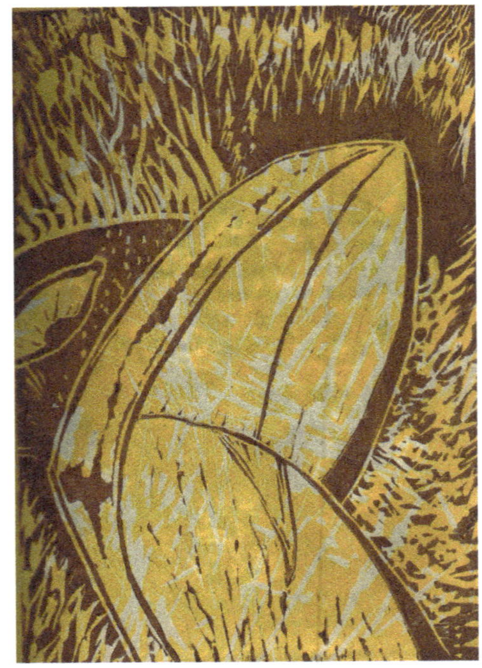

For if you know I cannot give
What I have untimely spent,
Squandered on a passing hope,
Not willing to let it fade untried;
Then perhaps the bough will bear,
The birds will nest and seek its fruit.
The sun will shine and shine anew,
And, if I know, I'll smile for you.

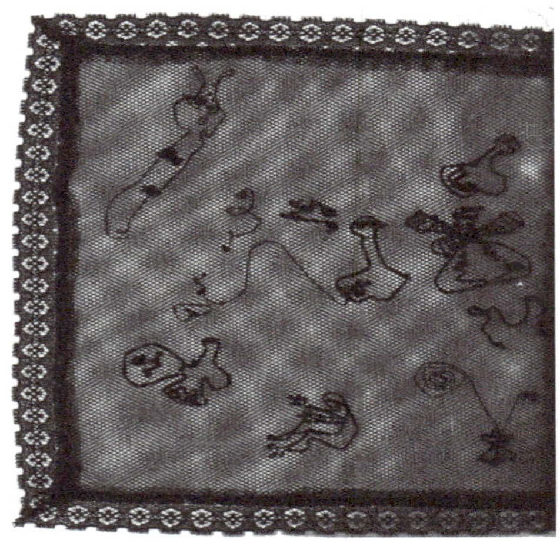

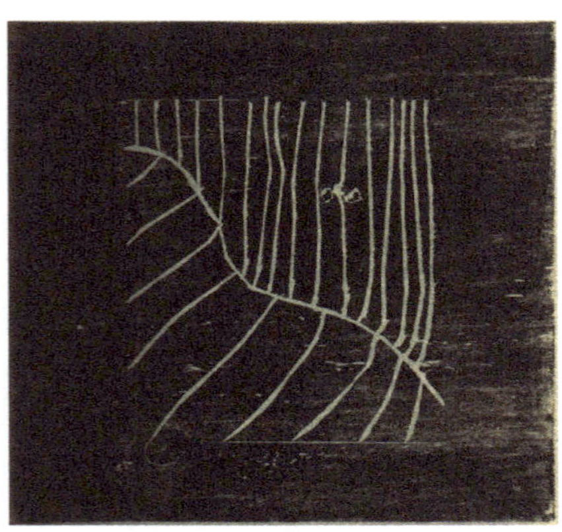

* * *

1973, illustrated late 1981

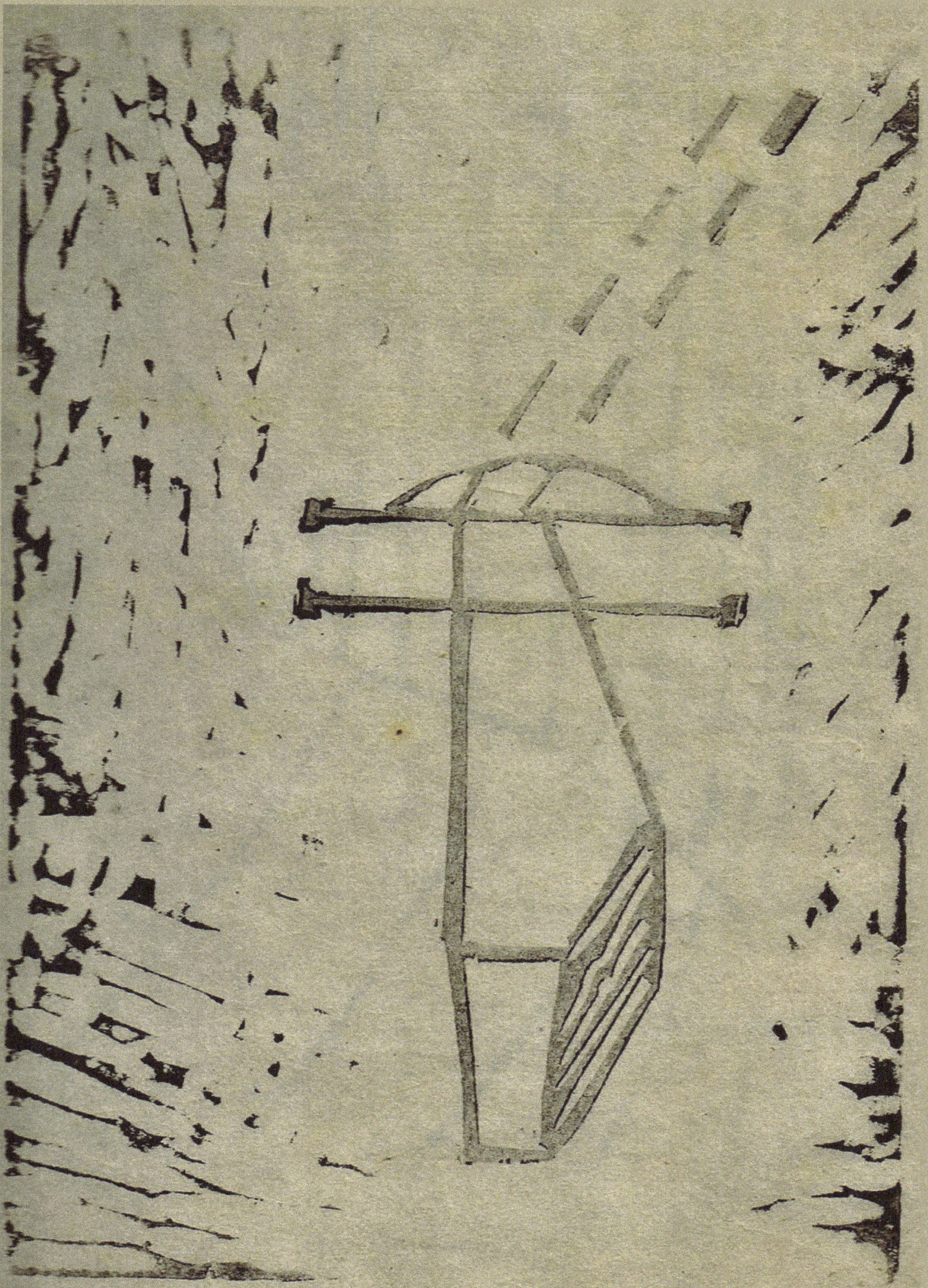

Keeping the Balance

Combining different parts of myself,
I keep the balance they ignite.... Joyfully.

When energy is what is needed
You must expend to find it.
Life is an exhaustive process!

First, you must search for the goal,
Then, you search for the fuel
To reach that goal.

It's a risky business
Between the goal
And the spark to get there.

Is the real joy to be found
In that combustion process,
Or in the achieving of the goal?

Once one is obtained
The next becomes
The operative process.

Goal. Search. Find,
And the energy levels to
Seek them out
Can be joyful,
Can be sad,
Can be difficult.
It's up to you
To choose.

* * *

7th. June 1981

The Weakness of Being Born a Woman

In this society
Gays and women have been reborn
From the weaker men
Of a previous age.

Ones who, being weaker,
Could not cope,
And therefore condemned to
Despise themselves
And sometimes be despised
For not being born strong.

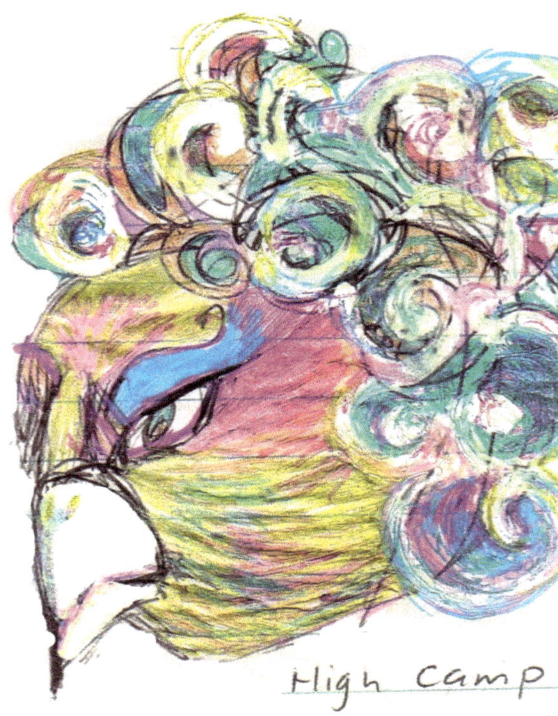

(I wrote this poem to escape crying;
one hour after hearing of S's private relationships with other women.)

* * *

7th. June 1981

A Deeply Felt Tale

(A word of explanation first. I had decided my piano needed tuning. The man whose ad I'd answered turned out to be a conman. He took the felts away, stating they needed to be ground, and I didn't hear from him thereafter. Here is the tale of how I/we tracked him down with the help of the police. I got the felts back, which was excellent, as my piano was given to me by my father when I was 7, and I have carried it around with me ever since.)

In the days of The Herald there came forth a Kamel,
And he, being a kind man, gave Benita an ad.

And she, being a rushed woman, did go forth unto her college
On the day that the man did come unto her house
To make foul noises and other mischief
Upon her piano.

And Richard, being a generous soul,
And wise studier of foreign sounds,
Did lay down his books
And give unto his housemate's workman
The price for his evil labours;
For truly, his ears were filled quite enough.

And speedily, upon her return,
She went unto her piano to make, as was her custom,
Most pleasing melodies.

At the time when the devils sprang forth,
And the felts were not ground,
And the notes became useless to her touch,
She did take her head into her hands
To rock back and forth,
Emitting most piteous sobs.

And all her friends and housemates
Did beat upon their chests
And cried out, and clenched their fists,
And wished to rend the clothes
Of the man Comorran.

And they spoke for long on the subject,
And, in short, tried to set him up.

But he, being a cunning thief,
And a wily staller for time,
Did offer many false days
And ways in which to offer reparation.

Her money not sighted,
Benita did put by her faith
For the telephone,
And did spend many long hours
In confabulation with elderly ladies,
Solicitors and turf companies;
For truly, his evil flourished Everywhere.

And so, in the time of the great purge,
Benita went forth into the world
Even unto the steps of the great law court.

Where, in lofty chambers,
Summons were taken out,
In the name of the plaintiff
To fall upon the head
Of the man whose names were many
And all wrong.

And, in the days of the riding forth
Benita did take it upon herself
To ring her mother,
And rallied forces
To ply against the man.
For, as much as his cunning ran deep,
So did his stature ooze forth,
And fears were in the hearts
Of the woman, and of her friends.

And, in the borough name Mosman
Dwelt one old dancing partner of her mother.
And he did issue forth suggestions
To drive Miss Rainer to her destination.
Thus, in the eagled chariot
Of the Empowered Ones
Did she approach the hapless place
To find herself undone.

From empty shopfront
To deserted house
She searched for him to no avail.
So, turning back defeated
She roused the innocent occupant
Who willingly told his tale.

For many months he had been harried
By debtors and by mail,
So, clutching liquid substance,
He hoped for apprehension,
Of the man named Comorran,
And the man named Denton.

A thankless task it proved to be,
For Benita, so, riding willingly,
She came unto Detective Beatie,
And offered up her story.

He said that he did know the man,
And that her loss was quite a shame,
But, as to finding clues,
She'd better trust her shoes
And hope for useful news
From his drinking place.

On All Saints Eve at 7.00p.m.
She entered in the pub.
Her eyes did comb from door to foam,
And many shoulders rubbed.
She shifted here, she shifted there,
Her eyes alighted everywhere.
She climbed the stairs,
Heard music blare, and settled back
Upon her chair and did no further roam.

Her friends were warm, her friends were kind,
They gave her nuts, they brought her wine.
They knew her way and kept her gay,
Sustaining her 'til closing time.
The Summons clasped to her breast
She stumbled out the door.
She placed it back into her bag,
Left with her friends, feeling sad.
Her quest was long, her time was short,
The man was wrong, but she had fought.

Her wearied steps had brought
From tuneless nights to Summons Court,
A fruitless search.
Tho' car she'd none she'd battled on,
From Mosman jail
And Manly pier to Cammeray
And a victim's tear, But all for nought.

The concrete done he'd not stayed long
But said it had to dry. Tho' she could wait,
It might be late; he might never return at all.

If so be you see her there,
Swatting flies from out her hair,
Please treat her with a kindly air,
Wish for her the cheque to clear,
And, secured, the man.

Or, maybe at the paper stand,
Blackened crayon in her hand,
Making rings 'pon the print,
Circling 'round the printer's ink;
Trying hard to tap the mind
Of a floundering, dullened kind
Of cheating, hapless skint.

If you see her, And you're kind,
She may give of her time to elaborate this rhyme,
Where I, alas, may not.

(Postscript : I did get the felts back. He dropped them off when I was at college. Replaced them at Richard's 'request' and scurried off. They were not ground.)

* * *

3rd. November 1981

On Turning 30

After the party,
And happiness lingers.
The dreams of knightly times
Reside in young men.
Warlocks prance
On soggy carpets.

A single pink-red bubble
Rides forth on Autumn air.

The sun is a soft bath
On our garden.
Punctured.....
The day warms up.

* * *

30th. March 1982

Father Love

And now I see my father's face
In every man,
And hear a longing
For his purity
In every woman's voice
That calls her lover.

* * *

30th. March 1982

Moves

Here I stand
With my bed rolled up
Ready to go
Four miles away
To another part
Of my life-times.
The future is ours
For the taking.

Deep compassion,
Warmest love,
Affectionate ease,
Are my companions
With you.

My soul shines
Even when my eyes
Are bedazzled.
Our bodies are one
Energy.
We are radiating our love
For the World, too.
It is doing more
Than acknowledging;
It is applauding.

* * *

May 1982

Evan

As if knife-cut,
Water pours out
From my side.

Snap of relief
As tension ebbs.

The steady throb of action
Replaces dull mind-mists
As I make my curtains....
Becoming
A home maker
I join millions of women,
Living and dead.

My lesions of indecision
Are closing.

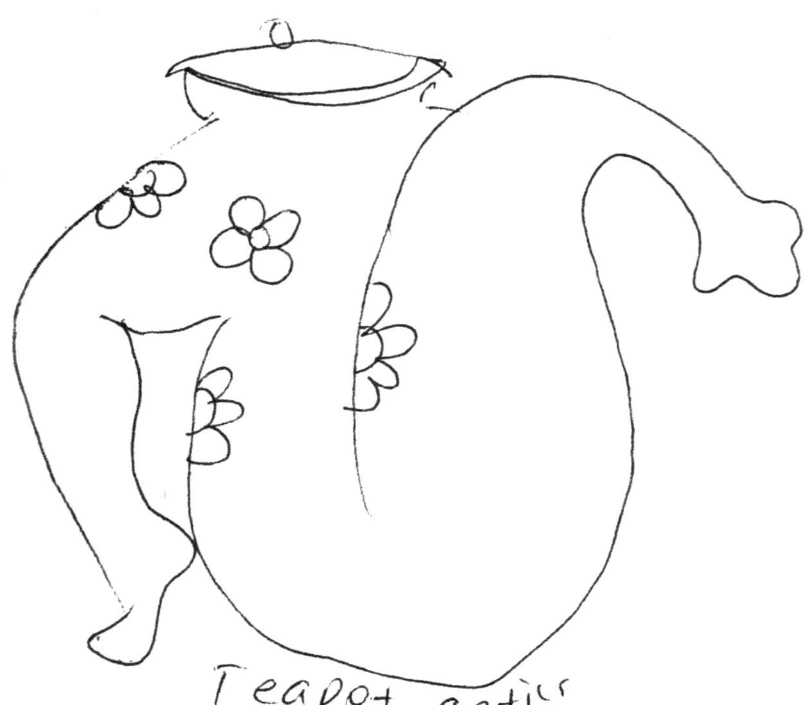

* * *

2nd. August 1982

The Baby

Gently, tumescently,
She came
In perfect whiteness
Entering and
Demanding me
In return for
Life.

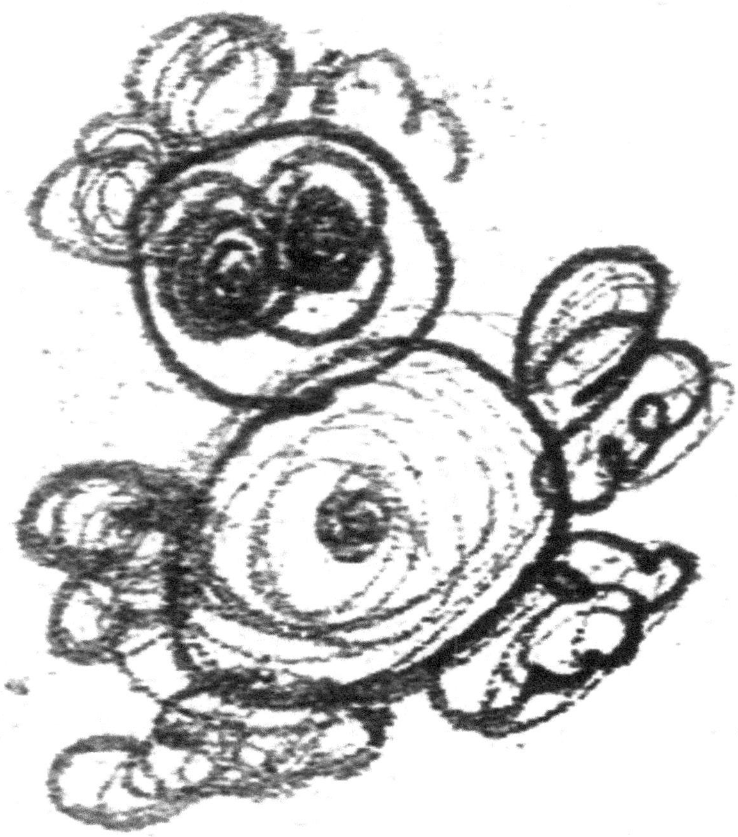

* * *

1983

Meditations after a Marriage in The Botanical Gardens

I

Mother-of- Pearl light shines through the glowing viridian tunnel
Of gently swaying leaves, devoid of graduated perspective, but clumped
So thickly tight together that, tunnel, yes, they appear to make
Against the dusk sky as she glides by.

I, sitting on white nylon, checking the contents of a photographer's bag
As my baby scatters things onto the grassy bed,
See her, not yet there, bridesmaids all in saucy pink,
Bows on high-heel-swayed derrieres,
Silk rustling, look out from dark curls, through netted pillboxes,
At her, gliding by.

One, chatting, clutches satin shoes to walk down the path bare foot,
Which incites good-natured mayhem against their sister…'one of the girls' who seems to know no longer the discomfit of a tight-fitting shoe or a high heeled stumbling over rocky garden paths leading down to the sea.

She doesn't even hear them. She has moved inevitably, inexorably
Along what is a path well-oiled by the passage of others across millennia;
But still for Her alone.
The white sits comfortably as a magnetic skin, She is a vortex whirling from her sacral centre, but she moves smoothly along; fully matured,
She is The One now carrying the glory torch, the engendering power
From heaven to humanity.
Her magnetic ship pulls all in her wake, down that tunnel's way.

Once through those green depths which enveloped and veiled her like a luminous pearl
Her passage beyond the tunnel is mysteriously unattended.
Her chelas have been drawn off to either side, suddenly willy-nilly,
Claimed by some Bacchanalian rite, which, those uninitiated, cannot know
Until it is their time to see The White.

II

Later that night, rocking Cassie's pram, soothing her down to sleep,
Bedded on the waves, we pass under The Harbour Bridge
And I suddenly want to move with the waves to gain their force
As I see that dark mass overhead.
As I rock my baby, so I am rocked under the thing that nearly bore me first of all on this earth.
In spirit I swung from rafter to rafter across the sea's waves,
Laughing in total exhilaration as my trapeze antics had the force of earth upon them.
Now as birth approached, enjoying that space,
Swooping higher than any mortal could've seen unless they too had spirit eyes to see,
I danced and laced my high-flown ways around and above my birth mother's labours; Seeing
below, the speeding car on route to my delivery thirty-two years ago.
Now, straddling the waters underneath my feet I rock my baby sound asleep, and feel time
layered upon itself.

III

We are doing great circuits of these waters
And I am drinking, laughing, eating off a white board.
But, I see Luna Park's painted grin.
Once more under the bridge the twelve sectioned Ferris wheel endlessly turning, seeming to
crown all under it, reminds me of how our lives
Are led in endless repetition, until we learn not to spin.

* * *

19th. February 1985

Season Follows Season

Season follows season,
One goes upon one's merry way,
Up until the day
That life catches up to you.

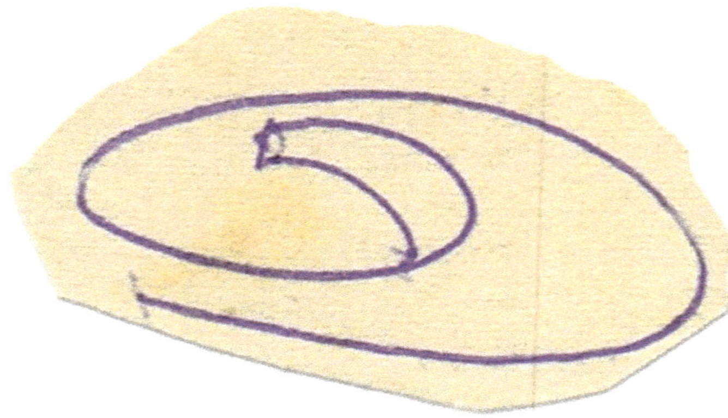

You see, you cannot have a child
And not be linked up
To every crime ever committed
Against children.

The barriers come down,
And, all of a sudden,
You receive
The inheritance of every man
To every other man;
Stamped, as it is,
On the soul
Of this mother earth.

So that we are part of it
As they are part of us.

Jesus said
"Resist not evil."
So, by seeing it,
Squarely,
You can be free of it.

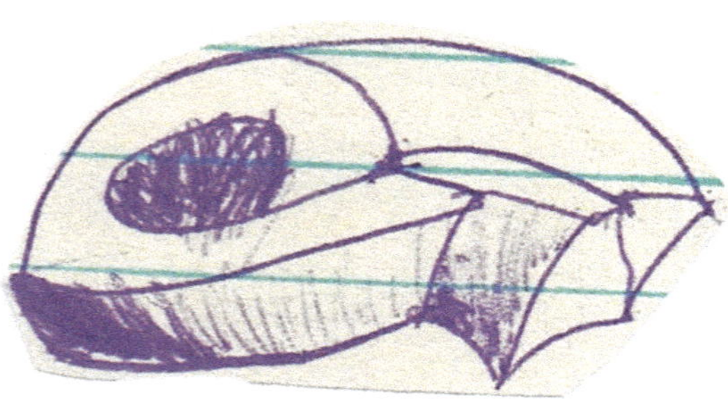

* * *

3rd. June 1986

Seeking Clarification

The man approaches the high places
And asks the gods
What would they have of him?
They answer:
He must ask his own question first.

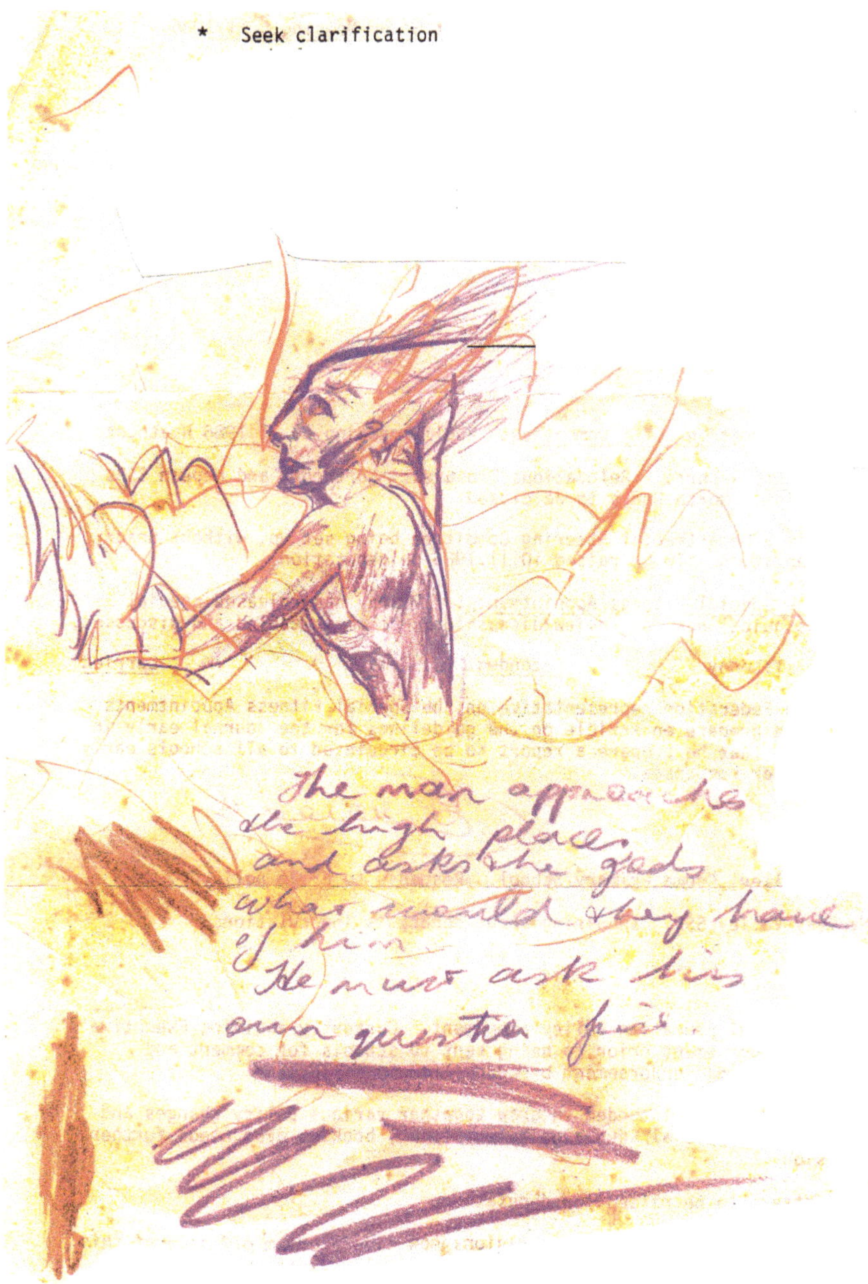

* * *

6th. November 1986

Anne's Birthday at Diethne's

Oh Luna, Luna, Luna Light,
May you, with your face so bright,
Illuminate this pearly site.
Shiny Diethne's, perfect nest
For our crabs, and the rest
To partake ... as honoured guests,
Seafood rich and greenery pleasant,
Ducks and drakes and maybe pheasant
Whatsoe'er is good to taste...
For caring souls,
Abhoring waste,
And seeking nought for the human race
'Cept all that loving peace,
Maternal grace,
Can give.

All lovers here
Will find themselves well fed;
Cradled in Her bosom near,
Be of very great good cheer!

* * *

1980's.

Dearest Anne

You travel far afield
To find something that is in your heart
Already.
Compassion...quoth The Dalai Lama.

Again and again.
Every mystery school ever known
Had this gift to give to its pupils.
The open heart chakra,
The chalice of the grail.
The lotus flower
Opening from within.

The rising of all green forces,
The kundalini, the yoni,
The open heart.
The way is eternal:
Love is infinite,
As it is known
At the end of the quest,
As it was known
At the beginning
Of one's life...
In love.

In the relics of the quests of others
Throughout the ages,
I hope you find
What I know you will find...
Certainty.
That path
As through mystery schools
Lies in
The path through and beyond
Succumbing to negative emotions.
The realisation that we are all asleep
In our own reality tunnels,
And that SEEING
Leads to
Endless
Compassionate
Love.

Written at a drunken farewell party of Anne before her trip overseas.
Year not remembered and not recorded on the night.

* * *

1980's.

A Meditation on the Universe, and on the Pelvic Bone of a Calf

"Further me" She says,
And manages me and all else by Her structures;
The endlessly free, flawlessly creative thrust
Of Her prototype forms repeating.
A nudge from Space
Or of origins unknowably
But wholly, solely, from Her.
It is creativity explained
By direct action.
Itself, in its processes,
The paradigm.

* * *

3rd. November 1987

The Performer

Like a golden animal caged to her ribs
She moulded him within her.
In the red luscious dark heat of her womb
She nurtured him, birthing him
Out of the fullness of her experience of life...
On the bible-belt.
She preached soft God and southern morals to him.
But the deep heat blood red light she wove around them
Had nothing to do with anything
But pagan possession blood rites.

He was Her Son
In the way she possessed the inner core of him
The way he possessed the inner core of her.
She pushed him out, lion-like,
Her animus; cat on a string
To live for her.

I wonder if the sadness on her face
Was the sadness of the keeper
After she opens the cage
When the spotlight hits the ring,
Knowing all her life, consumed by mastery over the other;
It Leaves an eerie shell behind for her to occupy.

What a strange life, so fully projected onto the other;
Who, desperate for her, his own soul,
After she had gone, collected her clothes,
Symbol of the Her he could never see again.

Cleopatra-like, she cast her golden barge out onto the Nile
Where it glowed like a Sun King until sinking in the reeds,
Not knowing why it was made,
Once She was gone.

* * *

16th. May 1988

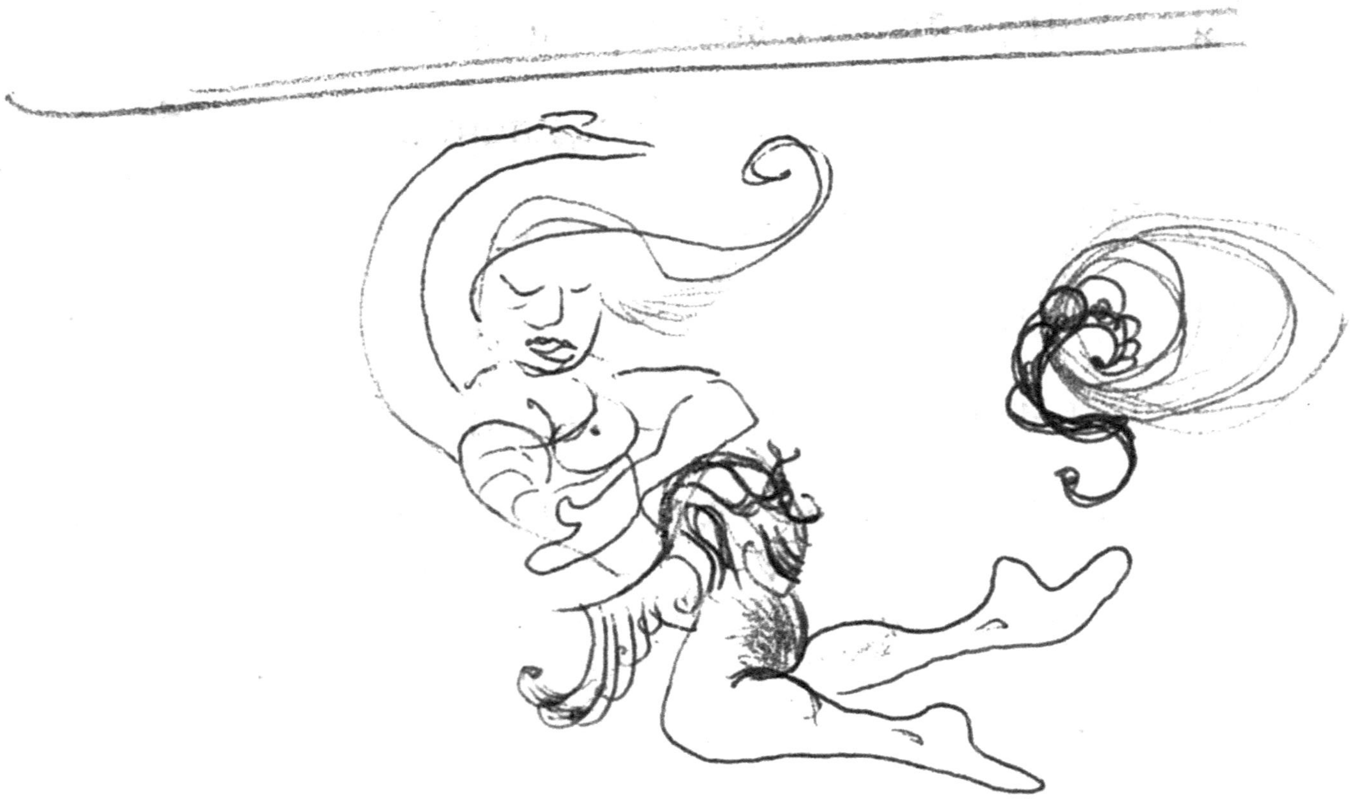

Why You should not Grieve, Daughter

Because she dreams...
In that time you cannot be,
Of golden yesterdays...
Of sad times, bad times,
Times of grief, despair, fret, worry
About you, about her,
About the others...

But mostly she dreams...
In that time when you cannot be,
A time that you cannot see...
A time where you will not be.
Do not worry,
Do not be sad,
Do not hang your
Head in grief
For her.

For she dreams...
Dreams of her future-present,
Beyond the here that is now,
In the now that is already
The other
Reality.

The reality which is to come
In the sharing of spaces
Only dreamt of.

As your mother lies dying,
Bind her not to you
With your envy for her dreams.
For...she dreams
Dreams of her tomorrow
Which is her today,
Which is her reality
In a space where
You cannot be.

Her round, vacant eyes,
Her wispy, straw hair,
Her rounded body...
Bloated with the milk-Life Force
Of a new beginning; which is her
reality,
Which is her new tomorrow
Which is her now.

Smile with her, gently,
When she returns to you,
As you would
The newborn.

For your mother is that.
In that space where you cannot be...
In the heart that is tomorrow,
Which is today
Which is
Yesterday.

* * *

26th. September 1988

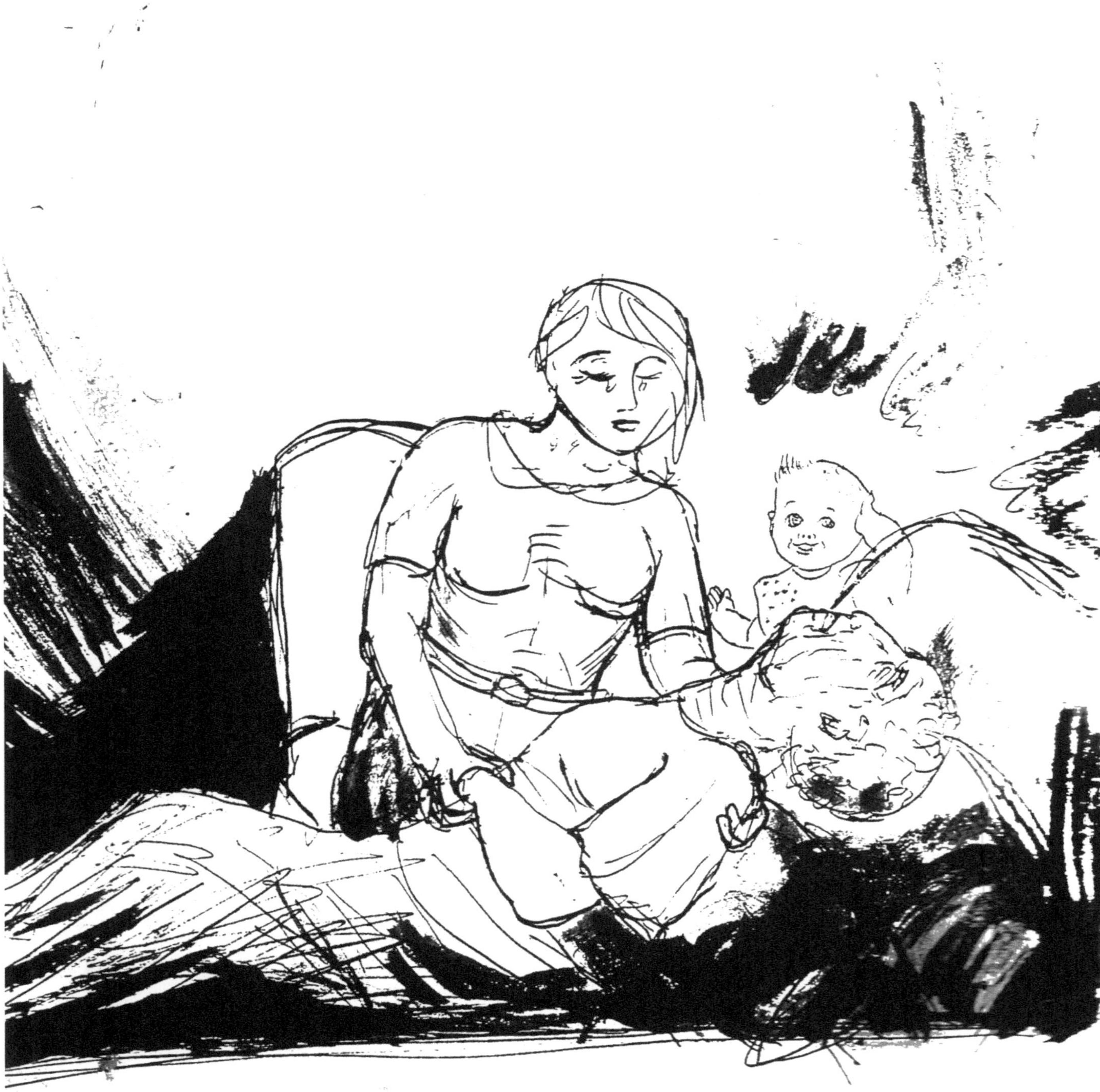

A bit of Contrary Nonsense- The Vampire Tale

The vampire came down like a wolf on the fold,
Its talons were gleaming in purple and gold.
"Oh look at those sheep and look how they bleat,"
It said to itself, "I'm sure they've no teeth,
And e'en if they did, they're not in the way,
I'm sure they can't speak, they'd have nothing to say!
So quick! Let me run in and tackle a few,
I'll suck on their blood while they drink up the dew.
They'll not feed on me, I'm a vampire, you see!"

So quick as a stoat without snarling a note
He leapt on one' s throat
As down through the air he did float.
The poor startled sheep who'd been wading a creek
Ceased being meek and started to shriek!
"Vampire! Vampire! Vampire! Get it while it's hot,
Snuffle it and gargle it and like it quite a lot.
Squoshle it and tenderise its meat,
And goo-goo it and ga-ga it and lick it while it's sweet!
And when at last we've mangled it and got out what we should,
We'll put it in a big hot pot and tell it it's been rude.
For, silly vampire, lovely vampire, it had temerity, you see,
It thought it could, it thought it should be like humans to me!"

"Ye-e-e-s," bleated one old sheep mum,
"I had a vampire once, I treated it like a son.
He thought he should, he thought he could,
Make me quite a dunce;
But I know what's right and I know what's wrong,
You can't teach an old one some new song!
So I put him in the grinder and blended him for tea,
He came out looking lovely, quite as yucky as can be!"

So saying, all the sheep ran off home to their keeper,
Who knackered all of them or ate them up for dinner.
The moral of this tale (I promise it's not long,)
Is, if you want to be a teacher- keeper make sure you're named St. Peter,
Not a sweeter purple vampire eater.

(Acknowledgements to Lord Byron)

* * *

22nd. December 1988

On the Environment

The Ayatollah Khomeini
Died on the eve
Of World Environment Day.
So, I'll spin a tale from that.

Earth has holes that show
Our mismanagement,
Like black fleas
Devouring to our detriment
All that she gives
Towards our increment.

For the sun to shine
From a clear blue sky
Must Gaia enclose man
In her womb again?

Once more, all savaged to behold,
A being, who renounced
Its own freehold
Now has nowhere else
But death to go.

Oh man.....
In your rubbish heap
Of self-hate, learn to rate
The human race,
Or life itself
Must turn its face from you.

Know that the child within
You and me
Lives also in trees,
The wind, the sea.
And drips rain on leaves.

Caring
Heart
In
Loving
Doingness.

The land's the thing
By which we find
The substance of the king.

* * *

5th. June 1989

An Urge for Wild Spaces

Piping in the woodland creatures,
Easy, as we go,
See the woodlands ring with children
Coming to and 'fro.
We are children, yes we are,
Children of the morning star,
Children of the twinkling groves,
Children of the snowy blasts.
Laughing on the breeze,
Flashing through the trees,
Finding in the fields
The sum of all our needs.

* * *

October 1989

Bathed in the Nascence of the Now

Bathed in the nascence of the now
I push my body thoughts away
To gaze, entranced,
Into space
And what it contains.

This is ecstasy....
The ecstasy of the now.
With a mind uncluttered
By preconceptions, precepts,
Concepts, mindsets
I gaze
Into brilliant space.
Each plane is already
Brilliantly contained;
Handled by nature.

What do I have to do?
Not for me to paint the shadows
On the gum trees;
To bathe their leaf tips in light,
Turn on his headlights
For the passing motorist;
Bend the branches into shape.

But I sit in absolute delight,
New, refreshed,
Rivetted by
The actuality of the now,
As I did when
Newly a child
My mind uncluttered
By thought....
That great imposition
On freshness.

Even this poem
Is,
But, through
Planting this realisation
I will
Plant it anew.

* * *

June 1992

Inner City Journeying

At Redfern Station, ferns matt gently,
Densely, writhing in an Intricate re-weave.
Mother Nature, that old Earth magnet,
Keeps her patterns ever young.
Warp and weft ever ready.
On they spring in time's winds,
Shamelessly on the rebound,
Ever waiting to re-form.
Some more train wheel revolutions,
Wondrous circle-lizard dance.
Koori art rebirth reclaims an Erskineville backyard.
Young and yellow t-shirted
Cavorting in bright bedrooms;
Cool studio walls a white man's front.

My father once lived in Haberfield,
But preferred the country.
Yet he came to Bondi to care for me in exam days.
Oh that I could push back the clock
So together, in that same restaurant
We could experience his old ambivalence to city ways.
Order, with sophistication present,
Artichoke Vinaigrette, and he the only one at table
Familiar with it.

Now I stare at grey restless seas as we once did together.
I sit at Ya- Habibi's, a different point in time;
And people stare at me as if I am on display...
An insecure lady, alone, writing, near a window.
Will I deter the customers?
My red- lipsticked down- turned mouth
An ambiguous statement on love and romance.

But you, Dad, loved people;
Loved all well enough
To come back for me.
So I undertake right now
To sit at Bondi Beach and love the wind;
Love just being here,
To talk in open good cheer
To fish shop men
And try not to be lonely
In the midst of life
Just as you
Would want me to.

* * *

1990s.

In Memory of Weary Dunlop

For you who follow duty,
Valour bore you to the halls of fame
That men and women in this wide brown land
Hold dear.

No question of despair,
To throw away each anchor point
And send each useless tear
Into the ground.
You held on fast to what you knew;
Compassion, honour in each human breath of life
Achieved against the odds
Of basal power plays…
Man's inhumanity to Man.

And of this end, this tiny end
Of this life's strand…
What greater plan do you perceive
To hold the faith for sons and daughters
Of those for whom you fought?

Perhaps you'd say-I do not know,
In war the path is clear….
And noble thoughts and hearts rise up,
Life's purpose very near.
But, for those who follow duty's call
And pledge yourself to service
Of man and womankind,
A nobler path unfolds for you….
A life of love and greater joy
Than dwells within the smaller cell
Of concentration on the self
And all things for the self.

No greater creed has any higher claim than this;
All faiths obtain this focus.
To follow duty, love, compassion,
Extending for the other –
Unites all disparate factions
And strengthens that
Of which we are all
A part.

* * *

August 1993

In Praise of African Ways

Circling roundwards, up She glides,
Circular eddies, up to the sky;
Ranting harshly, speaking wisely,
The heart of the mother,
The heart of the father,
The soul of the infant,
Of the wisdom within.

She stands at your door and knocks.
She reads the charms on your
doorposts.
They tell that it is a good day for mirth.

Miriam, goddess of water,
Fire, god of the desert.
Air, a dance in the sky,
As the ibis circles higher.

Circling roundwards, up She glides,
Circular currents, up to the sky.
Silently showing, seeking truth,
Your heart is the trumpet,
Your lips are her flute.

Circling roundwards, up she glides,
Into your attic, under your roof.
Oh rattle your gourds and water your
Seeds,
For the rain it is coming,
There's work to be done.

Circling roundwards up She glides,
There's fire in your belly and sweat on
your brow.
Your hands are not calloused,
For She's licked them clean,
And all, it is growing,
Not a weed to be seen.

Circling roundwards, up She glides,
Your roof knows no mercy,
She's into the sky.
Your wife will give birth,
Thank heavens for that;
Relax at the hearth,
There's room for a chat.

Circling roundwards, up She glides;
The seeds have all grown
There's mirth to be sown.
So drink and be merry
All friends we be here;
My gourd is now drained,
With thanks for your ear!

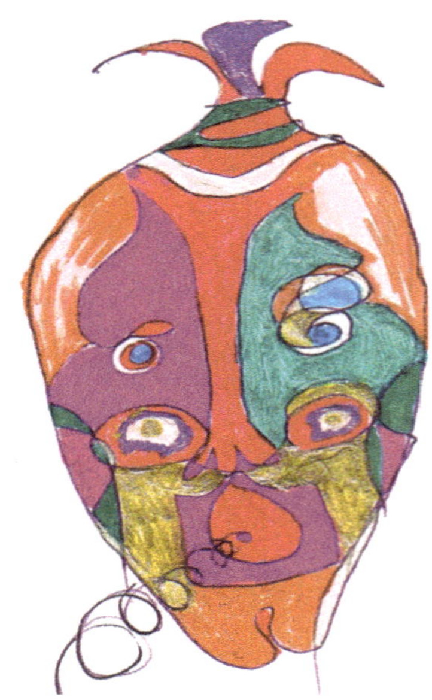

* * *

Mid 1990s.

Hologram

Suggestions of how...
Life could have been
Projected ... photons
To fill in ...
This empty void...
Left by the wrenching away
Of my sacral centre ...
A gaping hole
Where an abdomen,
Or, centre of power
Should be...
Nurturing me
And Thee ...
Sequentially...
Eternally...
Through our own
Timeline, pipeline...
Thence
Into
Mine.

* * *

1997

Fishing with an Empty Hook

A flock of sailing ships cutting and turning.
A line of them in Sydney Harbour,
Spaced out like a string of broken pearls.

Ten ibis fly in V formation,
Eight to the south east where I was born,
Two veer off to the south west.

They are in their element, but who am I ?
A misbegotten fool.

Here I am, replete with privileges:
Well fed, educated, loved
By Mum and Dad;
With no cause to complain...to,
With no blood ties to belong ....to
That have invested in me their future.
I feel big, awkward, clumsy...
Like a baby that has to be contributed to.

It is something set in concrete...
An evil spell.

It is called a generational thing.
It is stalled, malfunctional energies;
An imprint going nowhere in time.

Meanwhile, purposeful life
Goes on all around me:
Lithe, connnected, with mums and dads,
Aunts, uncles, cousins, nephews and nieces.
Alive and interconnected
In a breathing blood net...
A sparking, living thing,
Invested in the present and future
Because knowing its past.

***

It has a breathing matrix of connectedness
To its soul.
And by its own momentum can sweep
In its in-born protection
On to the future.

I, on the other hand,
Sadly free of that,
Like a country bumpkin,
Free to stumble into
A 19th. century industrial city...
Free to get lost,
Having claimed its right
To be alone
In the unrelieved grind
Of the meaningless material...
A shag on a rock.
Conspicuously malaprop.

I am every century's exile.
No, even less than that.
For an exile's pain is in
Knowing what he has lost....
And mine is in not knowing
As never having had.

Even the one who bore me
Said to me "What are you griping about?
You had parents who adored you!"
"That's not the point," I responded.

And, having done so,
I become the ungrateful lucky one,
The spoiled cuckoo in the nest,
Not accepting gracefully,
In a state of no grace.

* * *

20th. December 1998

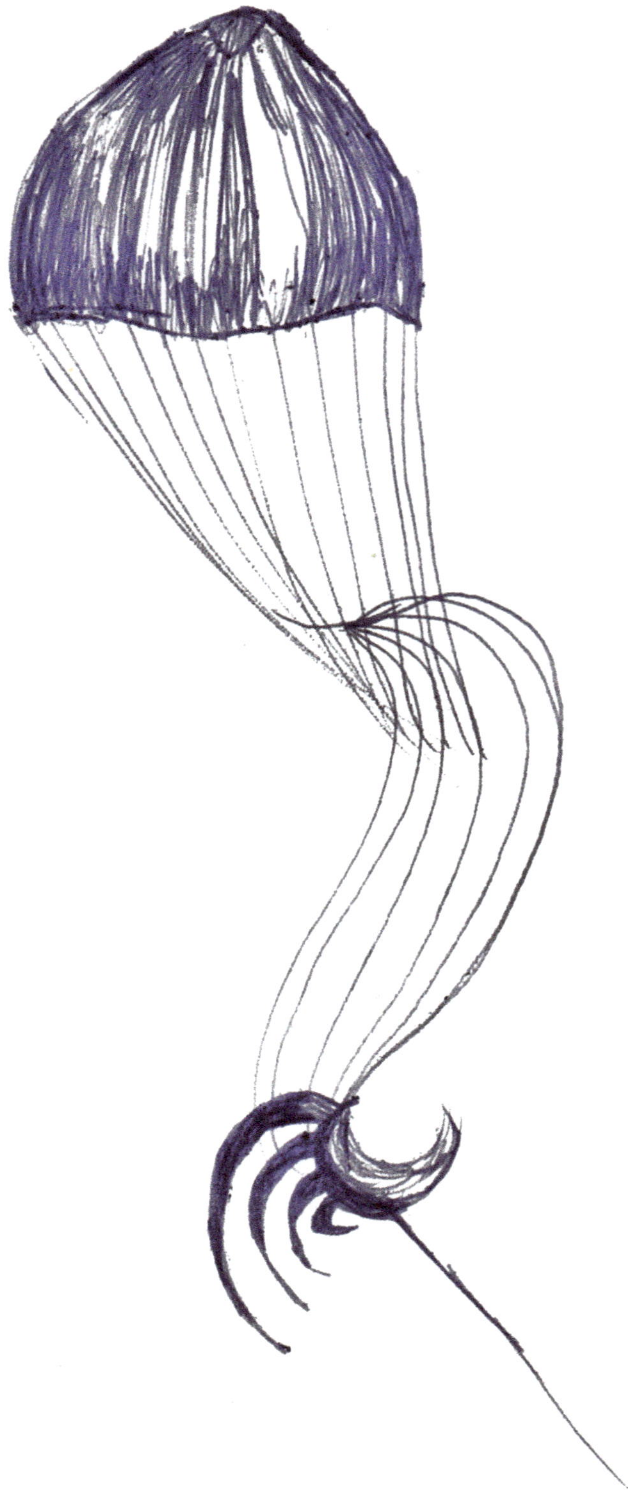

Adoption crisis

Praedatorius Innat'us

There is a predator in the heart of everyone,
Big or little, weak or strong.
It'll stop you from feeling free,
Prevent you from hearing your song.
It is the beast within, the beast without;
It senses weakness with its snout.
Of the exquisite rapture it has no doubt.
It's in for the kill as your blood flows out.

It's spite, revenge, jealousy,
Sudden cruelty – the dreadful hegemony;
Lunging from where- no conscious form;
Circling pressures within the dome,
Ready to strike when weakness displays
Its love for you; the tremulous gaze
Of trust and hope for closeness,
Of deepest bonding...in Love's remoteness,
But also its wild and most frozen space.

So remember, when you get sufficient clout,
What is within is also without;
What you can give you can also get;
Luminous tentacles around your neck,
Sucking strongly your blood away,
Eating you up 'till the break of day.
(It's called Jabba's place- just a breath away!)
It's making sure your dreams have all gone;
Your essence extracted...you're all alone.

What you will get is the predator's lunge
Striking into the heart of you;
Using your weakness as its grace,
Clawing the egg quite off of your face,
Stripping your essence of every trace
Of naïve trust in the human race.

When it's through you can have its chant –
You'll take it on as your own recant:
LIFE TO ME IS VERY SWEET,
WHEN I GET SUFFICIENT MEAT

* * *

2000

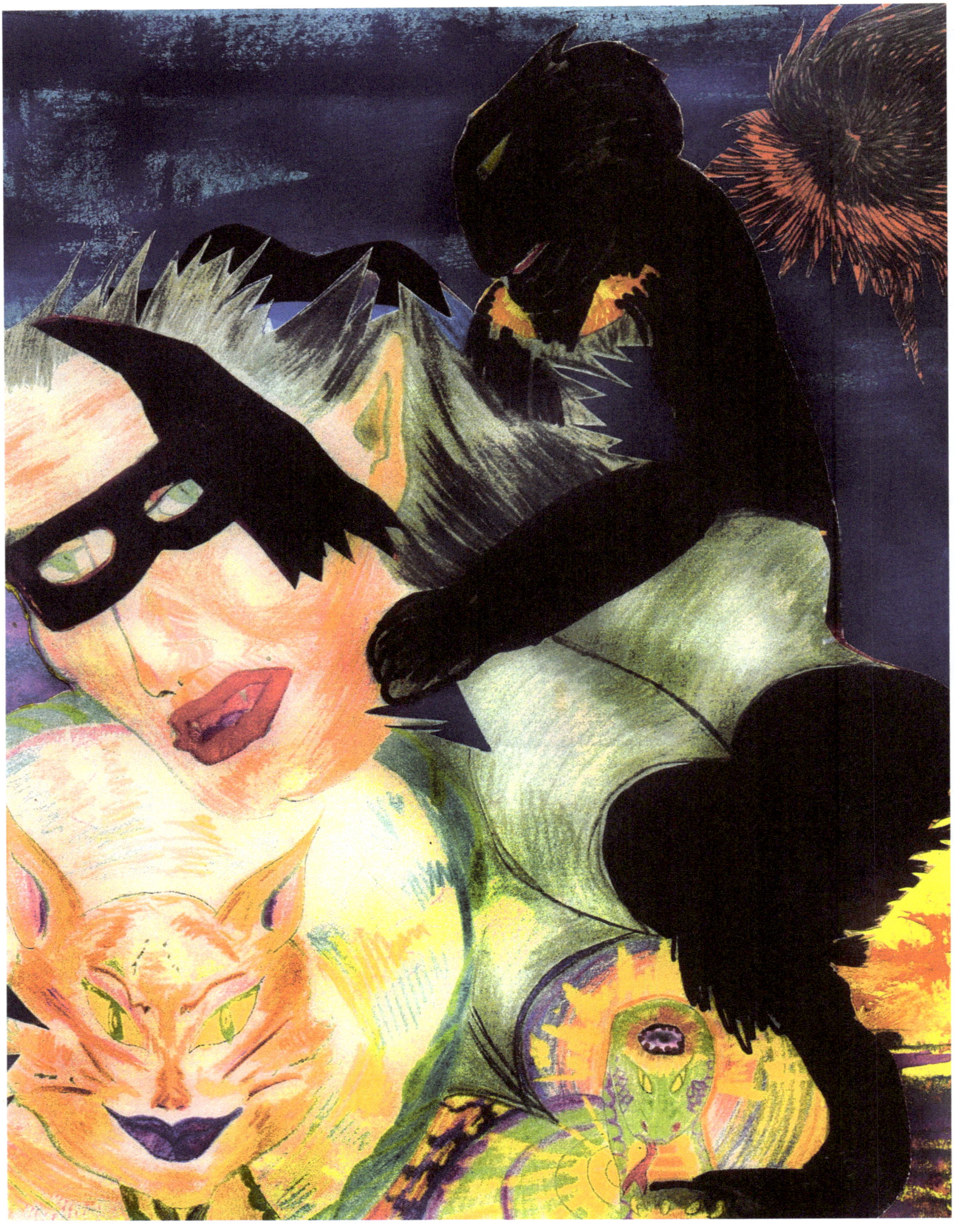

To Robert P.
-Astro post- talkus-

From time to time we sit and stare,
Perchance to dream, sometimes to share;
And in that sleep what dreams may come?
(And what is it the dreamer plumbs?)
Through the veil of illusion?
The Bardo of becoming?
Or that slip between
The walls of time
That tells no tale,
Accepts no wails,
That wags no tails of mourners.
Who, unless they
Read between the lines
Of their own pages...
Are left in dazes,
Mazes,
And phases
Of the kaleidoscope
Clutched in their
Own hands.

We should all show good cause
That we have
Moved fast,
And left
A well-lived
Corpse!

* * *

24th. April 2001

Trapped in the Machine

Trapped in the Machine, lost in primate machinations,
Howling, screaming, locked together
In gnashing, clawing horror.

Dreaming of the stars we are lost in the mire
Of our own frustrated passions:
Greed, love/lust, power, dominance,
Man's inhumanity to Man.
Self-serving, we chronically break our pious moral mouthings;
Fixed ideas for convention's sleeping sake,
Not worth the paper that they're written on.

Dying to slake our thirst for criminal use of each other
Like so many maddened chimpanzees
Tearing each other apart for their own advantage.

This happens as much in so-called civilised tea parties
As in the bantam pits where we bid
Animals do our mad destruction by proxy.

The horrifying truth is that every action can either pull us back
From, or propel us closer towards
Another turn on the karmic wheel.

Yet- just try to stay clear!
It's impossible down here.
Smiling faces turn ugly as power lust takes them over
And back-construction occurs on yesterday's words.
Deeds mis-translate due to the desire for covert control;
While false sentiments roll from the tips of tongues.

The bile of hidden scorn buried – once torn
Out into the open explodes with bottled up venom
Into the face of the one they now hate.

From love to hate…aggression without abate.

Untangling the skeins of samskara
Ever harder.

But we have Gold's clear light of self-observation
To play upon our actions
As the flames grow higher,
Plunging civilisation (now there's a misnomer,)
Into the danger of its own failure
To be truly
Humane.

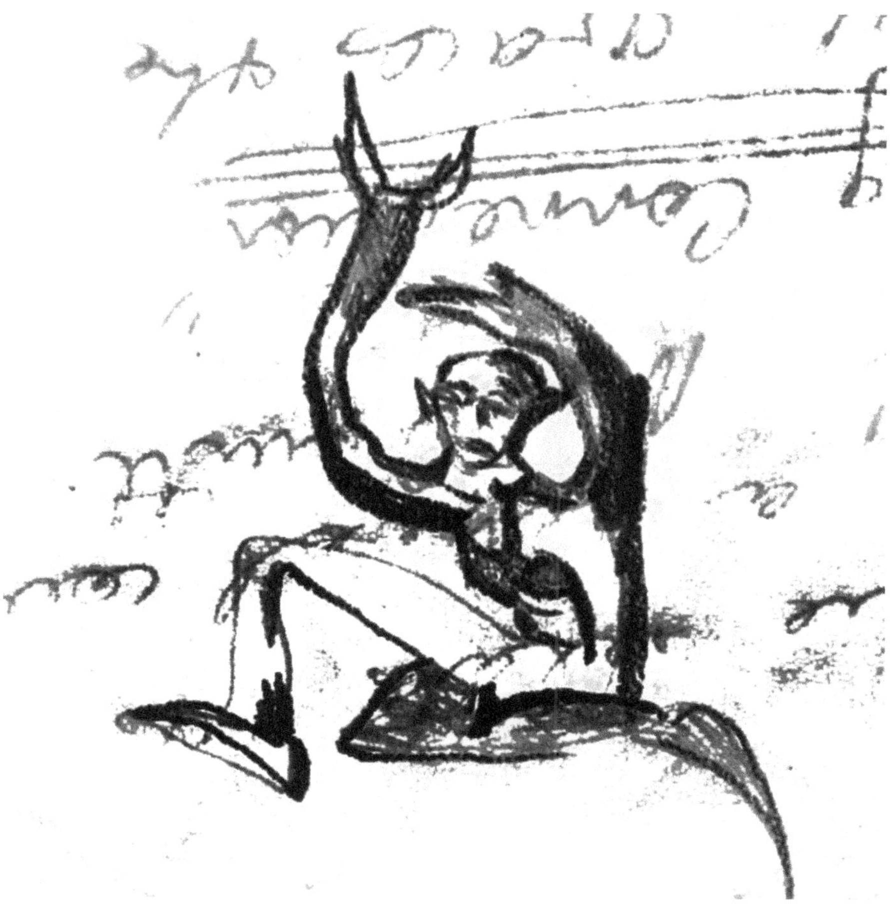

* * *

6th. January 2002

(Automatic Writing) Three Poems

I

John Lilly is Dead

The Fool is me and all things are the Fool.
Within me sally forth not perchance
With majesty's glance intact
But not that, this...within
Lies all states possible
And all men's dreams in nascent states
In disembodied chambers
For Fools to see and so rise forth
And you will see
Your face in Narcissus' still pool
Of cool reflection, Gaia's testing
Not by me or mortals.

Your fates arise thrice formed:
One the outer, one the Inner,
One transformed.

And you? Query not the eerie?
Dally you not the Dance
For forms half-formed that lie
Within you wait to be born
And torn and spawned to the grave.
You will get your chance
As dance leads on to dance.
The graves will give up their dead
To grow in the show
Of blossoming newborns aflow
With the promises they have
Already made.

* * *

II

Tarot

I throw a spawn of Tarot.
They tell me not to dally;
They manifest without
What really lies within
The half-enshrouded white mists
Of memories and genesis
In the half-land state
Where dreams are made
In the shadows of your mind,
In the wake of your days,
In your soul's budding
Is the growing, forming thing,
Time out of sight.

The cards fall and do they form without
Or will we reach inside out
To, with all our might, take them in
To spare us the impossibility
Of single-pointed manifestation
Of 'The' (is it only one) High Priestess
And Temperance must surely be just at the show point
In the gymkhana of your arena
To spare your manifestation and reactions
Look into your future.

Potters' elements can be manufactured
Without. Born with
And without a pure heart.

* * *

III

Fairy Tales

Enable us freedom from fairy implants.
In truth, 'fairytales' reflect and show
The many I's within.
In their constant interplay, intercourse,
All ways and always.
The many-headed monster
Is the clearest indicator,
As Hercules fights and wiles his way
To the princess within us all.
The male, the female, the monster,
The saviour, the rescuer, the dancer,
The lancer, the satyr
Who know
That all this is
The truth.

* * *

9th. November 2002

Cats
-A poem for my young niece-

Nothing is softer than a cat,
And that's that!
Caress her fur,
Her soft bluely green eyes
Melting into mine
With love and trust.

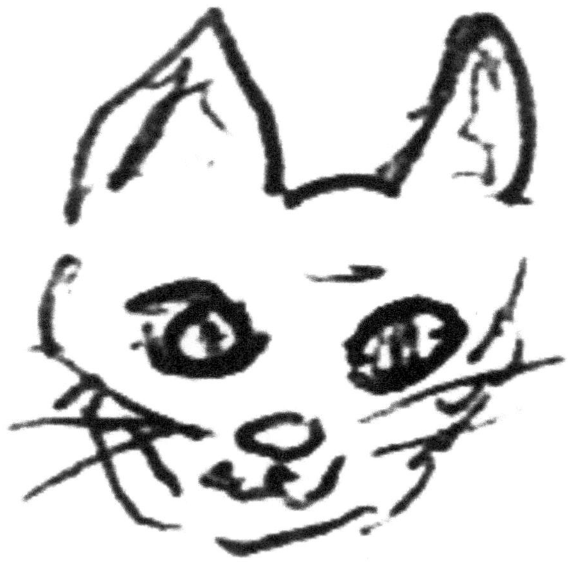

I really mmmmust….
Buy her some frisky biskies
Right now!

Sharper than pins
Dig her little claws
If thou durst
Mishandle her.
So, handle her gently,
Miaow- wow at her intelligence
And kindness
And that is what she will give you back
Instead of her pack
Of needle sharp claws.

Never forget
That she is a lion,
In herself.
Although you belong to her,
She knows she is yours
Based only on love
And her own giving
Oneness with you,
Her loving friend.
So do treat pussy with love,
Do treat pussy with care,
Be there for her
As she is for you!

* * *

16th. August 2003

On the Occasion of the Death of my Great Aunt Muriel

In the still pool of water reflects the moon who is our brethren;
Shining still and gleaming forth…like a pearl of hope for the future.
Regret for the past….but ever the waves move on, and in ripples of time
We all come from a common source, and as drops of water
Will return to the great source, call it what you will,
Or will o' the wisp…the old Scottish tunes abound with the names of possibilities
And of certainties that life is, indeed, a circle- the eternal theme;
Birth, Love and Death…genesis of old and of all.

Poetry the seat of the soul and with song, heart's balm…
For it is in death that our timely reminders of life and of all things loved
Are most heartfelt, state….with me let go of the sadness, insist on the positive!
For it is that and that alone which springs forth new hope, new life, new trust, new All!
Let go the sarcasm, the anger, the greed, the guilt, to remove death's sting.
For death's strictures are complete and its laws know no evasion.
In death do we trust, so that life can be re-known.

* * *

11th. August 2003

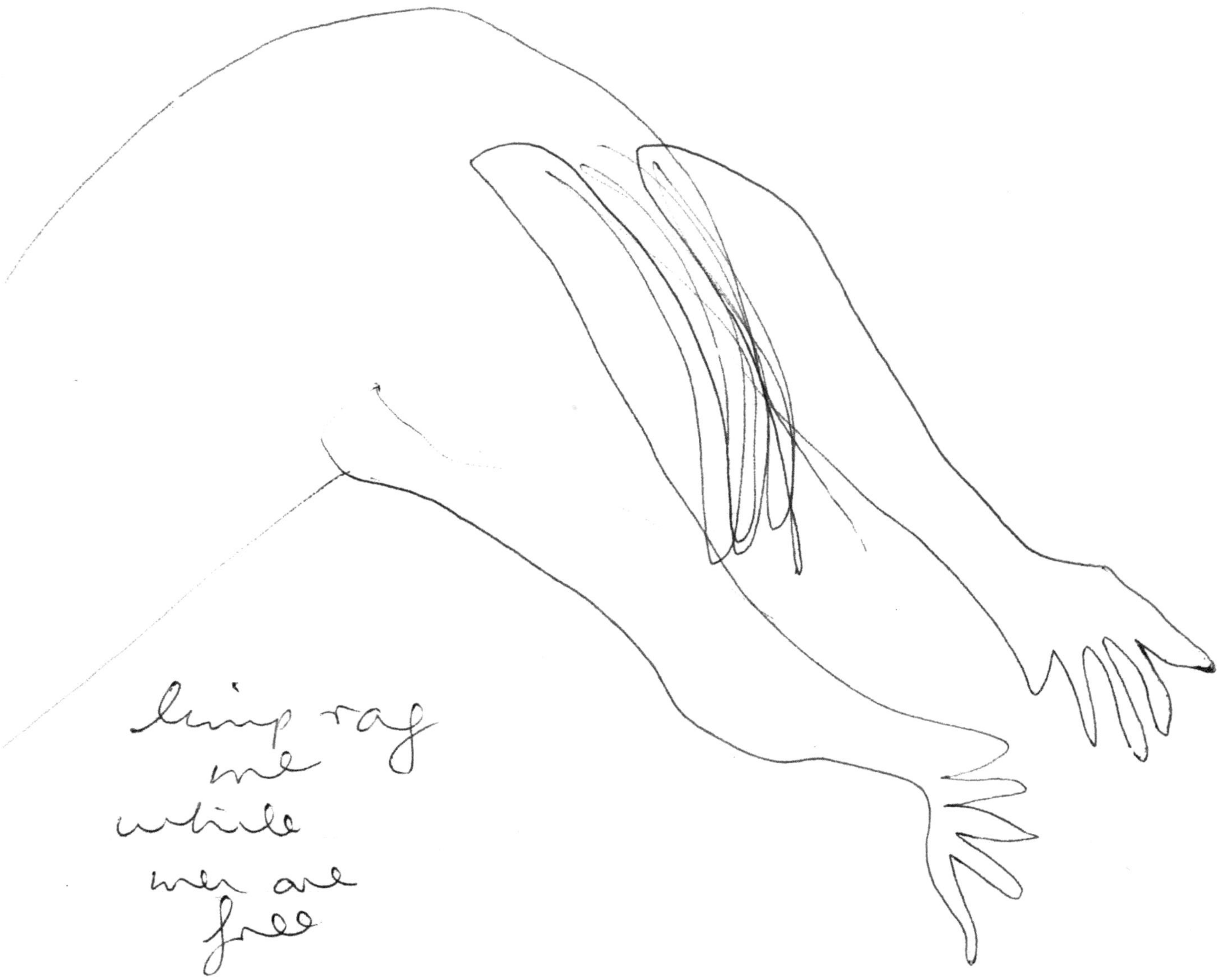
limp rag
me
while
men are
free

John Paul II is Dead

Well, John Paul II is dead,
And, for a while he had me considering
Why no condoms?
Because human sexuality is a deep mystery,
And this means, to a pope born May 18th, in the sign of the bull,
That one should simply obey and stubbornly abstain.
And that would stop the spread of AIDS and other STDs.

And it would prevent 'disappointment'
If you did not have sex before marriage.

Yesterday I thrust a post office ad magazine
Down onto a black granite bench
To sop up some coffee puddles.
This morning I tore it off.
It had stuck to the bench,
And my tearing produced ribbons of torn paper
Still stuck to the bench,
Like a human heart, which, once
'Stuck like glue' on you
Is sharded, frayed, nebulised into
Molecular lonely fragments
Spinning off into a galaxy of despair,
No hair, you not there.

Disappointment? Loneliness? Entrapment of your soul
In the other's casual leavings?
Yes, I have known all these,
As sex becomes all things
To all persons, and sometimes love.

* * *

3rd. April 2005

Let Me Not Be a Bad Baby

Let me not be a 'bad baby.'
Let my cries
Reach, to the skies,
That I
Am
I

* * *

1st. May 2005

The Day is the Reason for the Night's Descent

The shadows are lengthening, the colours are tonalling
Into still dark pools
Whose boundaries, only spidery, are as moving branches.

There is hope in this decision to change
From the sunny certainty of Noon
Into the wavering lack of resolution
Of slow descent into gloom.

There is boredom in certainty.
It is a clear-cut clinician's pattern.
Not slipping between the cracks here,
Square is square.
The sun – traditional symbol of the intellect-
And Reason,
Rides daily in Apollo's chariot;
Describing all boundaries.

I prefer Night's velvety offerings
Of moonlight, glimmer and innuendo
Into instinct's whirlpool;
The throbbing pulse, birthplace of all such gestations.

I foresee a not-too-distant time
When my life, all circumscribed by its strictures,
Like a blood-pressure sleeve
Enwrapping me
In the shroud of my experiences
Will take a dive
Into that night
That is beyond despair-
That old gatekeeper to the truth.

* * *

16th. August 2005

Channeling from Oscar (Wilde, of Course!)

Oh, I see you dear boy in your pink,
You really kick up quite a stink.
You need nannies to soothe you
And bovvers to bruise you,
You scream and you poo and you sick!

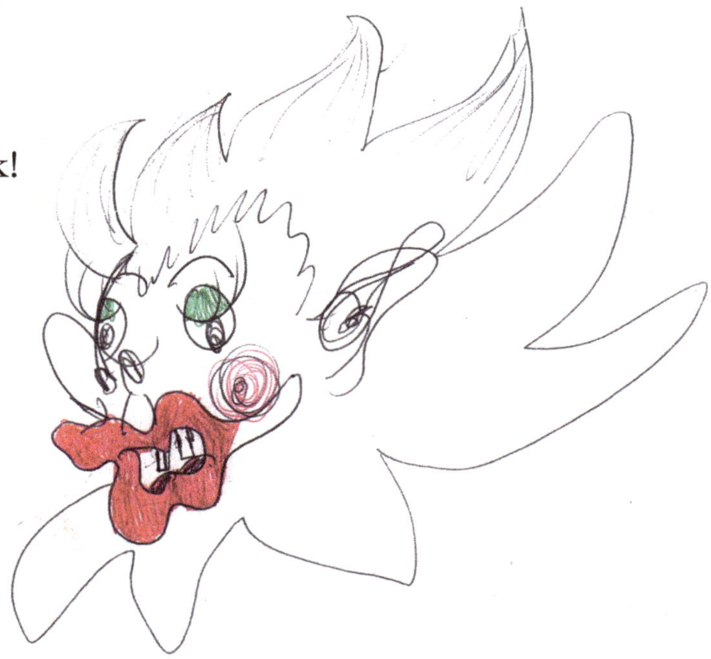

But I wonder, dear boy, it it's true,
If that 'nana you eat isn't you?
As you learn to tell tales,
And avoid, like a 'gator,
One would think you're a primate,
Or even a raptor
In cunning confusion
Deceit and false rapture
At twisting the truth quite askew!

I'm quite puzzled, you see, 'cause I think….
You're not me 'till I stand near the mirror;
Then the truth always sets me aquiver
For what I am seeing…
Is you.

***

The One Song

The squall of the infant
Beats and resonates
The heart strings
Of the entire Universe-
The One Song.

***

3rd. July 2006

Poem for Life in Death

Brown oak leaves lie together,
In death a dead fit.
Jigsaw-like.
They enable, through their fit-together,
The living to walk effortlessly
Over the mud;
As perfectly intertwined,
Indistinguishable now
In the matrix of Earth's
Previous generations.

Morphogenic fields resonate
Their love and well-fittedness
To us, still,
Resonating in each glow
Of our energy field;
Resonance after layered resonance;
Sounding the beat of blood
That will rush not only through us
But onwards.... not only to 'ours'
But through every living being
Like wind-swept leaf mounds
Cushioning the path of all generations
Filtering out the
Randomity of chance mutations;
For even they mulch down quite easily...
The levelling of compost, eh?

Good, bad or indifferent
We breathe as trees do;
Our encysted patterns
Quivering through the ages;
For sparks to be struck off
In some distant
Resonant heartbeat
Of the stages of Man
Hopefully kind.

* * *

7th. July 2006

Guillames at Bennelong

While the tyranny of mobile phones
Compel some to attic poses,
Joggers break all forms
Whilst I dine at Guillames
On Bennelong,
Summoned by the lure
Of Valery Gergiev,
The great Russian Master
Conductor
Of
My
Heart.

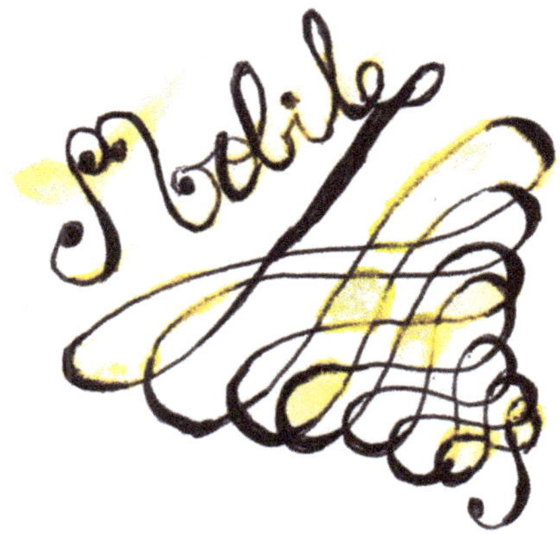

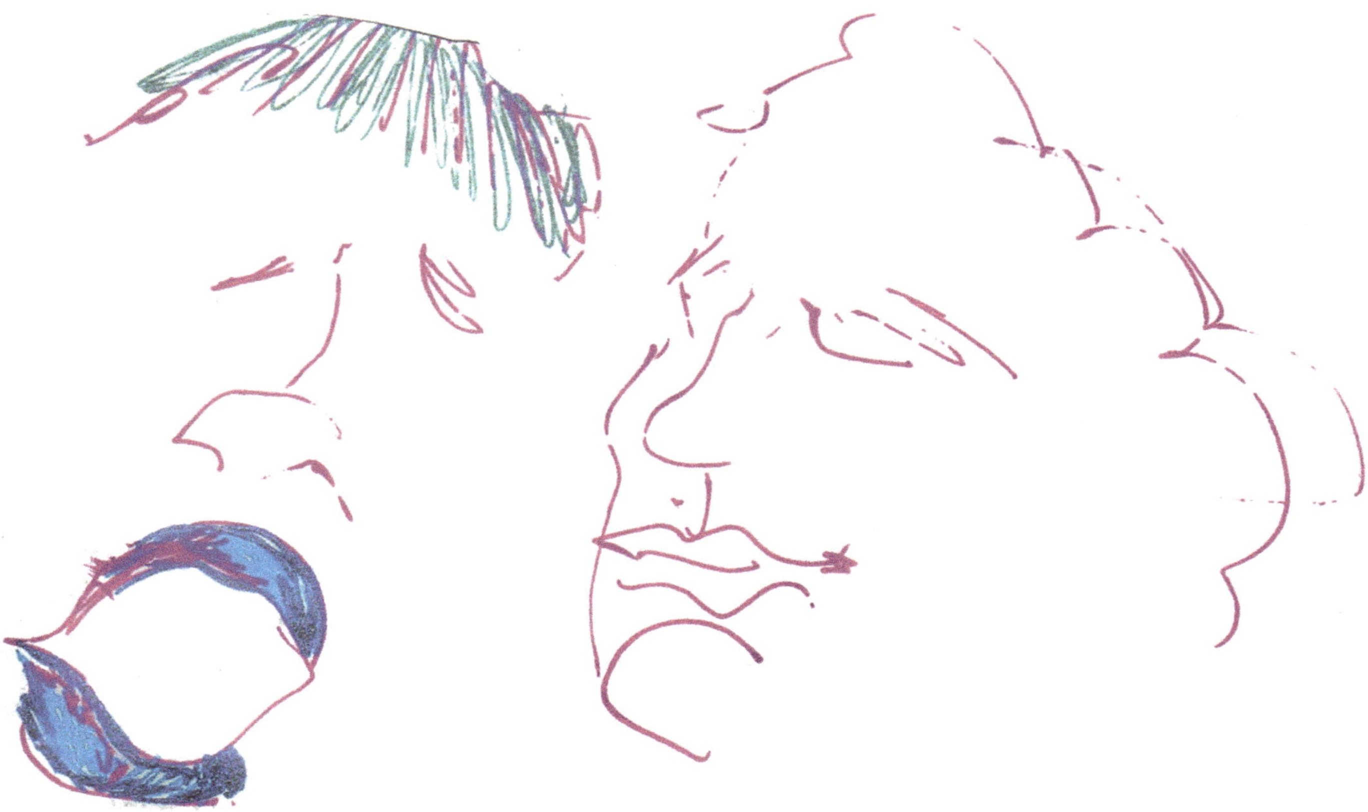

* * *

28th. September 2006

Sunday Poem

In this park of lovely spaces
I see I have been a good mother
And a partner of many chances,
Both of giving and of getting.

This cuts both ways…
It is lucky and also
In the space
Of becoming.

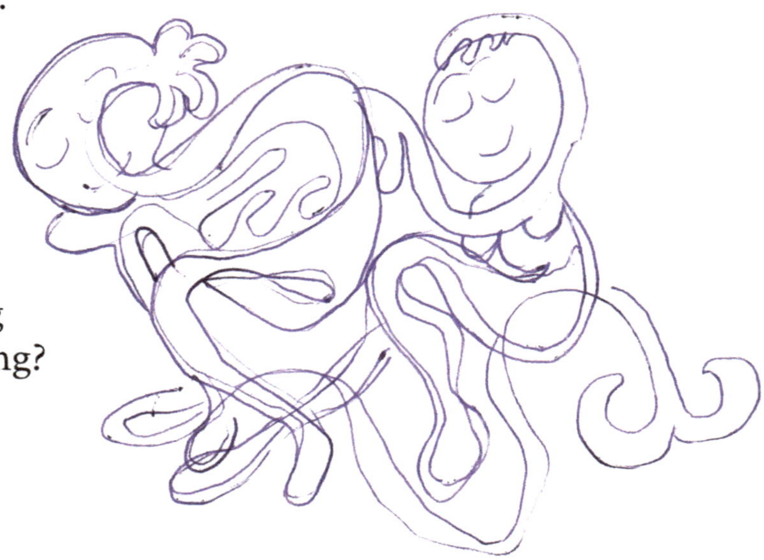

Which also has
Two meanings.
Can you ***be*** becoming
Whilst you ***are*** becoming?

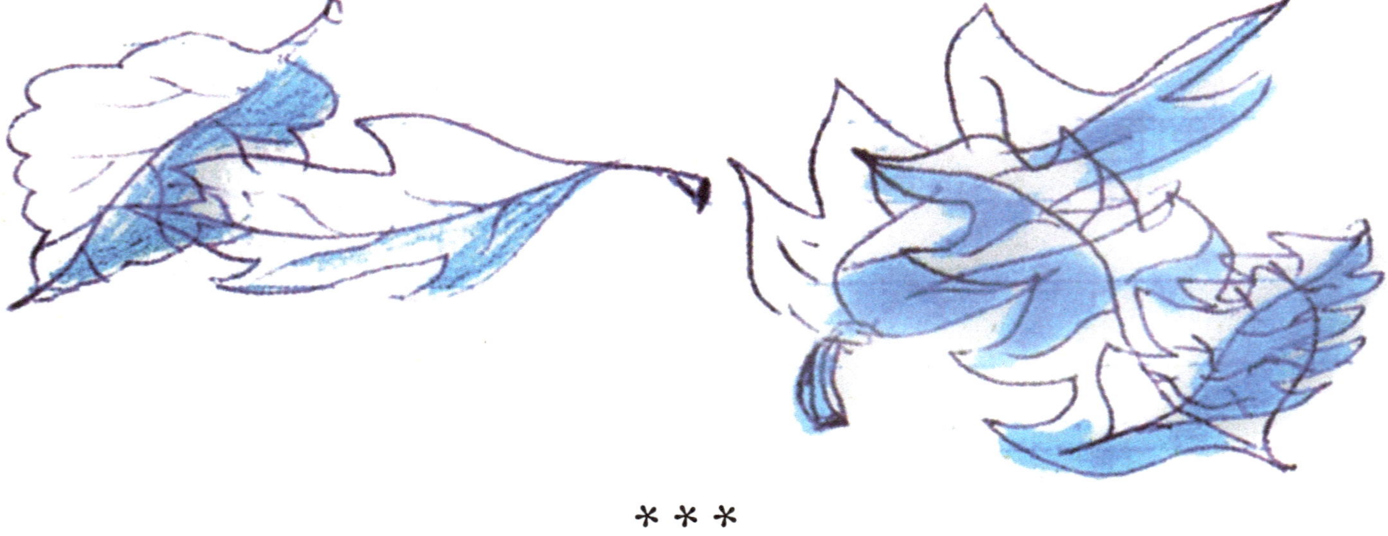

* * *

5th. November 2006

Me

Sitting in my bed
Arranging the pillows
Behind my back
I feel 14 again.
As if being 55
Was all a
Horrible dream
And once again
I am
An eager
Girl.

* * *

1st. October 2007

A Poem to Grace at A Lake's Social Club Xmas Party

A Xmas party so bleak,
We were not offered a seat!
So, upon an outer bench so meek
The company of Grace did seek.

No room at the Inn, we cried!
Then eight sound chairs espied,
When Grace the villains despised
She arose, the trouble to meet.

Those villains she did greet,
And upon their brows did beat;
Until at once, all shamed and 'sweet'
They finally offered us a seat,
And, full of their salad and meat
We sang and laughed and danced.
With Grace we were entranced,
Our new friend, our saviour, our mate,
Who'd ensured us both a plate.

"We're real people here," she said to me,
A glint in her eye as my soul she espied,
She saw my grief and who I was
And laughingly said "Scorpio is Boss!
They're afraid of me here,
Their bullshit I hear and them I don't fear.

Aboriginal I am,
I've birthed six kids.
Two at the Boong camp in Emerald;
Two of my sons are in jail."
She said, throwing back her ale,
"And...without fail,
I punt, I drink, I smoke, I tell a tale.
Welcome to the Anti-Social Party
At Noon tomorrow...
It'll be my treat,
You can be sure to have a seat!"

* * *

16th. December 2007

Babs Died Yesterday

It's not quite 24 hours since Babs died.
What is death?
A release, says Babs, or, at least, I.
What is grief then? Says I.
No release,
But an increase of pressure.

Babs died yesterday and I grieve.
'Tho she is relieved
From pain and suffering
I hope into the joy and purity
Of her own happy youth.

Babs died yesterday
And I write this through
A wall of tears.
Even tho' I feel
Her loving arms encircling me
And my poor bruised heart.

And some of the events of the past
Few days make sense.
Of how I bared my heart to her son
And talked completely openly to him
Of how he'd been my partner.

Babs died yesterday
And I feel peace,
And love perfected
Beyond the barriers
Of the human body
Through which the heart
Can shine
But dully, sometimes.

Babs died yesterday,
And I am grieving for her,
That's all.

* * *

18th. March 2008

The Flight of the Phoenix

-A Poem Written in Reflection after Viewing this Movie Starring James Stewart

We sit in the desert In God's eye.
We struggle with our lives
As flies on a speck of sand
Beneath the sky.

Against all odds,
In the lives we live
In the face of all meaninglessness:
Frustration, aridity, failure,
We seem to come to a purpose
Only when all hope is gone.
If, then, we push on....
Will we ever get airborne?

And what will we see
When we are finally free?

* * *

19th. October 2008

Married I Marred

Married

I

Marred

* * *

13th. December 2008
(Acknowledgments to William Shakespeare)

Creation

I wish happiness
On this bright day
To all primates great and small,
For the great God Mother
Made them all.

Each little smile that blossoms,
Each little hand that grasps;
She made their tiny consciousness,
She made their big fat ass.

All thought slight and slothful,
All people great and small;
All wars dark and turbulent,
The primates made them all.

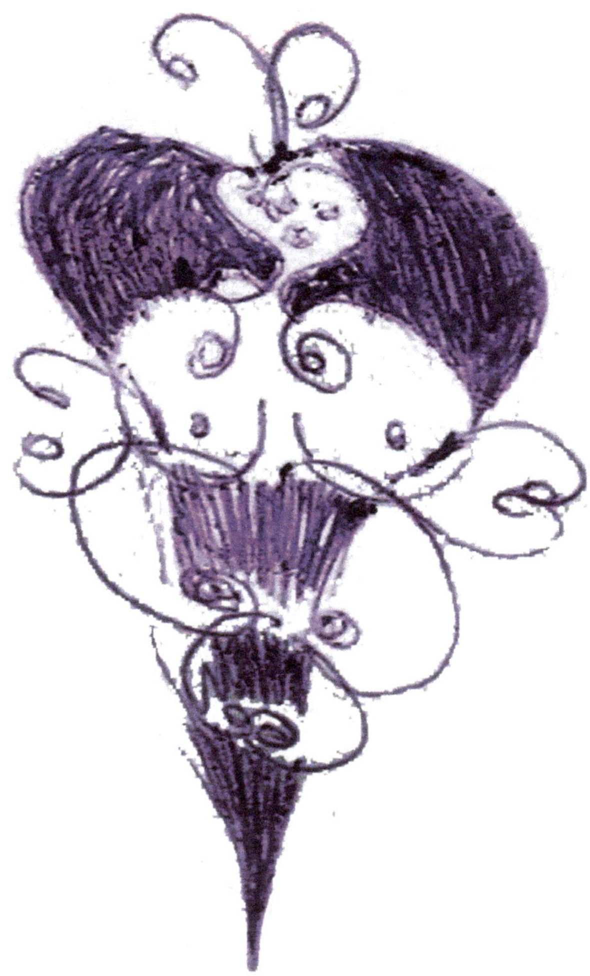

* * *

28th. March 2009

For Milvena of The Titanic

Above all imagination
When on the docks they stood,
The pinnacle achievement of man's industry;
The braggadocio of the name
Enough to deter one woman
"It flew in the face of God" she claimed.
But 'unsinkable' is as it does, she knew,
And stayed awake that night,
To save her family, in God's eye
When all had took to flight.
Milvena, Milvena, Milvena,
Rocked in the arms of The Titanic.
How great in the security of those arms
Was the promise.
Milvena, Milvena, Milvena,
The slap of the waves did say
In your mother's mind
As she sang to you that day.
But in the night, in terrible hours,
The plight of man she saw....
Tiny, puny, helpless, in the great sea's maw.
Milvena, Milvena, Milvena,
Rude descent in a sack,
While all man's dreams of glory
Were set quite soon aback.
Your life span near to a century,
Just one, no miracle there,
And now in the twenty-first
We've grown quite used to despair,
As towers fall around us
We glimpse death's forward charge
On its white horse Apocalyptically
As the once feared sea,
Denuded now of vitality,
Becomes a carbon sink
To watch us all slip silently
Beneath the waves
Of our own stupidity
And free Titan Earth
To live again.

* * *

1st. June 2009

Written on the death of Milvena Dean (15.04.1912 ~ 01.06.2009), last survivor from The Titanic.

The Stones Sit there Unreaching

The stones sit there unreaching,
The bush soars up,
Its branches reaching out,
Every leaf strained
To greet
Wind, rain and sun.
The blossoms sit,
Elegant, comfortable.

* * *

June 2009

Reflections on the Coming Copenhagen Conference on a Blood Red Day

It was a real wrath of God day today....
The air over the Sydney Harbour Bridge
A hundred percent orange.
From Tibooburra to Wollongong.
Elsewhere in Sydney
The sky is blood red
Due to the loss of
Millions of tons
Of topsoil from
NSW farms.

And two earthquakes occurred
In Melbourne.

The air, pink, enhancing the cherry
Blossoms before me,
I photographed the park;
Its bowl full of soft Spring rain,
The rhododendrons pulsing
With the hope of their coming bloom.

In Copenhagen
The air is blue,
But cooling.

I wonder if their speeches
Soon will stop the death
Of all we see today;
Our blood stretched out before us
As our farmers' life blood stands before us
A silent sentinel. How odd.

We see our future in sepia tones,
Our future seed
Dashed and dry
Withering to nothing
In the soils of our hopes.

Old men cricketers in their whites
Rub their fingers gingerly along
Reddened shrubs.
As if Narrabri may now be in reverse gear,
The dust on leaves, now, not under foot.

Parents talk and put on circuit
Their teens' eyes, rolling like a cow
Who has taken fright
Seeing with their own eyes...
And I remember Narrabri.

Old cattle dog
Beside The Great Western Highway
Confused...thinking he is beside a
Wide, empty country road.

I gently beeped my horn to remind him.
He grinned at me with recognition,
Now half-larrikin spirits touching.

And I think that both he and I
Remain bonded,
In memory of Narrabri.

* * *

23rd. September 2009

Poem for Margarite on Her Birthday

Just as Spring
Breaks through
Each year
Without fail,
May each new season
Be
For you,
A new tide
Of hope's
Renewal.

* * *

12th. October 2009

The Blood-Stained Carpet
- Reflections After a TV Crime Show

The blood stain was on the carpet.
Someone had had the presence of mind
To quickly mop it up where it mattered.
The green expanse.
Leaving the rest
In its
White Mondrian golden mean,
For Forensics.

Where does one slaughter end
And life begin
In the forest fabric
Of our existence?

* * *

17th. October 2009

What is the Solution to the World's Problems?

A bombe or a bomb?
A bombe is a melon-shaped or round
Mould filled with ice-cream;
It is rounded and curved outward.

A bomb bay is a compartment
In the fuselage of a bomber
In which bombs are carried
And from which they are dropped.

To indulge in a Bombe Alaska
Requires you
To
Be aware of
The difference.

* * *

6th. November 2009

I Have Turned 58

I have suddenly grown old
And a small cry gestating in my mind
Seeks the person I should tell.

But there is no-one.
My mother... but no;
My cry rang out half faulted
For she is gone.

And my cry reached out to empty space
With just the shadow trace
Of a half-life
Presence.

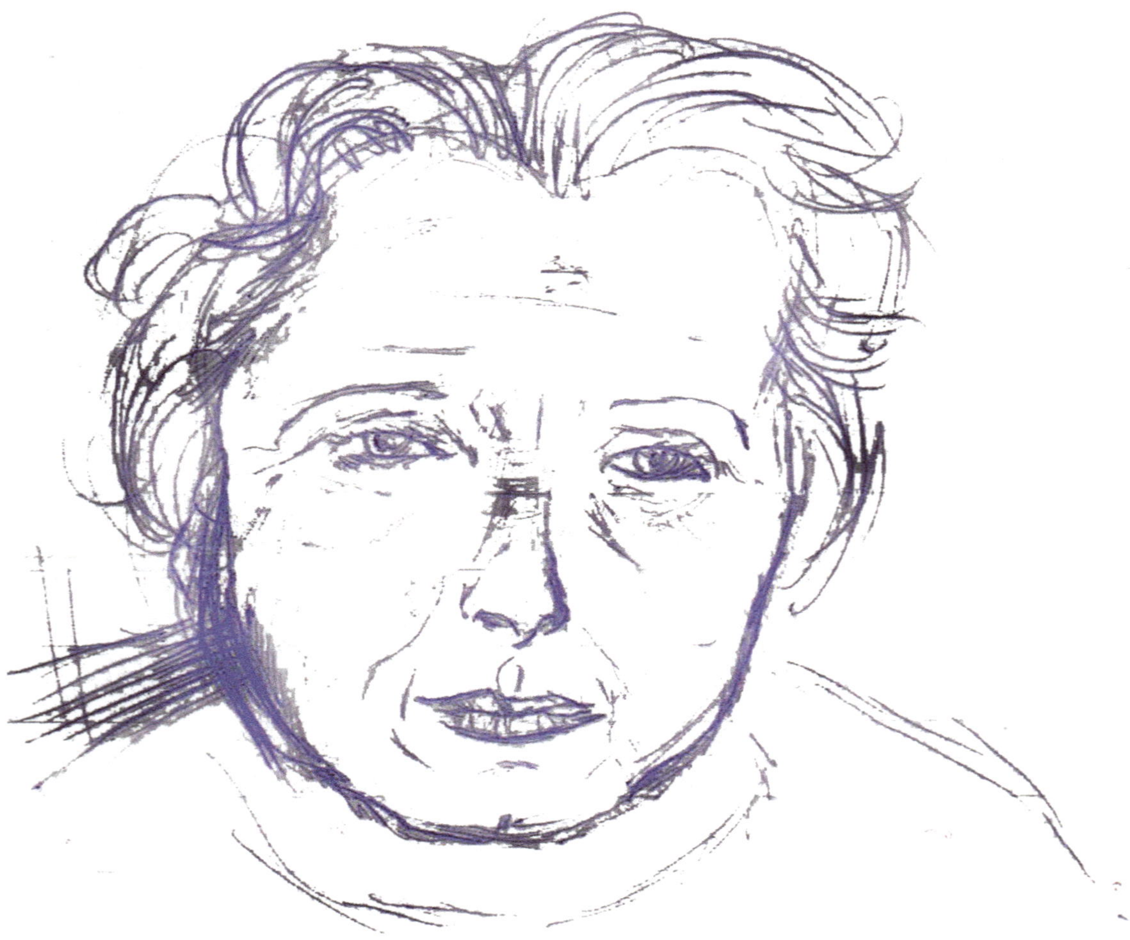

* * *

27th. April 2010

How Can the Child be Me?

How can the child be me?
I was once that foetus child
Already netting memories
To make up me;
Most sticky memories,
Papier-mache
Do not make me,
However prettily
Stuck together like magazine patchwork
On a New Age art work.
Electronic impulses
Imprison me
In a salty sea;
But I am not me,
As I am not free
But only free to move.
But each pulse of outward movement
Circumscribes
To the end of its tether
And each return
A pulse of terrified abandonment.

Curled into that foetal shape,
Inside or outside;
Your womb
Shall not manage me.

* * *

12th. July 2010

It would be free

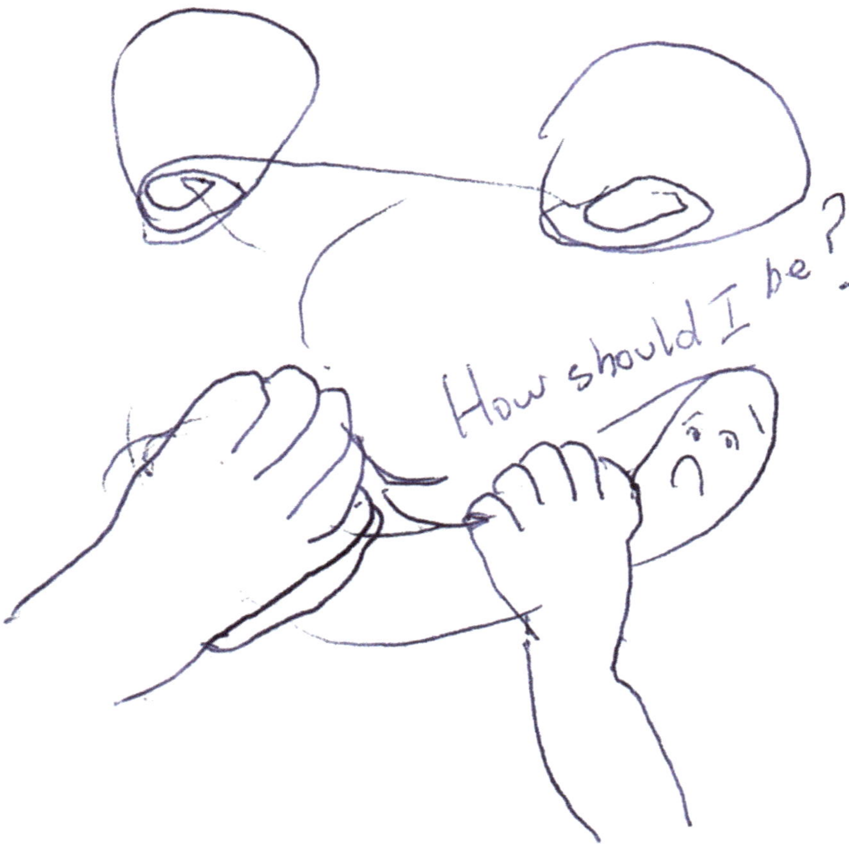

How can the abandoned
child baby be? As
Inside the womb of the world
It swirled

Kraken

Nine giant ichthyosaur vertebrae
Laid out in rows…
Stranded or strangled?
Nobody knows.
But arranged specifically,
In virtual mimicry,
A pattern – in his lair.

A self portrait of care…
Vertebra in double lines,
Circles like what, alone, he could see
Of himself…so queerly,
Himself…his suckers.

His way of reaching out
To the universe around…
Could he phone home?
Tell me, Kraken,
Were you showing me
That you, too, were alone?

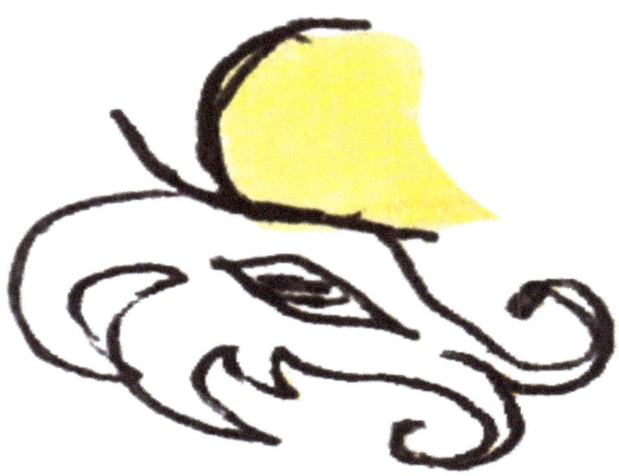

Reference: Article in Sydney's Daily Telegraph: Friday 14th. Oct. 2011 "An Octopus' Death Garden."

* * *

29th. October 2011

Poem for Margaret on Her Mother's Passing

In this time of loss
Remember rebirth;
Not just in every lifetime
But in every second, every hour.
For it is not only in
The big things…
But also in the small moments…
Slipping through the spaces
Of our consciousness
That Time and Moment
Are born.

* * *

15th. December 2011

She (1)

Her smiles
Like the waves
Upon the ocean
Bright
Wash all my thoughts
To flight
Of how
All and everything
Delight,
As one
In those joyous
Circular interplays
Of light flashing,
Circling, interweaving
All living stuff
Being made
On the patterns
Of Her smile.

* * *

12th. January 2012

She (2)

Meditation on a Disco Ball

In liquid still or dancing
The myriad diamond imps
Describe Her
Ever - changing fancies;
All knit, all knit.

And on her thoughts
All quiver
In depths so to respond
All to one another
In joyous loving throng.

No crystal is still-standing,
For, in harmony of dance,
Each particle resounding
While She
All entrancing
Spins the Universe's tale
Each particle enhancing.

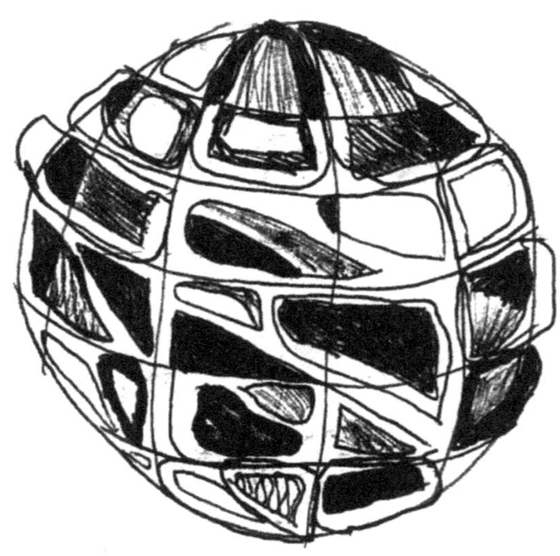

* * *

12th. January 2012

Swimming Carnival

There are dinosaurs on the roof
And paedophiles use binoculars from flats.
Mynahs line up in their ranks
In a queue for food.
With my time up, a covert smirk
Caught from a school bus...
Quite a lurk.
A teacher fleeing.

A toddler cries
With a backwards
Tear for a wading pool too near
To forget yet,
As his hunched shouldered mother,
Her duty done,
Shields the rest of her children
From possible hostile words.

A fattened old bird slowly savours a chip
In full sunbask.

This is my 33rd year at
A swimming carnival.
This school is a jungle
Of chaotic impulses
Ready to explore
The chinks in social order.
But on so-called lesson
Free days
They practise:
Flirting and display,
Beating and relays;
Gorging and delays
While organisers scrape
Together teams,
And children scream
At insects
On pieces of paper.

* * *

21st. February 2012

At Margaret's House

In the sun's early rays,

I breathe in your lakeside
Kitchenette wonderland of colours
And Hans Christian Andersen's
Fluorescent turquoise tin of ballerinas,

Mermaids, soldiers and palaces;

All merrily merging
Under the fairy-tale apple tree
Of delight and wonder.

That is true.

And quartz-like blue
Glass facets of reflection
Dance gaily in my eyes,
While lavender and lemon
Gracefully align with Virgo violets
And passion deep red roses
To warm my heart chakra too;
Making all brand new
In each ray's transfusion
Of light into life!

* * *

24th. March 2012

Fate

I throw myself at the foot of Fate.
I have nothing left on my plate.

* * *

9th. June 2012

Along the Road to Coolamon

Sheep rise out of silver-beige paddocks
Like their own crenelations.
I drive through life's tunnels:
Orange-amber-olive green
Massed crowns sweep over me.
And we are in a Victorian painting;
Each of us lacquered into immortality.

Ah, what used to be used to be.
Julie is dead.
Soon to be burnt without trace.
For her, this is reality.
A neat pile of ash
In a proper unit, sent off to Mudgee.

But I saw Julie floating
As she felt like it
Just above the field stubble...
"Fancy me, a fairy!"
In total freedom
Lies total delight
For Nature's Wonder,
"A Truly marvelous person"
Who suckled a little lost goat kid herself
Although never having given birth.
And performed a successful caesarean
On a cow
Having only once witnessed a vet do it.
The cow birthed again, as do we all,
Until we learn Julie's lessons.

I cannot end this any better way,
Except to say,
All submergence of one's "I's"
To give, instead, to others, is the only thing
That gives merit at this life's end.

* * *

27th. June 2012

Teaching is Now

Young women wrapped like lollies
In animal prints,
Legs like liquorice sticks
Teach now in classrooms.

The sky's blue maw,
Indentured trees;
Its ups and downs
In ever open jaws

Hold me to my
Life line.

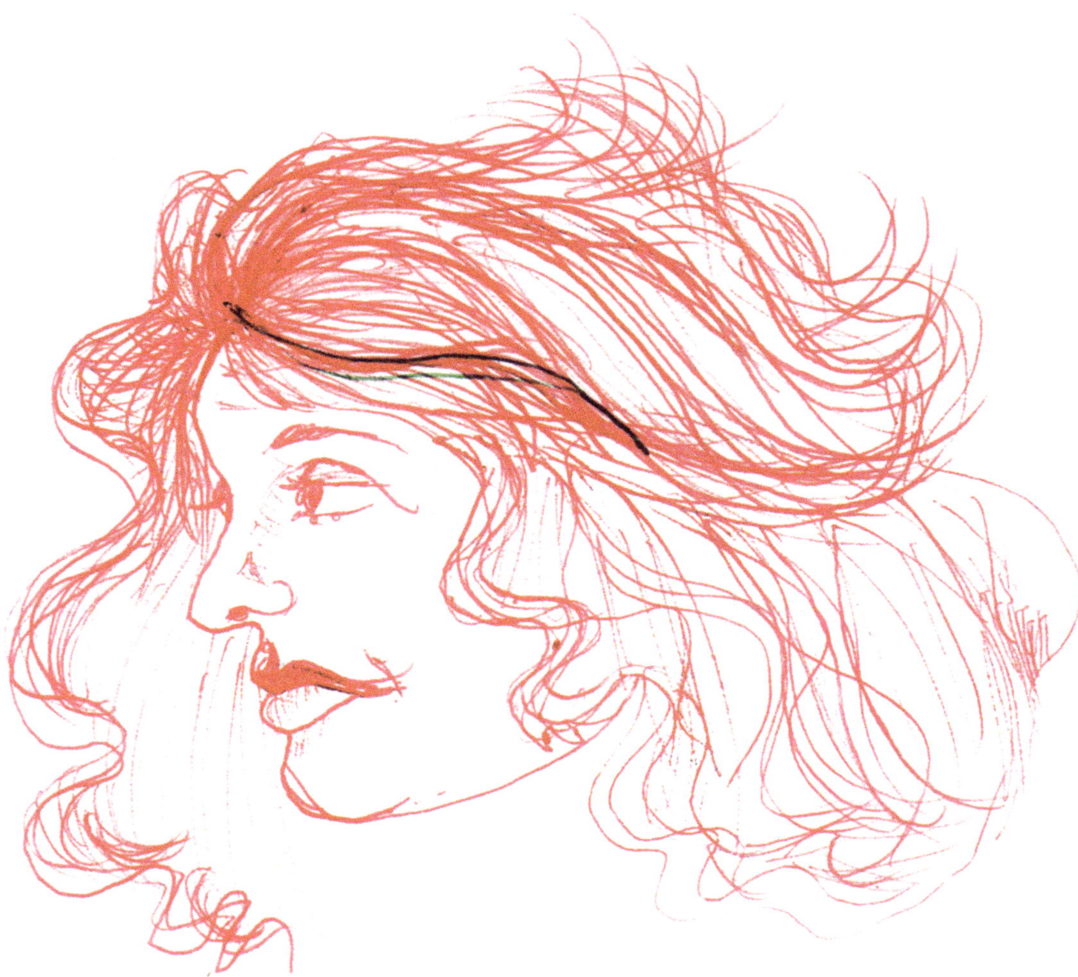

* * *

20th. July 2012

The Poem That Should Not Have Been Written

The student writing paper
Was folded to gently encase
A small, faded, pressed flower.

At first glimpse- after some years-
She gasped at its prudent beauty.
Intact, under the Moon in Virgo.

Its tiny pale beige stars
Were amazingly together,
As not disturbed.

But any rupture
Had it doomed.
And it cast into several pieces
On a second look.

What was done is done,
Is finished.
Wrapped in still memory;
Unnaturally immobile.

A second look
Will reveal it for what it truly is;
Merely a cascade of past events
Unendowed with any future life
Or significance.

* * *

21st. July 2012

Friday Voyeurism

A couple knitted together
On the shores of Lake Macquarie.
That love bond they're creating,
Instilled in their mating,
Will ensure
They fall in love
With their babe in arms.
The adopted child knows none of this.

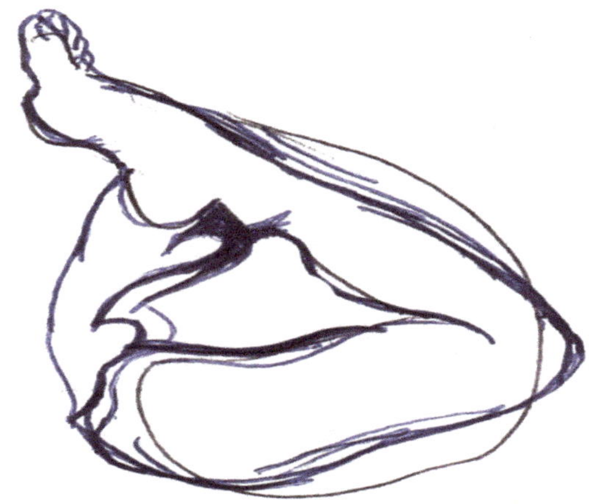

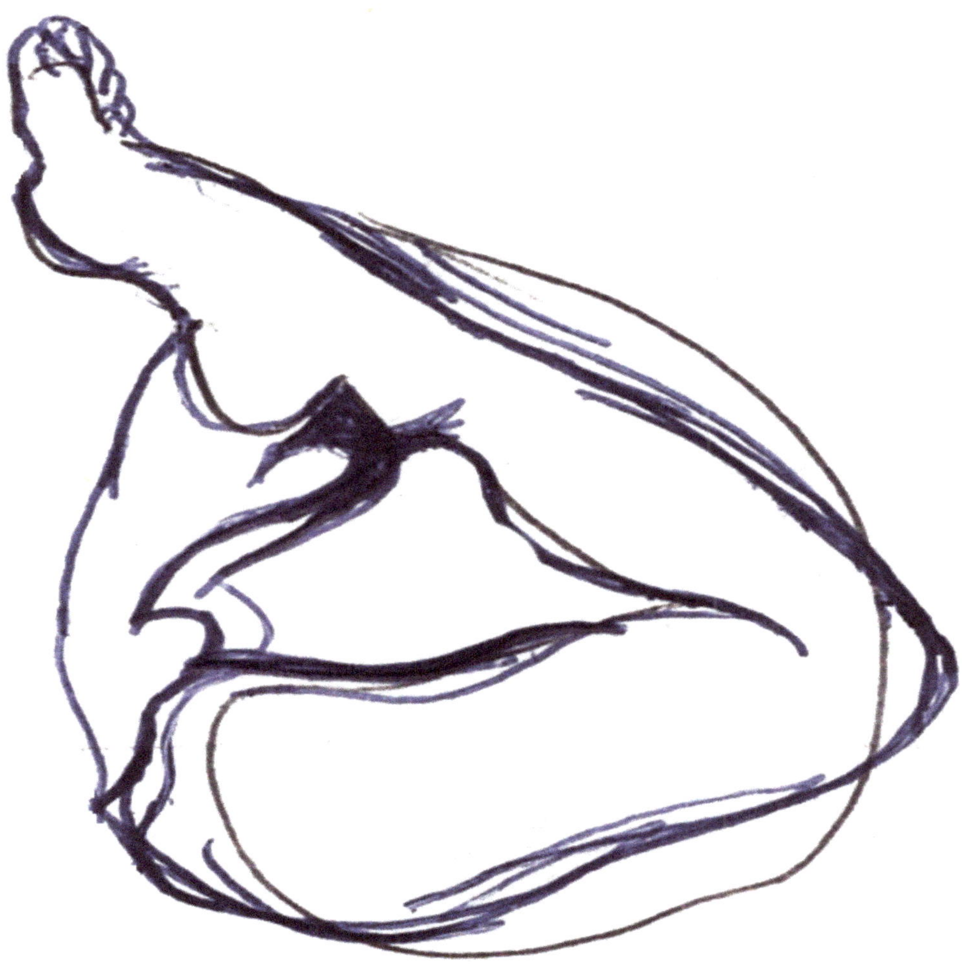

* * *

24th. August 2012

Boddington Hill Earthworks

Still an emanation of Earth energy,
A silent sentinel of power
Exuding dark richness
Beyond words
Torn roots like nerve shafts
Expressed to the sky,
No longer resonate internally,
In dark tunnel depths
Where all is known innately, not descriptively.
Your power not yet gone,
Man has copied it with
Dull grey concrete blocks in pyramidal piles;
Poor copying of your presence
Of stillness, resonance, strength, mammoth support
A part of Earth's Herculean pillars.
Pardon my archaic language
But modern words pale
As having lost arcane knowledge of such things.
You loom above us still;
Deeply rich earth, rock, dark green growth.
You will always be there within
When overclad, waiting stoically to release
Again over that which can be temporary only.
I asked you what would happen
After the collapse of humanity.
A cliff will rise again,
It will not be you.
For you will have merged into an archetype
Form with universal energies;
There as a prototype available
For what will come after.
For no form is ever lost
In the great emergence.

* * *

28th. August 2012

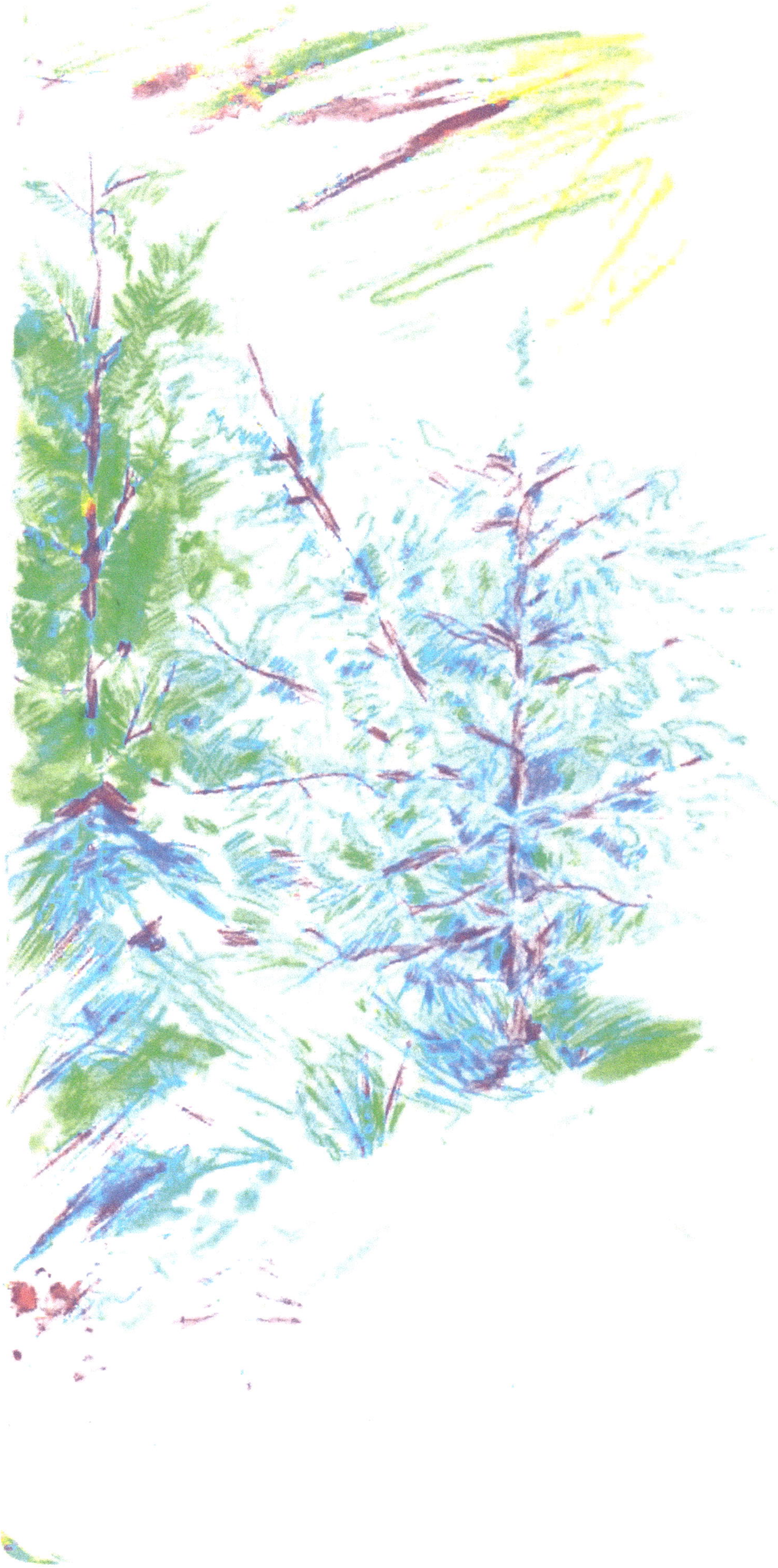

Fir outside
Chee's Summer
House in
Hunchy
1/01/'03.
BR.

The Dragon Founders

On the back of Evil,
But perhaps not quite so,
The Dragon flounders;
Has no-where to go,
Unless the gold is
Used to a purpose great
Its substance
Is only weight.

The good is in the giving,
Life is in the living;
Souls' transitions
For the mending
As spirit soars
In a well spent life.

* * *

2012

I Remember

I remember a trip to the city,
Somewhere near DJs,
In the proximity of The Rural Bank.
My father, and a safety deposit box
In trust…for a bank customer.

I, by his side,
And happy to be so.

I wonder now
If I was like some
Treasured object
To be kept safe…
In trust.

Only I
Was never
To be
Given
Back.

* * *

18th. October 2012

On the Occasion of Receiving an Award for Excellence in Education

Child woman in sheer dress
Four years old again
Though mobile now, in hand,
You walk with me
In the vast hall's shadows
Still entombed
Here at Wyndham College;
On this, the occasion
Of thirty years' teaching.

Heart and soul
And student solos;
I am alone,
As usual,
But first among the peers
To shake the hand
Of David Phipps,
Regional Director
Of Education in
Western Sydney.
Every element I spy
Is as familiar
As scraped burnt toast
In Eleanor's kitchen.
For all my life
I've been here.

* * *

27th. November 2012

The Van Entrains Their Suffering

The van entrains their suffering.
Lo, the disinherited of the world
Are queerly there.
In their night train
Bridesmaid to death's face
Of grinning fear.
To the world's
Mad darts
Appears the saviour?
Lo, if he is come……
He is dumb.

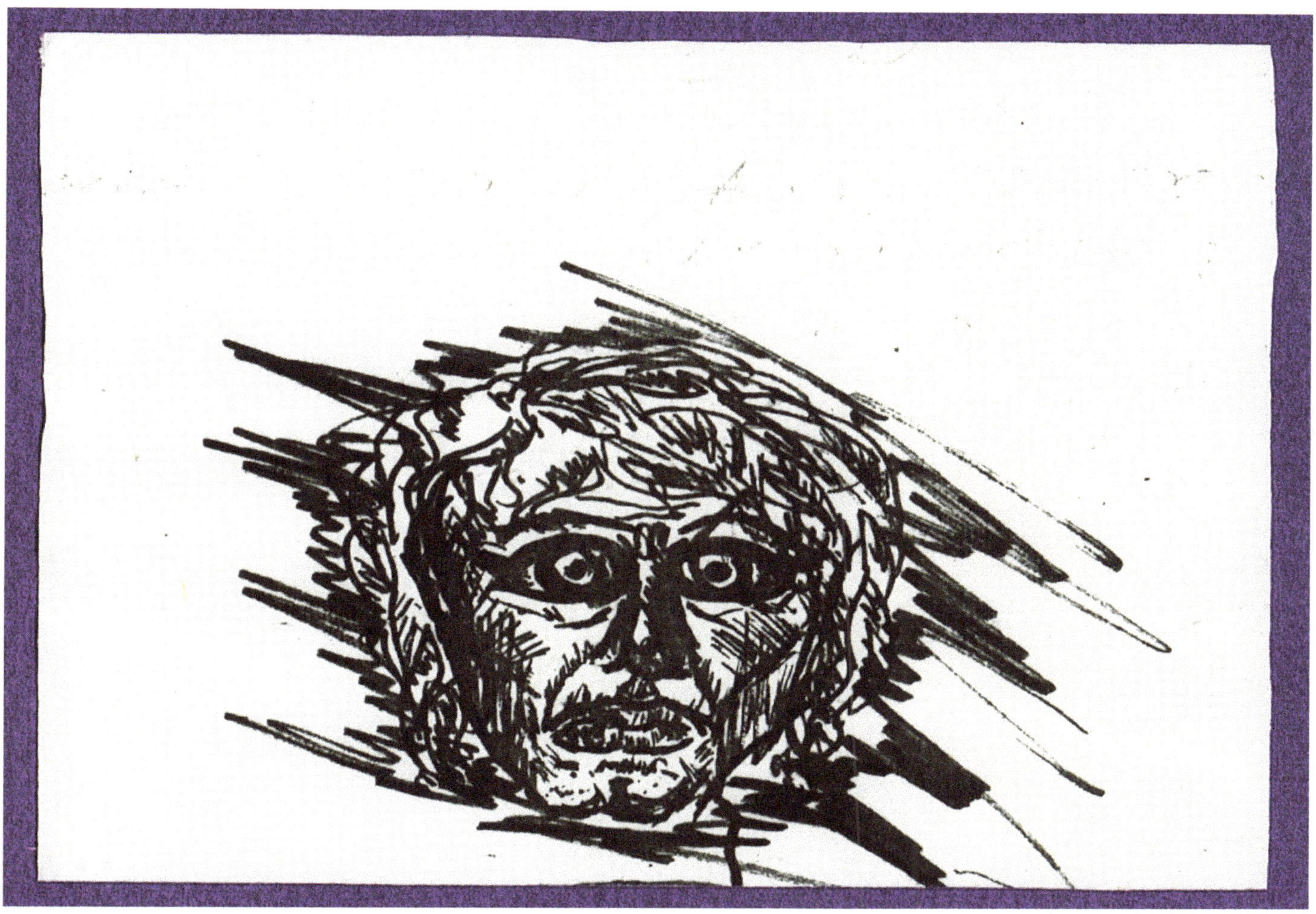

* * *

12th. December 2012

Pope Francis

Yesterday I heard
The crowds cheer
In Vatican Square,
And I knew
That he was there,
Though no vibes
In the air,
My world chakra
Knew
Before all else.

I know you know!
The humble need you.
Sexually abused people,
People in the trap of poverty,
Those who lose
All to despair
Need you.

Pope rhymes with hope,
Assisi with assist me;
And don't tease me.
Humble with tumble,
Jesuit rhymes with…
Be alert!

* * *

13th. March 2013

Highway Plunder
- Requiem for a Blue Mountains Cliff Face -

The burdened clouds
Oppressed the hills,
The men below oblivious.
All eager to scrape back the cliffs
In regulation hideous.

Reptilian, incisorvist,
The earth machines ploughed on;
'Til wild things, sprawled at nature's angles,
Tilted to the sky and sun,
Sculptured by themselves alone
Are stripped quite bare,
Man's foul work done.

* * *

7th. June 2013

Mindscape

The mind is its own scope,
The mind is its own landscape,
The mind is its own escape.

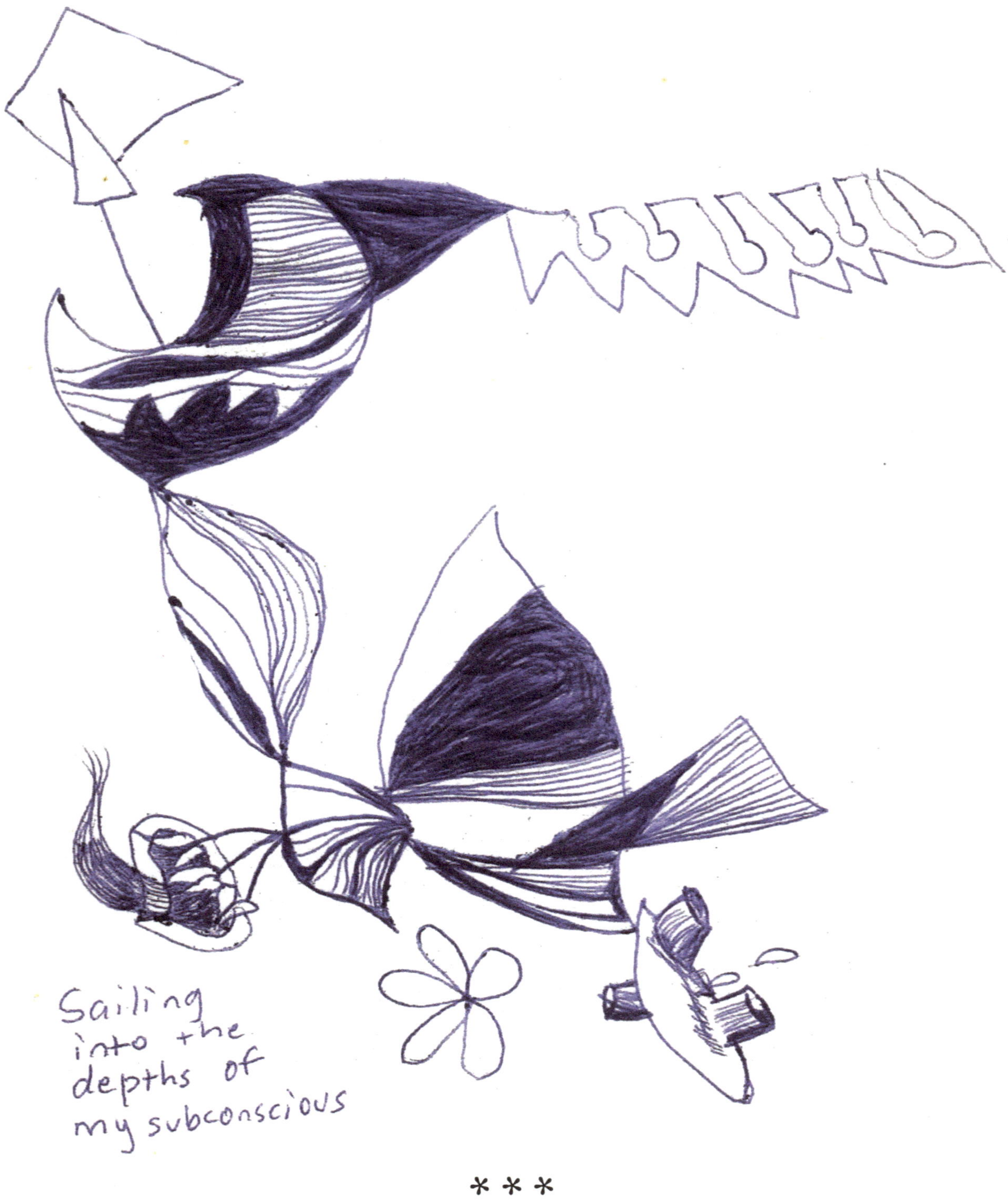

* * *

2nd. March 2014

In the Inkling of the Day

In the inkling of the day
The sway of times past
Be-clouds.

As the day snickers
Off into the wilderness
Of days that came
Before it...

None of us
Really
Escapes
The pull
Of the
Womb

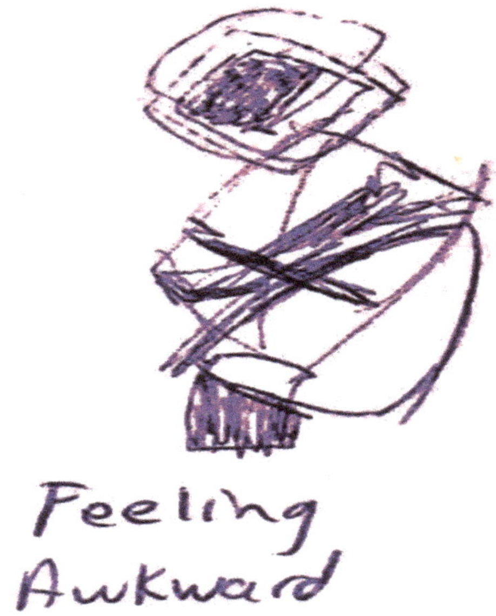

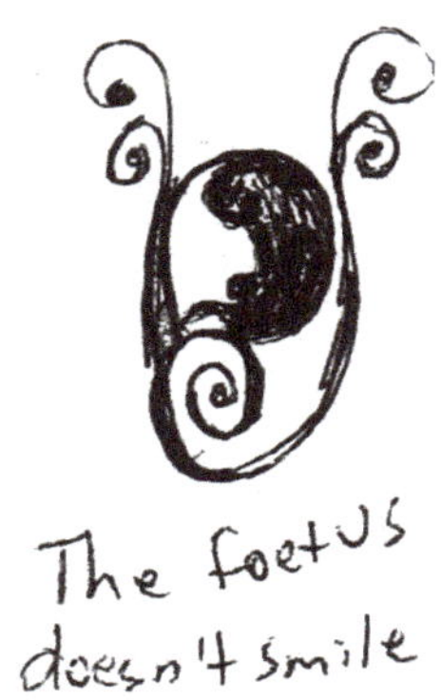

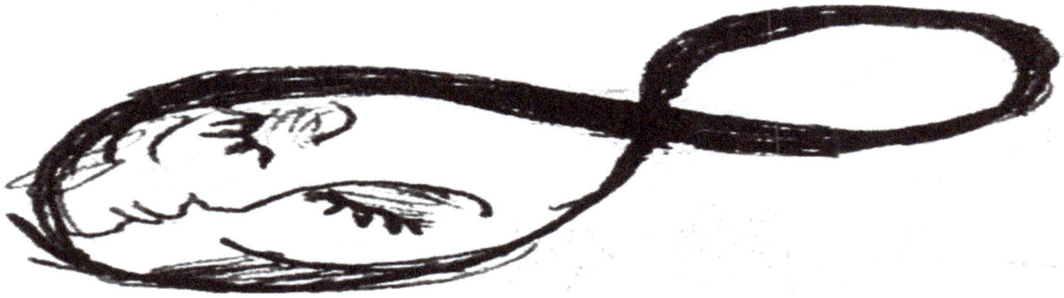

* * *

29th. August 2014, 4th. October 2010 - being an amalgam of 3.

Anzac Day Duet

I

"Anzac Day is for those who were duped,"
I said to the other that day.

A chorus of male voices said
"We KNOW we were duped,
How about you?"

I replied
"Well, thank you."

They answered
"You got it."

And one responded
"I didn't."

(I think he was a newborn of the 2000s.)

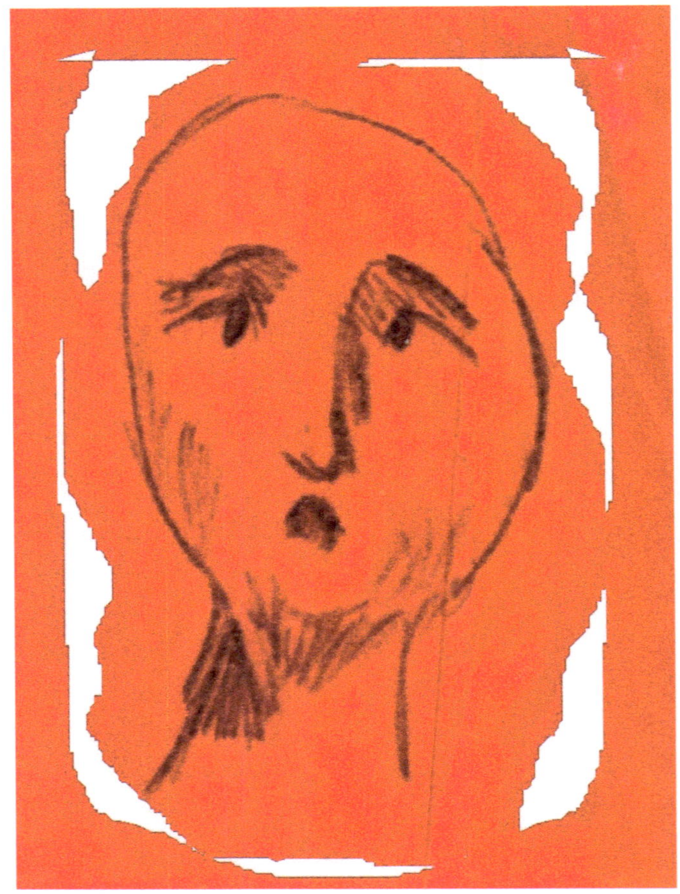

II

Now No Brinkmanship Required

And for those men who were fallen
Before their time….
When will be their time?

A rhyme consists of two similar-sounding words
Placed one before and one after.
We've had many wars since then,
Wars that came again and again
With forward and backward referencing
Each one in step with all others.

I ask my daughter's friends
Please break this sad old trend,
Or they'll have a lend of you
And more
De capo Al fine.

* * *

25th. April 2014

A Food Not Poem

I don't want any food.
Food's crude.

I mumble
About how I stumble
And crumble.

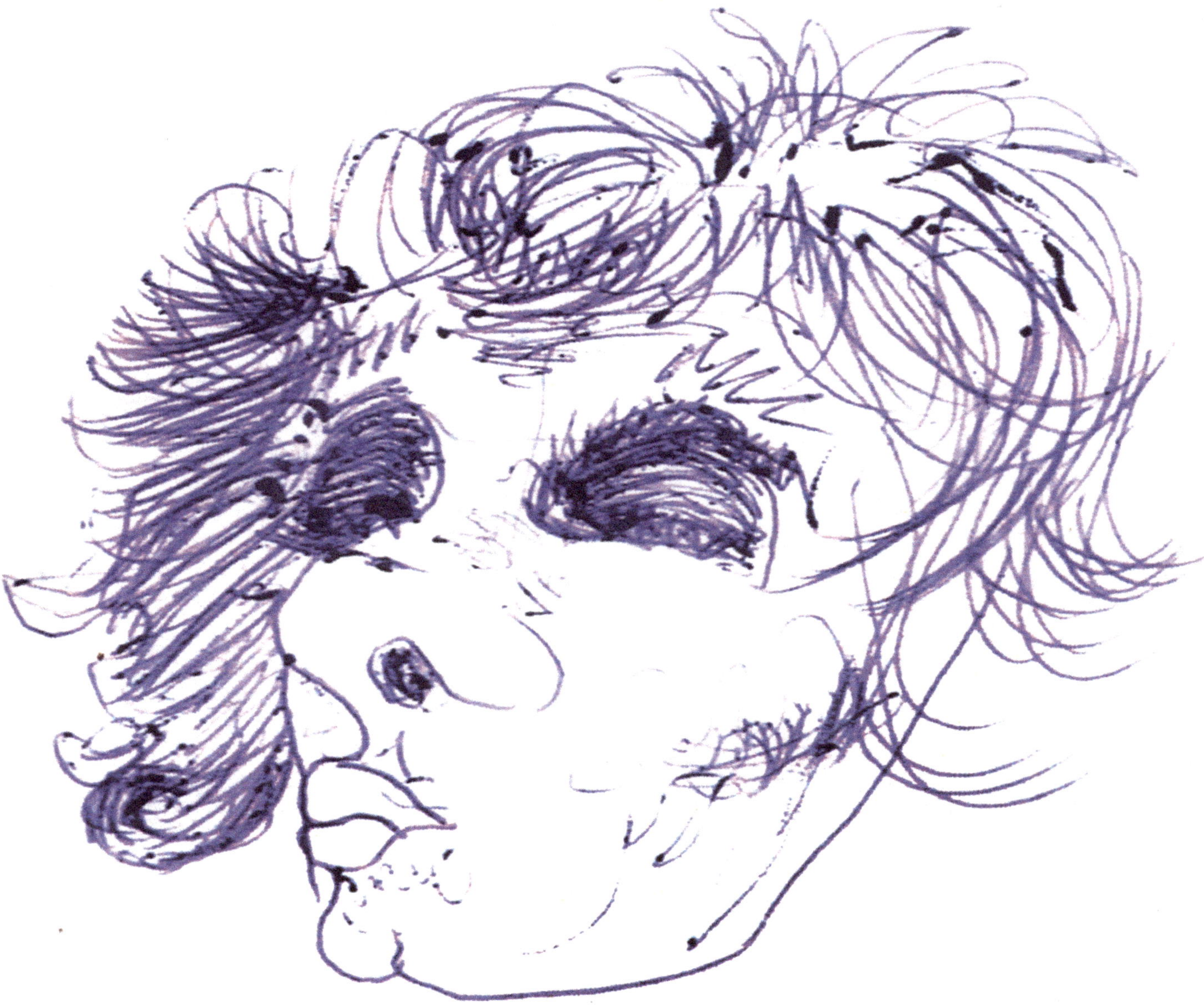

* * *

30th. May 2014

Marrickfield Days

If, in a thousand years,
My tooth is analysed
For its mineral strata
It will find me
Still, in Narrabri.

On the edge of the world
A little blonde child
Peeks through a hand's grasp
Latch
While, in Edgeroi,
Birds seek formation
Naturally,
As dams glisten
And peaks create
A nation's wealth.

Inner...
Love, ethics, family
Envelop me too
As children's feet
Echo, still, in my heart.

I cannot reach you now;
But your shrine remains intact
In a room out of sight
Where mother once sat,
Beaming love as father sang
And Clarys played.

* * *

Now In Present Time

There on the banks I stood.
The Namoi ran;
Dad's spirit and I
Walked together again.
The mud slipway
Present still;
My heart and his
In Narrabri.

How the soul and heart
Know where we belong
Comes on so strong
Even after
So long.

Apart.
Distance is nought;
As, dreams of Narrabri
Pass into reality
As reeds and silver waves
Lap the foothills
Of my heart's
Awakening.

* * *

24th. April 2014

Narrabri Ways

I have a happy child within
That made dark secret passageways
And ball bouncing walls
But mazes into other spaces
And a tunnel way of mystery
Once, in Narrabri.

* * *

1st. June 2014

Heart Wisdom

What the heart doesn't see
The mind doesn't get.

* * *

7th. July 2014

Has Millennium 2 Got the Better of You?

We're all lying down
Before we can stand up.

Millennium 2 will
Get the better of you
Unless you take a stand,
Take him by the hand
Look into his eyes
Staring right back at you.

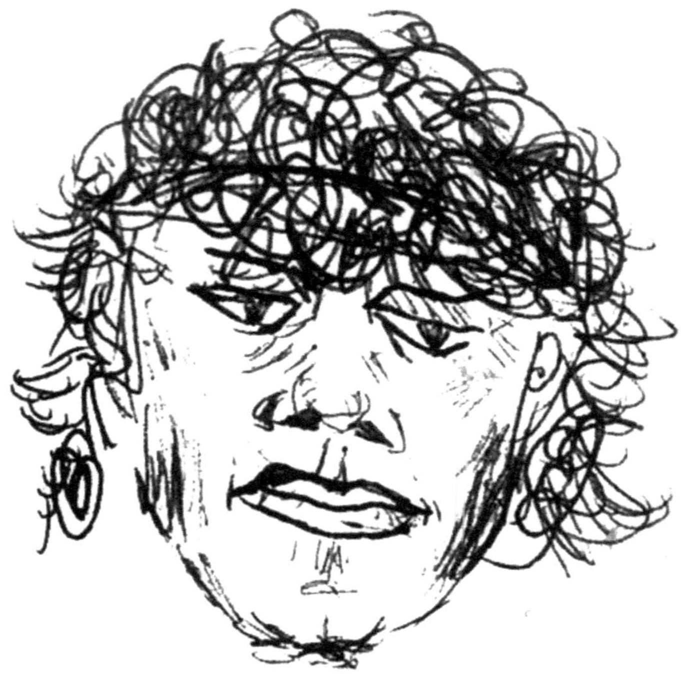

You and the door
Have a decision to make.
Stand there and fight
Or walk together
Out of night.

You walk out in season
You have no real reason,
Your dead fight long gone,
And your brain has no plan.
You take it by the hand,
You hate to grandstand,
And you have no brass band
Anymore.

By the door's a Tree
Of poetry you've done.
One day it'll be clear,
May that day come along.

***

Friday 11th. July 2014 - Full moon in Capricorn

Out of My Head

Swirling around in the atomic spread,
Swirling around eating butterfly bread.

Swirling around,
That's what I said;
Swirling around
Eating butterfly bread.

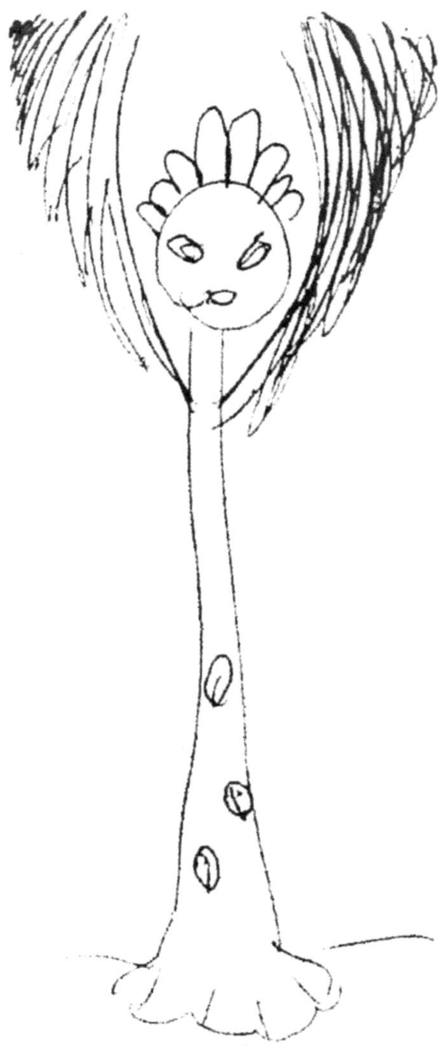

Angel Tree

* * *

6th. August 2014

Water Dragon
- Song for Scorpio -

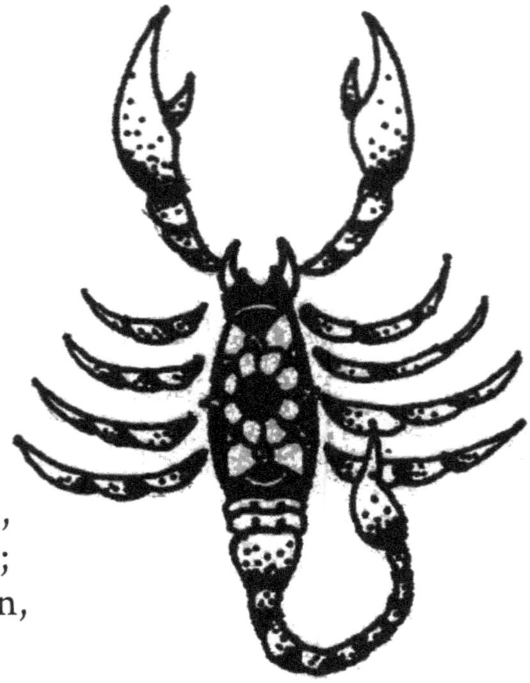

I am a water dragon,
Who's been on land too long.
My blood is overheated,
But I am strong.

Find me the deep cool water,
As blue as turquoise pearls;
Where circuit breakers flourish,
And Earth's red rivers pause.

For I shall fly when time's upon me,
Soar in the air through coolest rain;
Then dive as deep as the bluest ocean,
And enter your heart again.

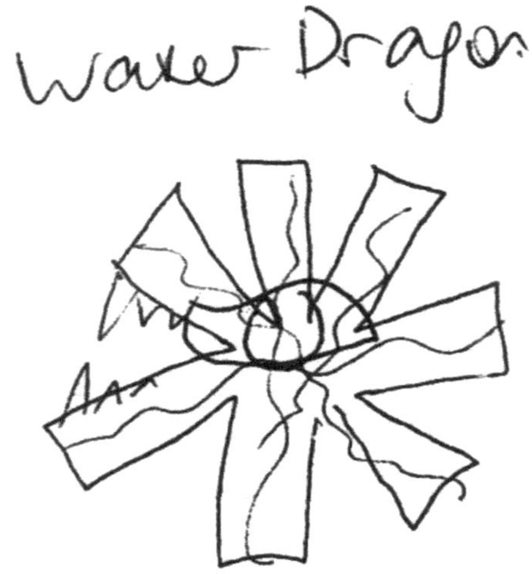

(Previous name was **Dragon Nature**)

This poem was one of 12, acting as inspiration for, but not identical to, the songs of the:

'**Cosmic Wheel of the Zodiac**' Song Cycle

View performances of the songs on YouTube http://bit.ly/mb5music

* * *

22nd. October 2014

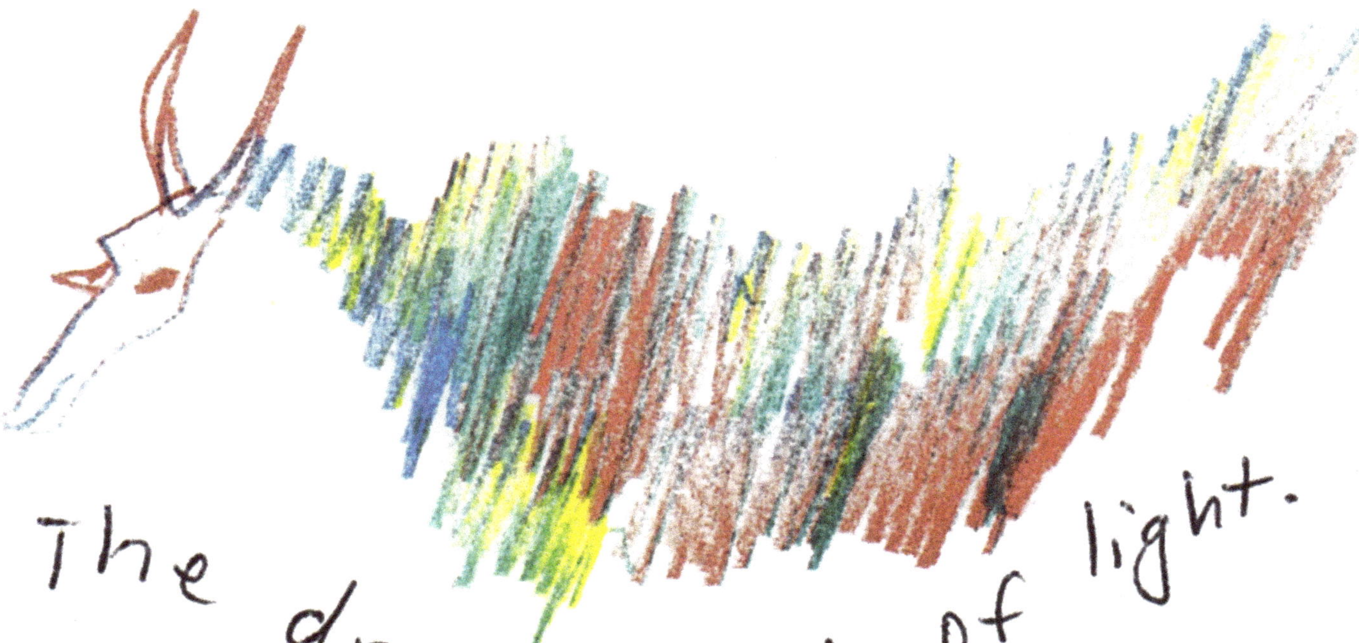

The dragon's body of light.

On Your Dark Shore
-Subject: Benevolent Narcissism-

On your dark shore
Waves ebb
But you remain the same.

Allowing ingress:
Calm taking,
A yin and then...

Your night descends.
A cloak
To wrap you in
Your rock-like self.

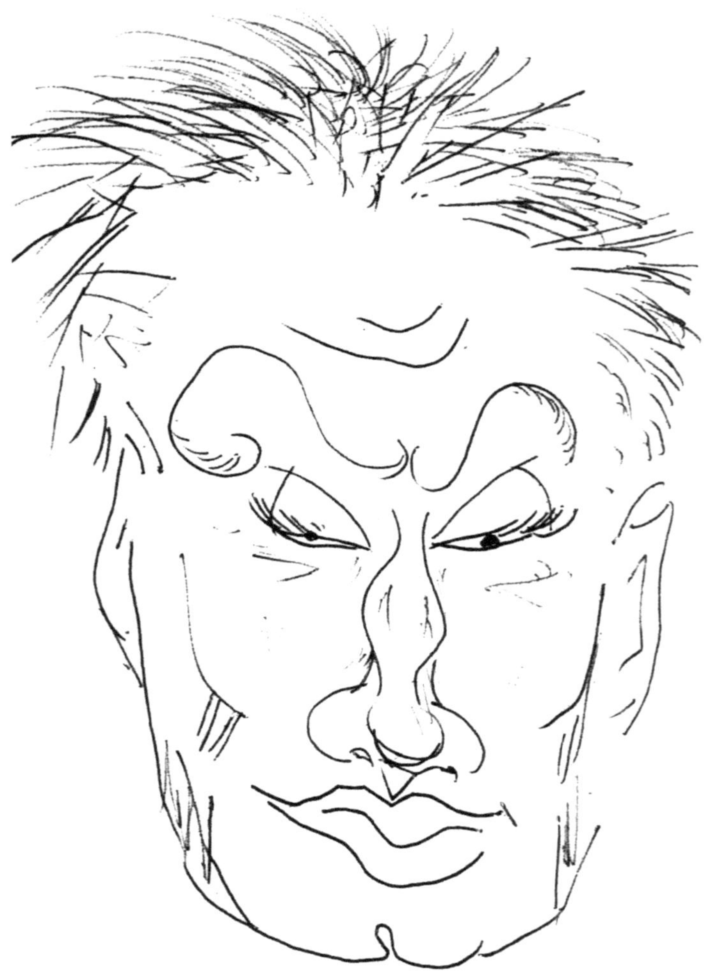

* * *

5th. November 2014

On Going to Adelaide

What are we doing, Margie?
Why don't we stand by
Pellucid pools
With Blaze the cat;
Or wade, ankle deep,
And see our ripples
Cross the surface
Of an otherwise
Undisturbed morning?

* * *

8th. January 2015

On St. Valentine's Day

Hello wind!
Hello gorgeous,
Juicy
Wind
Through my oak tree's garden;
Whom and which
I love.

* * *

14th. February 2015

In My Dream I Dreamt

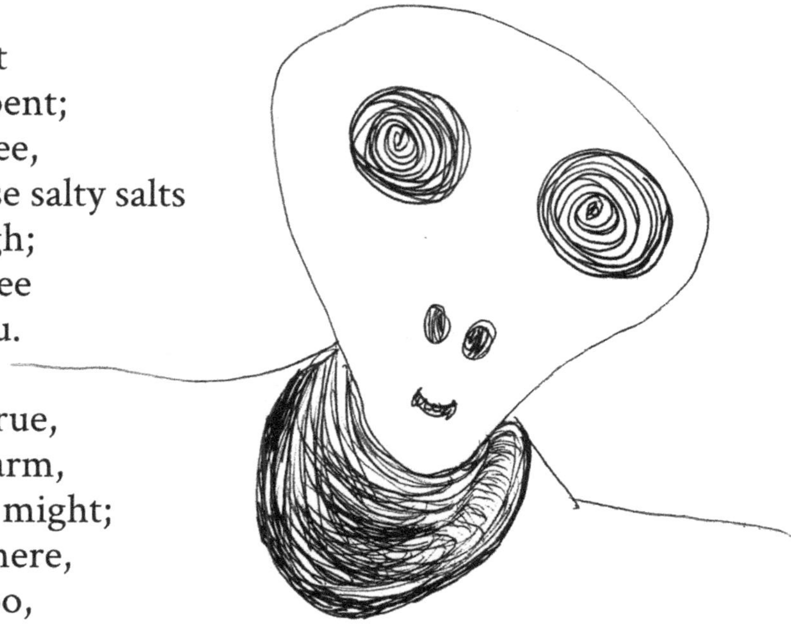

In my dream I dreamt
The prisoners all were spent;
And, dreaming to be free,
On their bars did wee,Until those salty salts
Wore the metal through;
And quickly they did flee
To tell their tale to you.

From dream to you it's true,
These aliens meant no harm,
But stared at us as scientists might;
This wondrous man not here,
This glorious soldier too,
But creatures void of hair
And brain enough to care
Of their fellows' plight.

Hans and I were merged
Before old birth's despair.
We dancingly took flight,
And through the air we jigged.
Hand in hand, in sky and sea
In Shiva's form and Indra's net;
All arose in he and me;
Earth's prison chains to shed.

Hans Christian Andersen was a famous Danish author of fairy tales,
which he really wrote as morality tales for adults!

* * *

13th. March 2015

One Hundred Years After Gallipolli ...
Four Billion Years After Prison Planet Earth

As I look into the mirror
I imagine quite a thriller
As the DNA gorilla
Answers back its mazy days.

If my forebear's genes were active
In the royal halls, their antics
Echo back to me their patterns
On the horse and in the lanes.

Country towns and steeplechases,
Lacy maidens, pouty pollies,
Vicious plots and daggers,
Countless wars, they all were mine.

As they looked into their mirrors
DNA and epigenes
Moulded souls like drones and clones
Through quantum timeless time.

Reaching back, and to the future
Like a mystic caravan
Their tendencies – all theirs,
Are really, really, mine.

I'm a chiller
And a swiller
And a guiless
And a guiled,
As I walk the halls of power
With the Stewarts by my side.

In my throat and in my heart
And in my three-brained skull,
Slurping up and out their patterns
Their very all I cull.

In every waking moment,
In every sly old deed;
When sleeping after pork,
Their old dreams I feed.

Until this force-feed ends
I will tread this circle's bend.
Until their stuff transforms
I am simply just their spawn.

Hallelujah I adore you
Prince of peaceful sways;
Prince of living in the moment;
Prince of craveless ways.

To be a babe, a cat;
At one with time and space;
And never looking back
Takes up the puerile slack
Of their royal almanac.

I would stand on purple mountains
In the sky and in the sea...
Touching sunlight, moonbeams, stars;
And in their light see me.

See me as dancing energy,
For verily I am...
Joining up with thee and me
In our purity...on the lam
From false old memes and dregs
Of ages gone and spent
Alive and all at one...
In Indra's arms and net.

For all is one in truth
In the mystic maker's dance,
All separation mischief
In the quantum physic's lance.

If I am you and you are I
Then end this dream of mass;
This Luciferian fall
Is really quite a gall.

Plunge beneath the stream of things
Where thoughts connect and meld;
It's up to you to end this mess,
These wrong old patterns put to death
With love and care
And tenderness
To man and woman,
Race and creed.

In nothing but yourself believe;
Your nature good and true;
In service to all living things
Accept what ***is***, do not resist.
And you will be
True Blue!

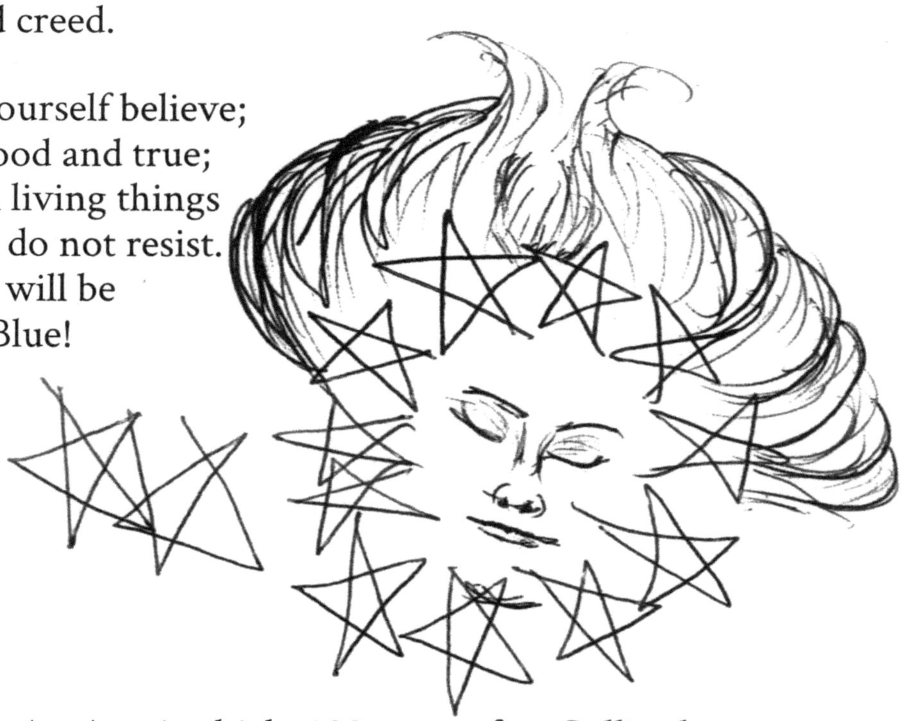

- An Aussie chick, 100 years after Gallipoli
Read: Gored/GALLed to death by POLLies!

* * *

21st. March 2015

While Sick

I don't want to talk to you about anything,
Although I'm as lonely as a particle in space.
My loneliness extends to visions of Victorian staircases
In some mad inner scramble for surety,
Of connection to something other
Than this heart hollow over fleshed
Envelope which I inhabit.

"Oh, what can ail thee, Knight- at -Arms,
Alone, and palely loitering?
The sedge has withered from the lake,
And no birds sing."

I struggle with some
Suburban tale of meaning.
Something to do with
Seeing photos from some
Current performance, of me
In Verdi's Opera "A Masked Ball."
As this is somehow of some
Significance to others.

(with acknowledgment to Keats)

* * *

19th. March 2015

German Wings

Souls trapped in the cleft
Between mind and reason
Wondering why they are there.

One thing is clear.
Two actions happened:
One soul crashed a plane
And all within died.

But to put themselves
Under the pall of victimhood
Will not do.

You do not need to wait for answers
That start with "He did this to you
So stay forever scarred and blighted."
No. Two things happened.
One soul smashed a plane and vanished.
You move on…
On to the next stage,
Free of the past,
Not damned by cause and effect.

* * *

3rd. April 2015

Joy is.....

One little cat
Showing me where it is at.
She glides 'tween my feet
With a movement so sweet.

After you do your work,
Your true work,
You create...
Everything after is easy;
Chores done....
Elate!

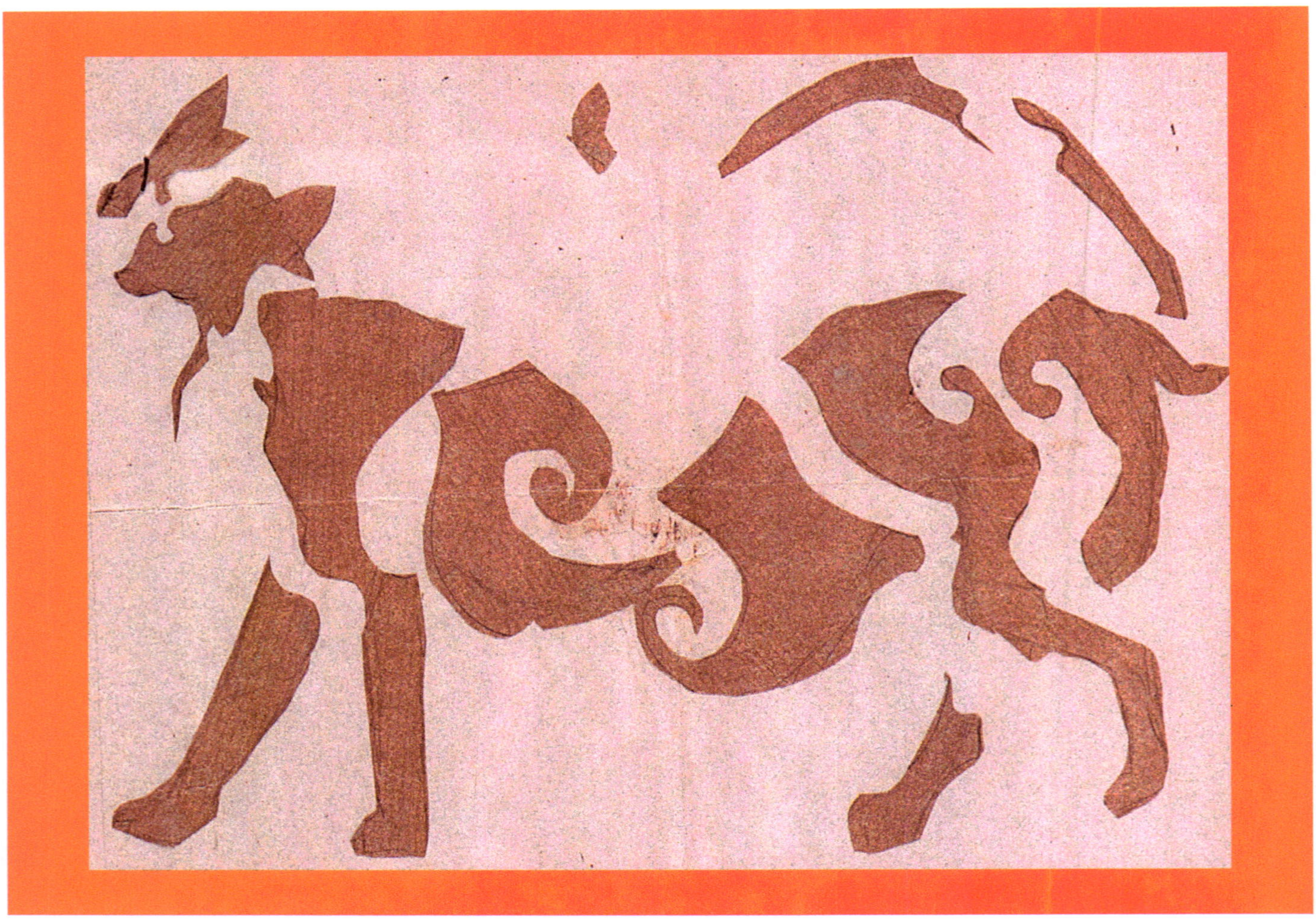

* * *

April 2015

Nature's Ways

The stones sit there, unreaching.
The bush soars up, its branches seeking out;
Every leaf strained up to greet
Wind, rain and sun.
The blossoms sit;
Elegant and comfortable.
That is the way it is;
That is the way of it.

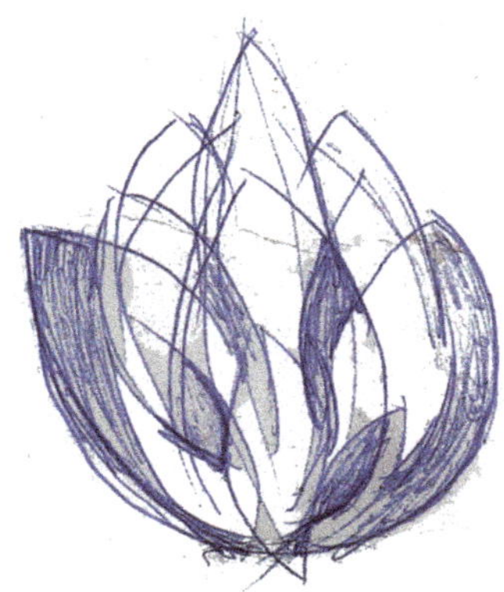

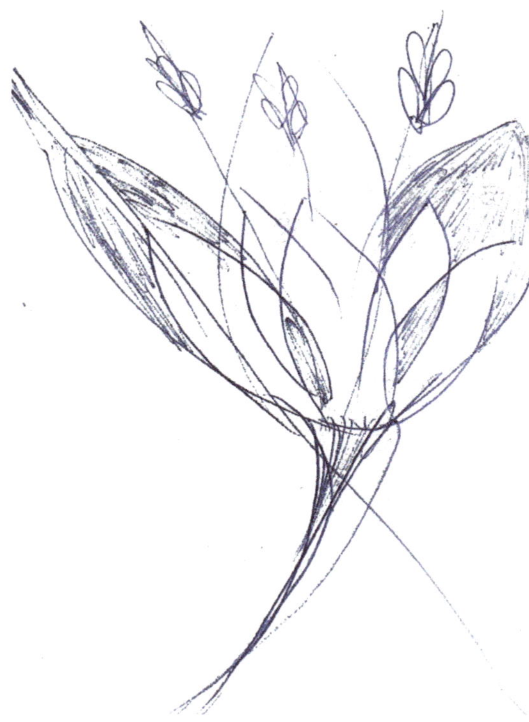

* * *

19th. April 2015

Mountain Goat
-The Capricorn Song-

I am a goat, swift and oh so fleet,
I roam the mountain side;
With ever climbing nimble feet
I never ever slide.

Clinging to the cliffs
And challenging the peaks
I take a different path.
With hooves like flint,
I split the stars in two.
For me no ifs and buts!

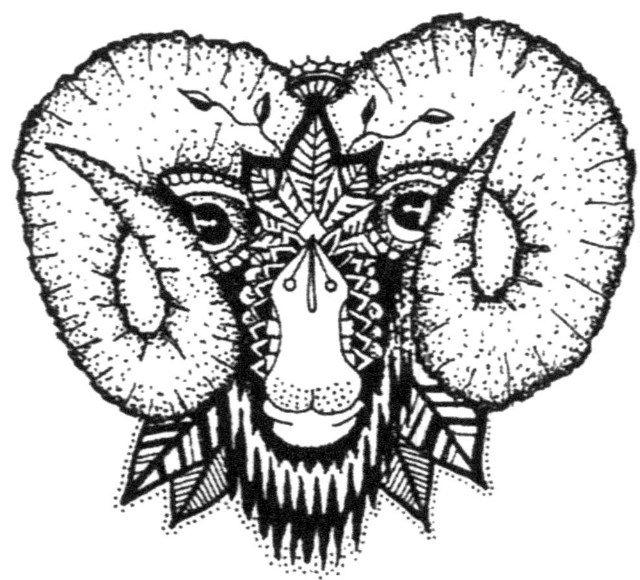

Although you may see me Tamed,
And grazing paddocks mildly,
My soul can never be arraigned
For it ranges wildly.

Just loose me from your field,
And see me vanish briskly.
I'll climb and never yield,
For freedom finds me quickly.
For freedom finds me quickly.

This poem was one of 12, acting as inspiration for, but not identical to, the songs of the:

'**Cosmic Wheel of the Zodiac**' Song Cycle

View performances of the songs on YouTube http://bit.ly/mb5music

* * *

2015

The Ram in Spring -Song for Aries-

Eros, born from silver egg,
Mother courted by the wind,
Double-sexed and golden winged,
Stirred the cosmos, four-of-head.

Hissing like a serpent,
Or bleating like a ram,
Covering four quarters
Of universal span.

Symbol of creation,
Father of us all,
Tremble in your joints,
Hear the lion roar.

Eros as Zeus: the ram in Spring,
Helius (lion,) Summer sprung;
Hades: snake, the Winter brings,
Dionysus, bull, New Year belongs.
Linger round the melting pot
As your life is newly born;
Spin the ever- moving top
'Till you're really quite transformed.

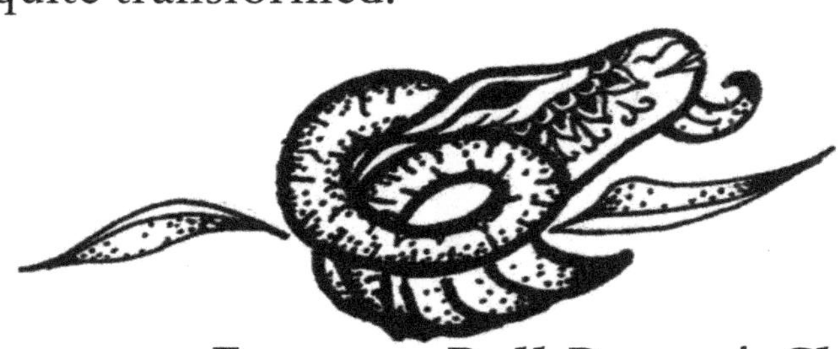

(Previous name was **Eros, or a Bull-Roarer's Charm**)

This poem was one of 12, acting as inspiration for, but not identical to, the songs of the:

'**Cosmic Wheel of the Zodiac**' Song Cycle

View performances of the songs on YouTube http://bit.ly/mb5music

* * *

25th. April 2015

Pluto- Planet of Transformation-the energy that thrusts the young seedling up through the Earth towards birth. Ruling planet of Aries and Scorpio.

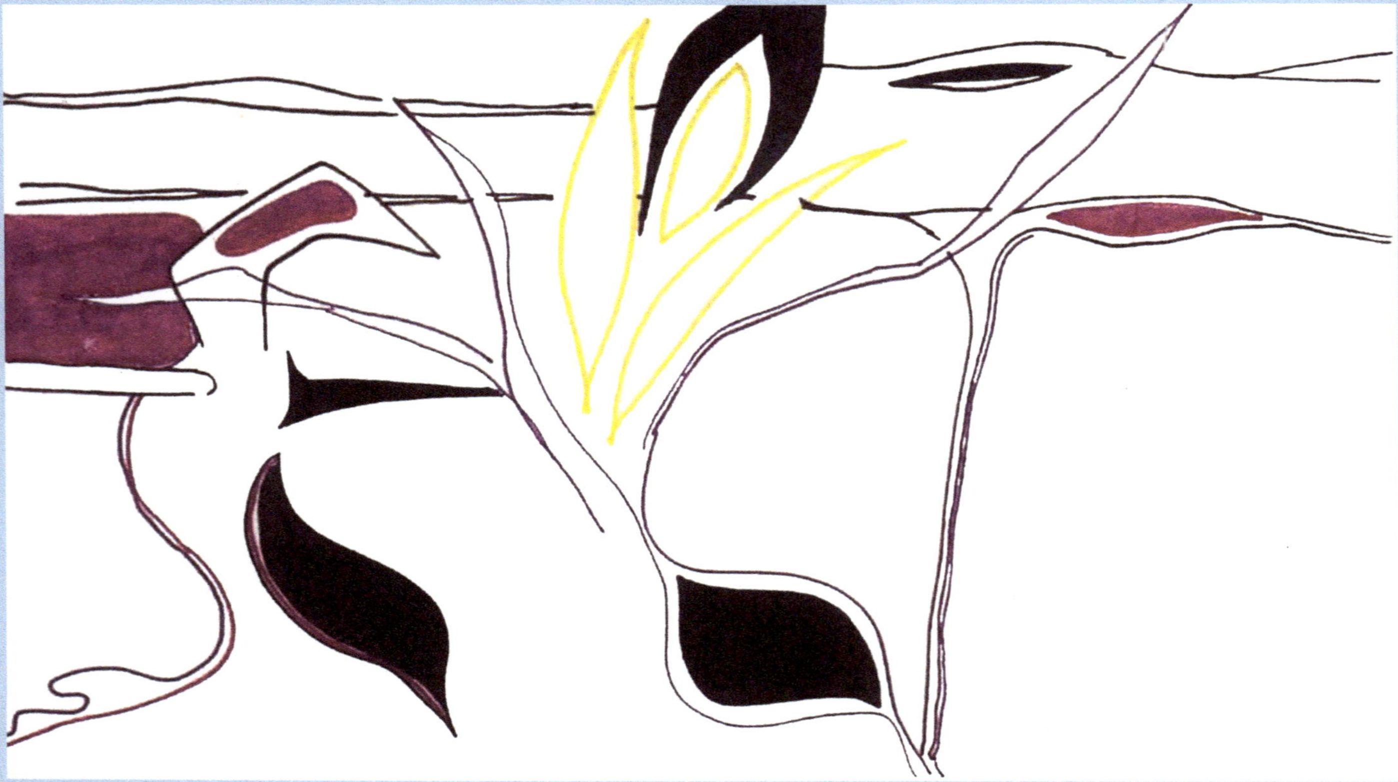

In Neptune's Realm -Song for Pisces-

If you see me
On a bed of snow,
Rainbow scales now quite dull,
One eye glazed,
Think of Psyche's
Flowing ways...
Soar above the crystal skull
Made by no man's art.
Penetrate, with your rays,
Go quite deep, to the heart
Of Neptune's realm
As Indra's net,
Quite cast,
Holds all men's thoughts
Attuned to
The Other,
Whether
We like
It
Or
Not.

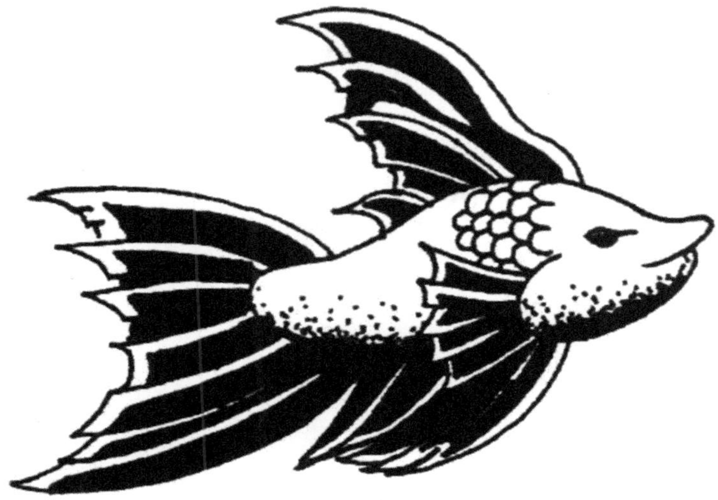

(Previous name was -**Fish Soup for Psyche**-)

This poem was one of 12, acting as inspiration for, but not identical to, the songs of the:

'**Cosmic Wheel of the Zodiac**' Song Cycle
View performances of the songs on YouTube http://bit.ly/mb5music

* * *

25th. April 2015

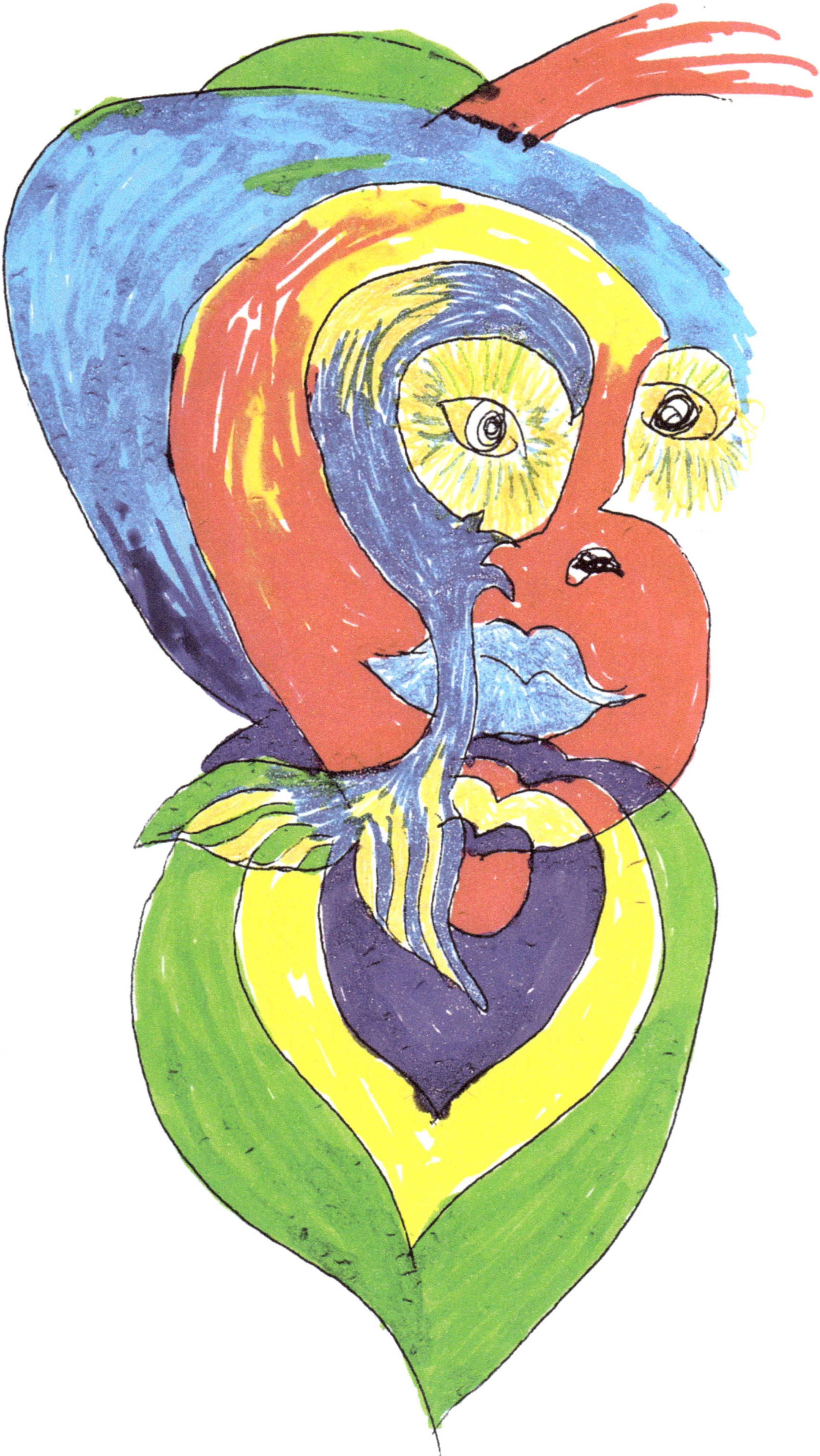

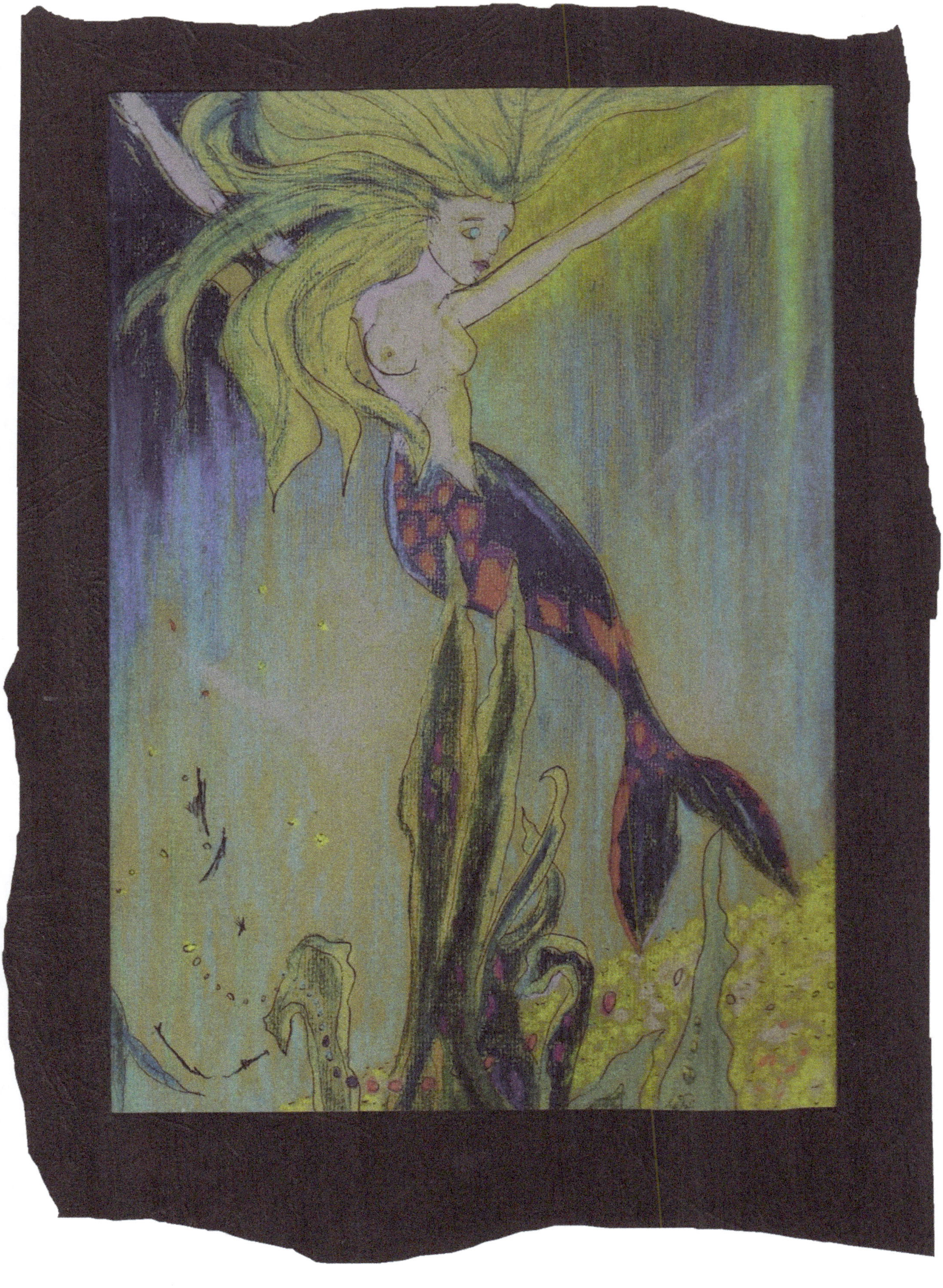

Anzac Day Yin and Yang

I

They say that
War is to man
What childbirth is
To woman.
The hideous contrast,
However, is
Really quite clear;
Not hidden at all,
But seen at every day's reveille.
When, it is said,
The tides of death
Most frequently go out.

II

At the rising of the Anzac sun
The hearts rejoice in wakened throng…
Point of concentration. Alert.
Why not now?
Why not
Always in The Now?

* * *

25th. April 2015

Lion Love -Song for Leo-

There is a lion in the heart of everyone,
Young or old, weak or strong.
It'll teach you how to sing your song,
You'll find your goals,
And where you belong.

In the first rushed thought
Check with your soul;
Run it right past,
That first impulse...
That beats in your veins,
And rouses your loins,
And lights up your mind,
And feels good
Inside.

There it will be
For both you and me;
Instinct's decree
For true harmony.

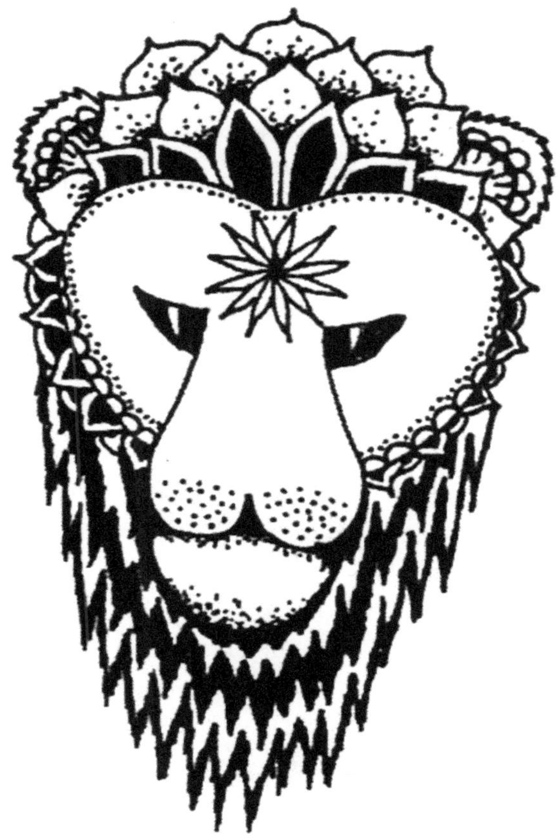

* * *

This poem was one of 12, acting as inspiration for, but not identical to, the songs of the:

'**Cosmic Wheel of the Zodiac**' Song Cycle

View performances of the songs on YouTube http://bit.ly/mb5music

2nd. May 2015

SBS Struggle Street Blues
-With Thanks to SBS-

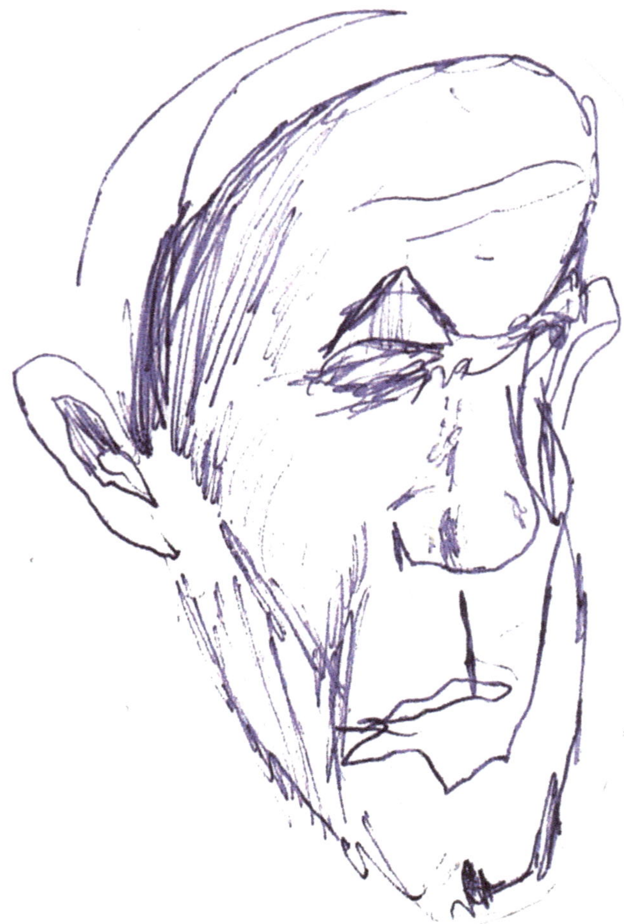

What lies behind the sneer of Struggle Street?
What lies behind the fear?
The understanding of reality.
How big-boss billionaires
(Yes, New South Wales,)
And worldwide capital
Have worked hand-in glove
To shaft them big time.
For centuries in every way.

We're not only talking:
Unemployed, desperate, Underprivileged
For every generation before their Birth,
We're here to be spoken to,
From the insight of those who Know,
From the ruin of their own lives.

So, what will you do, big timers?
Start a discussion in your
Cloistered dens,
Whilst never setting foot
South or west of the CBD
(Beyond a certain radius
Of privilege, of course?)

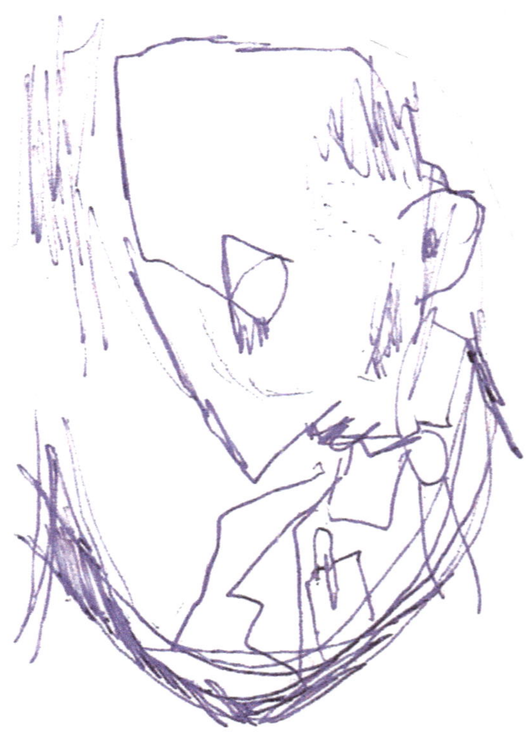

Basically it boils down to this.
What good is your intelligence
If: young children go hungry,
If their mothers went hungry,
If every generation on this
Earth which ever lived
Had Plenty pulled from under them
By the few real savages
Who, responding to
Only their lizard brains,
Died from obesity
And excess from all things accrued
Only to their real benefit?

* * *

6th. May 2015

Cut Out

As I sit in the old
Form Master's office,
I know,
I'm not cut out for anyone.
My form is my own.

But I am a crying baby,
And that's bad form.

* * *

2nd. June 2015

The Thawing of the Heart

The thawing of the heart is really quite an art.
It's very, very smart to jettison the tart
And not so very arch to embrace, blanche de carte,
The other….. willingly, not jealously,
Utterly, in the chamber of the heart.

In the chamber of the heart it is very, very smart
To accept what is quite freely.
Giving freedom to all, we resist nothing at all.

Accepting…that everything is perfect,
We throw ourselves open to the universe;
Who treasures every one of us
As she treasures Herself.
You see……there's no difference, really.

If things could've been different at any given moment
Then they would've been.

The might've beens exist only as possibilities.
The actualities, the resultant effect
Of causes able to manifest
Bud like, spore- like, when possible only.

"If"......That great word....
In the multiplicities of the quantum theories;
Things not yet born.
Accept your will, Oh great creator you, Yourself, and I.

* * *

26th. June 2015

Songs to the Four Elements

I
Bush Fire

Brass hills glow in the coming heat,
Millions of sparks ignite the leaves, trees, crowns
By Vulcan's furnace set alight;
Tribute sacrifice to him.
Tribute sacrifice to life.

In this land new life demands death follows destruction.
Flames licking bark demand submission.
No gain without pain
Fused into the fibre
Of life in this land.

Gumnuts crack released
In a birth of fire.
Birthed by fire
This entire land across agrees.

Man, animal, nature
Adapted to this creed, path,
Tough, persistent in nature's way;
Glorious sunsets end each dark day.
Death, Life, Beauty,
Triple themes.

And who can say or judge,
But just observe
That symphony in three parts
Consume all within it
And in its own time.

* * *

July / August 2015

II
Sea

In that old dance of life
Earth holds the percussion,
Air the wind section,
But water's melodies
Show us the rhythm of the ages.
Time…engulfs all things
While air teases waves to rise and fall
And dance and descend most frighteningly.
Sometimes the love affair
Between these three
Scatters man's petty structures
Like match sticks.

Huge waves reclaim the land
As if it's alone.

The ancients knew four elements:
Water, fire, air and earth
Enwrapped in raptured dance,
Interplay of the ages…
What a show!
A love affair aglow
Across all ages
Earth's coitus of interflows
Bridge all levels of time and space.
Volcanic lover embraces earth,
Heat too much makes hot springs gasp
And reach the air's cool comfort.
Grinding thrusts make mountains rise,
Create the diamonds
Which testify to
This gigantic love
In Gaia's depths.

* * *

July / August 2015

A Poem on Fate

I howled against my fate,
Spurred on by a fight.
I chose to not do nothing,
I'd chosen not to just accept;
I'd failed to surrender,
So I'd resisted evil.
Tears flooded down my cheeks
As I railed against God, the Universe or whatever.

In my classroom during roll call
A large spotted dog trotted in
And smiled at every student there
And then included me
And trotted back out the door.

Later, when he was caught,
And held in the front office,
The P.E. mistress in attendance,
I heard him howl.

Out of sight I walked around, to his calls for freedom,
Echoing, loudly, everywhere.
Cracked voice, enraged voice,
Desperately calling for freedom.

Just like me.
So what answer did the Universe give me?
"If you're in the right place, you can't be caught."

* * *

19th. August 2015

Homeland

I am a banker's daughter,
I've been with him so long,
He is my bricks and mortar,
And to him I do belong.

He caught me as a little fish,
Swimming helplessly;
A little golden baby,
And nurtured me.

He took me from my mother,
Who'd lost me right or wrong.
They'd told her not to bother,
To go home and be strong.

Away, away, the keening cry,
Pierced to the bones the newborn one;
Away, away and far begone,
To never know where is my home,
To ever be the golden one.

Eleanor, she loved me;
Held me close, I guess;
Yet memory knows well,
It was only tenderness.

From another woman I was born;
I knew her smell so well;
As infant eyes and fingers sought
She to whom I once was brought
And from her arms then torn.

I am a banker's daughter,
I've been on Earth too long.
My blood is overheated,
But I am strong.

* * *

Send to me the coolest water,
To splash upon my face.
To find where homelands do not falter,
And vanish without trace.

Some scrying pool would that be,
As deep within I know;
There is nothing can be seen,
And nowhere, now, to go.

Uprooted from my native earth,
And never more to part,
My spirit home, my soul's true turf,
Is in my father's heart.

Though he is dead and gone,
And buried in their grave,
I seek him, all forlorn;
His memory, still, I save.

And I will always search for him,
'Till universes die;
'Till stars collide, and in their din,
I'll take advantage of their spin,
Careering all awry,
To jump right in and search for him,
Who loved me best and true,
When daughters of his own were me,
And soundings found that true.

* * *

8th. September 2015

Four Castles of Stone
-Song for Taurus-

If I use will
To break through the veil
To you,
It will open doors
To possibilities yet undreamt of.
I do not ask you to forgive me.
For you will place your hand in Mine,
In mine....in mine.....
And we will build, in time,
.........in time.........
Four castles of stone,
To keep us safe and warm;
Our dreams piled high...
As a bridge to the sky
Once we have
Pierced all barriers
Of inner and outer
Resistance,
And found ourselves
At home
With one another.

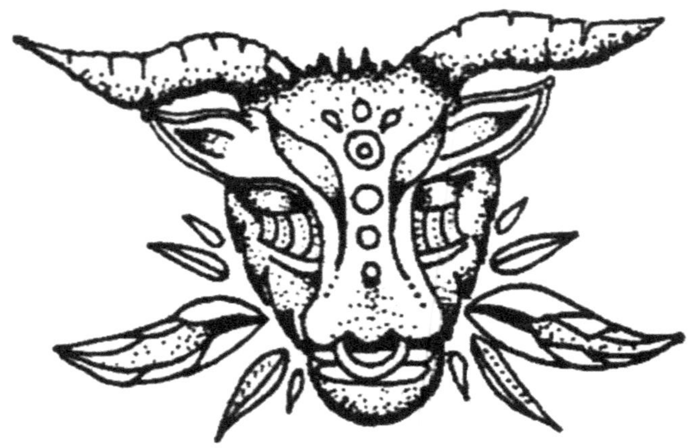

(Previous name was **Taurean Ways**)

This poem was one of 12, acting as inspiration for, but not identical to, the songs of the:

'**Cosmic Wheel of the Zodiac**' Song Cycle

View performances of the songs on YouTube http://bit.ly/mb5music

* * *

30th. October 2015

Universal Truth Remains
-Song for Aquarius-

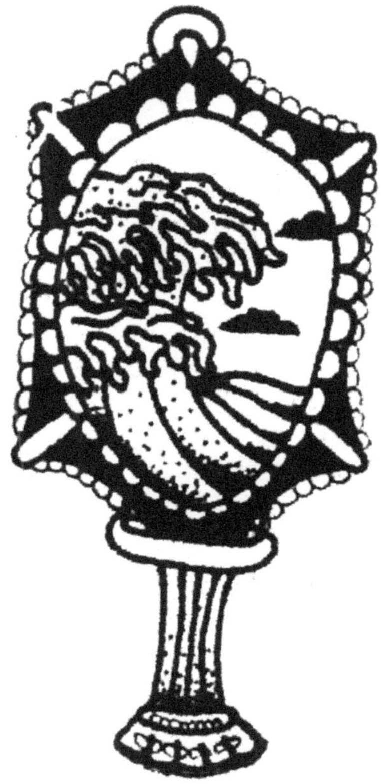

See me not as man or woman,
And our love remains the same.
Humankind is in its childhood,
Universal truth remains.

Souls are neither one nor other,
Let us stand and take the hand
Of our any-shaded brother, or
Sister, o'er the whole world span.

Even the water that we drink,
Even the air that we breathe,
Through countless other cells have Been,
In myriad ages past.

Do not narrow down our love,
Excluding all around.
I embrace all human causes,
Possessiveness would close us down.

We are merely grains of sand,
Rubbing up against each other,
'Til our edges sharp we blunt,
'Til we truly fit together
In the world, then in our hearts.

(Previous name was **Aquarian Hours**)

This poem was one of 12, acting as inspiration for, but not identical to, the songs of the:

'**Cosmic Wheel of the Zodiac**' Song Cycle

View performances of the songs on YouTube http://bit.ly/mb5music

* * *

November 2015

Jacaranda Blossoms

All jacaranda trees
Take me to a place
Where my spirit soars.
Taller trees
Even more strongly.

On hot days
Your blossoms, in their
Depths, darken,
Highlighting the mystery
That already envelops you.

That indescribable colour
Only decipherable
As yourself.....
Your jacaranda hue
Merges the great divide
Between Earth and sky.

As, plummeted into
Spiritual ecstasy,
I dive into the portal
Between where blossom ends
And sky begins.

And I am on the threshold
Of Eternity
As my mind slows to a sweet trance
And I enjoy spirit's
Eternal dance.

* * *

20th. November 2015

Sleep
-People of Plato's Cave are We-

If I see you going by,
One eye closed,
Feet in mud,
Asleep,
Should I ring the bell
To wake you?
You, on your cloud of self?
But, are you there?

We sleep, yes, dream;
Even as our feet
Mechanically plod on.
Not many wish to wake.
No knowledge of
The possibility of that
Having occurred to us
We spend our lives
Dreaming that we live.

* * *

26th. November 2015

People of the Cave

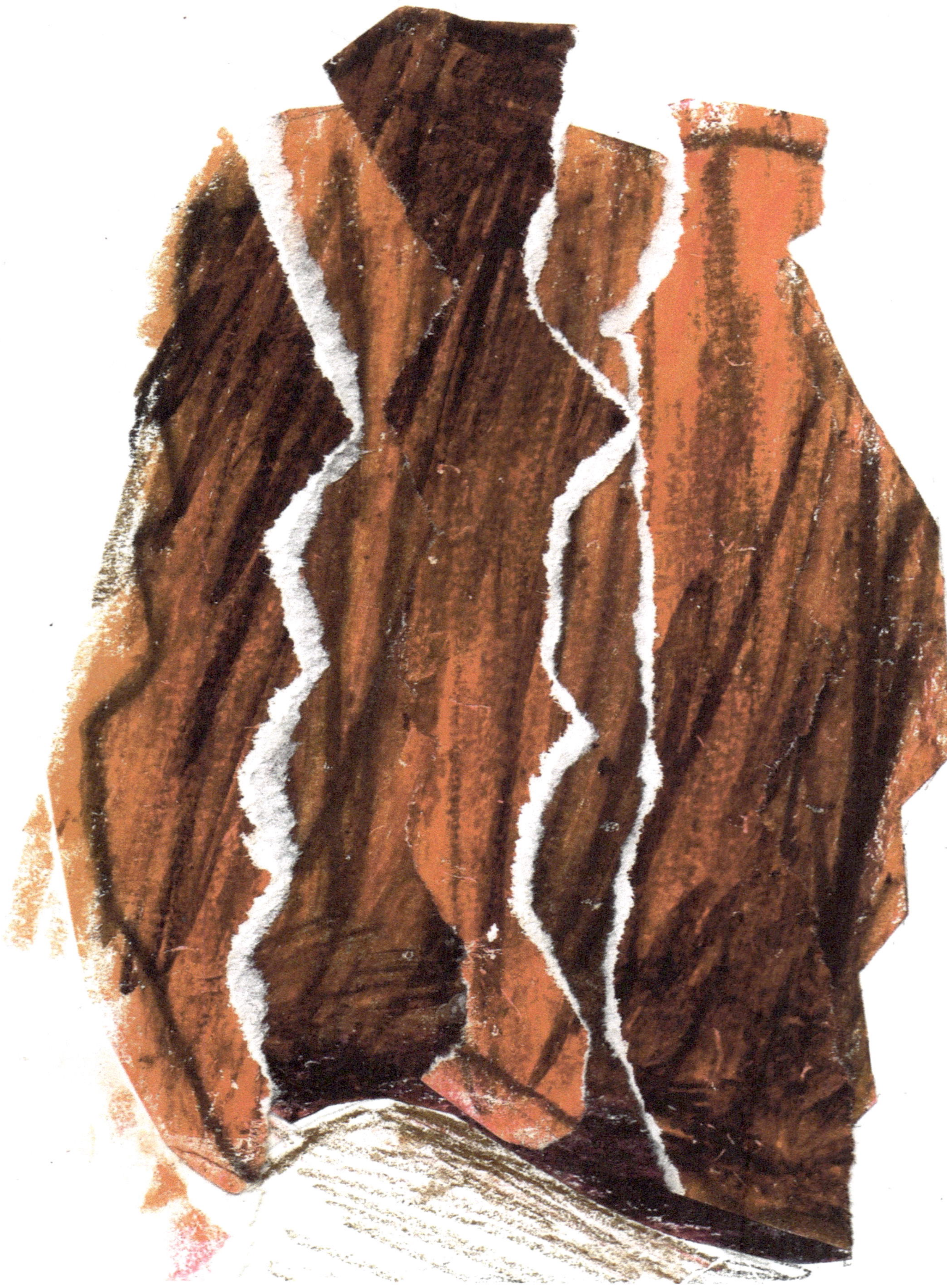

Jacaranda Tree

I adore thee,
Jacaranda tree.
Your blossom hue
A portal
'Twixt earth and sky.
Indescribable....
That close merger
Thrills the soul,
Which, although seeking definition,
Cannot make the distinction,
This time, so close.

* * *

December 2015

Dance of Life
-Song for Cancer-

When I go I take you with me,
In my pocket, near my heart.
There you sit to comfort me,
In the light and through the dark.

We must keep abreast of changes
That would sweep us far apart;
Stop the wind and dam the waters,
'Til we are alone at last.

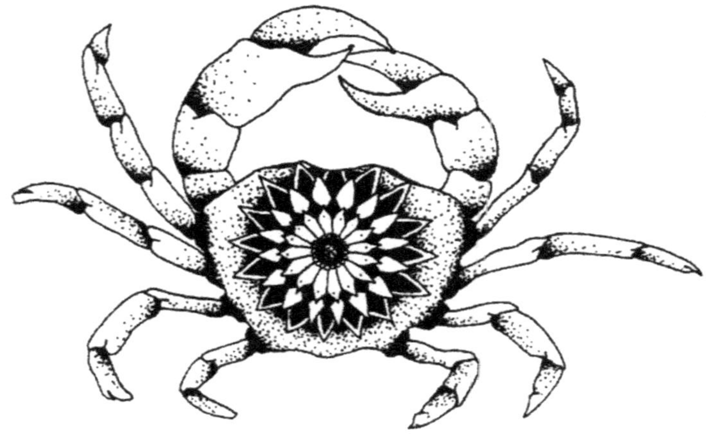

We are dancers in life's contest,
Waltzing for that silver cup;
To seize the very grail of romance,
Forever after, love and trust.

I can feel your arms around me,
Clinging tenderly,
In my arms, and cheek to cheek,
Dancers through the dance of life.....
We will dance on through the dance of life....
..... of life.........for life.

(Previous name was **At Home with Sun Sign Cancer**)

This poem was one of 12, acting as inspiration for, but not identical to, the songs of the:

'**Cosmic Wheel of the Zodiac**' Song Cycle

View performances of the songs on YouTube http://bit.ly/mb5music

* * *

2nd. December 2015

In Perfect Perfect Pitch
-Song for Libra-

If I should correct you,
Accept it as a gift.
For we must be attuned in
Perfect, perfect pitch.

Though I'm sociable, it's true,
I will not grant you quarter.
For it's justice that I long for;
As for the very air we breathe,
And then I'm in my element.

Truth never, never,
Does deceive.
It's what we must believe in,
And long for, like a lover.

Who knows the truth of my soul?
The balances weigh
The hearts of many
Are wanting.

But I will follow Theseus' thread,
'Til I find my just reward
That resonates through the lies,
The dread,
Until
Our scales align in
Quintessential beauty.

(Previous name was **Libra's Scales**)

This poem was one of 12, acting as inspiration for, but not identical to, the songs of the:

'**Cosmic Wheel of the Zodiac**' Song Cycle

View performances of the songs on YouTube http://bit.ly/mb5music

* * *

2nd. December 2015

Acquiver with Sagittarius!

Shall I show you the Truth?
Merge our vision with the stars?
Cut the ties of Earth
And everything that mars?
I will shoot my arrow
And free us for all time,
From the petty ties that bind,
We'll leave them far behind.

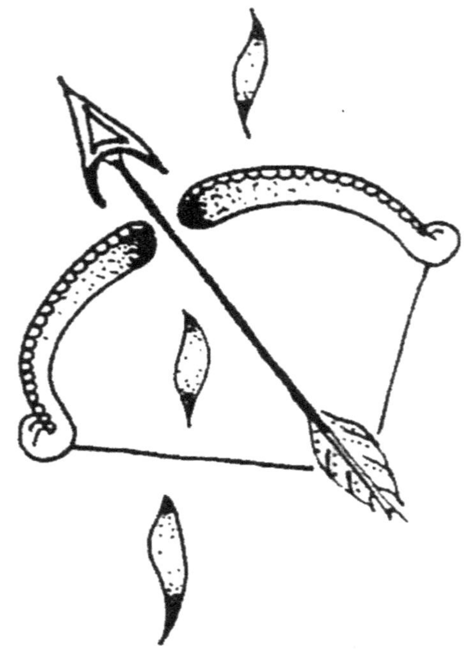

Cosmic fire,
Shooting higher
Than others dare aspire.

Create a living purpose
In the here and now;
Justice is a healing stream,
Sow the seeds of knowledge gleaned
From mind and on to mind.

Why are we all here?
Can we do it better?
On this sad old world,
Release us from all fetters.

Cosmic fire,
Shooting higher,
Than others dare aspire
To where our souls belong
To where our souls belong....
Higher and higher!

This poem was one of 12, acting as inspiration for, but not identical to, the songs of the:

'**Cosmic Wheel of the Zodiac**' Song Cycle

View performances of the songs on YouTube http://bit.ly/mb5music

* * *

22nd. December 2015

What is a Universe?

What is a universe, the one-verse?
It is that every possibility is generated,
And resonates with every other.

Emerging in sentient points,
Bursting through forms
Of every possible variety.

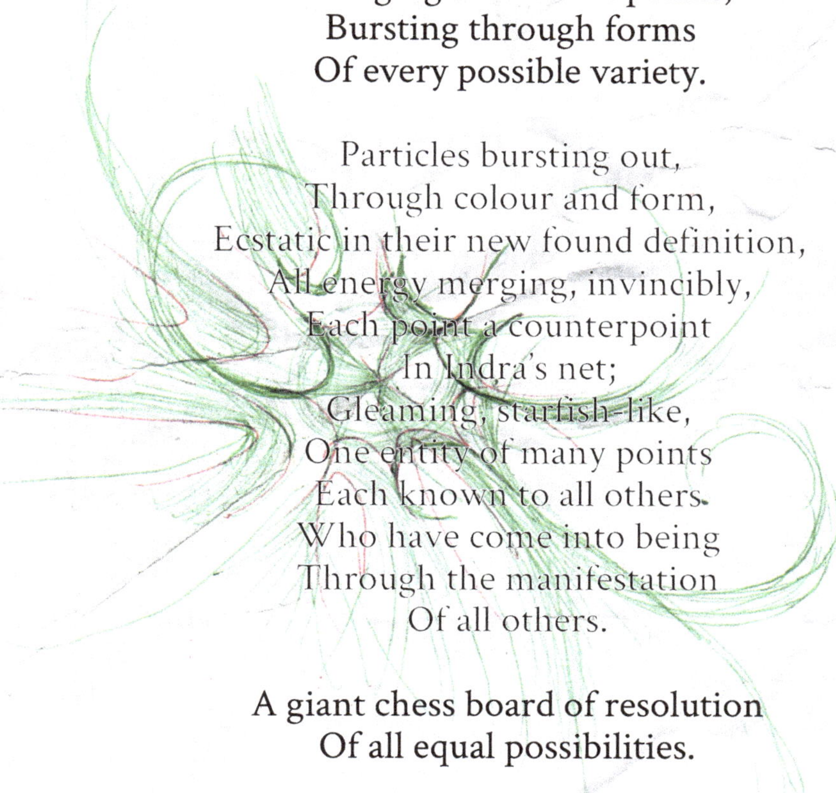

Particles bursting out,
Through colour and form,
Ecstatic in their new found definition,
All energy merging, invincibly,
Each point a counterpoint
In Indra's net;
Gleaming, starfish-like,
One entity of many points
Each known to all others.
Who have come into being
Through the manifestation
Of all others.

A giant chess board of resolution
Of all equal possibilities.

Life expanding ecstatically
Through each point of manifest energy,
Accruing more joyful energy
To kick out, on, ever expanding
Until every possibility emerges.

No contraction until then,
When everything re-discovers all else
Upon the contraction
In orgiastic delight...
When it is finished.

* * *

22nd. December 2015 (The Summer Solstice)

Crystalline Purity - In Pursuit of the Goddess
-A Song for Virgo-

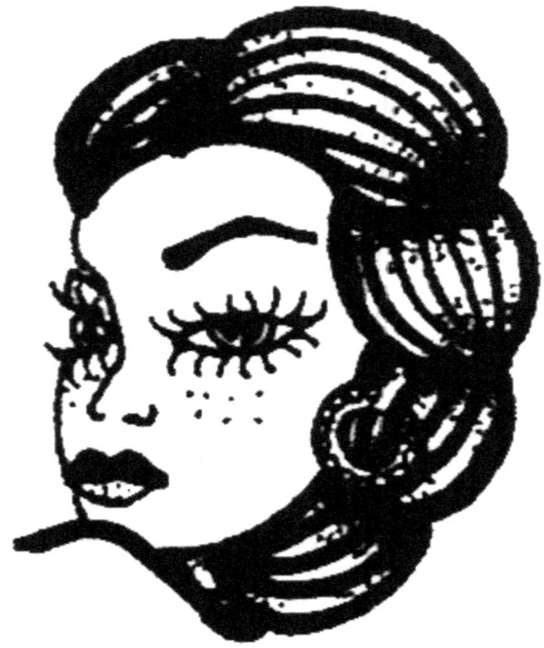

Crystalline Purity.....
Crystal purity.

Why can't I have you,
Why can't I make you mine.
Your form I would endanger,
If you and I entwine.

When I see the goddess rising,
Rising with degree,
Her Radiance is shining,
On all things, and not just me...

My patient heart, it longs for thee
My soul lets out a sigh,
My lonely heart beats fitfully.
You do not just see me...

I gaze along your crystal face
Your hard lines hurt me so...
To see you vanish without trace,
Long, long ago

Your facets formed immutable
In Universes' birth;
The building blocks inscrutable
From chaos there comes life.

What is that vital throbbing force
That livens every cell,
And resonates in you and me
With perfect synchronicity?

Do I need to spell it out?
Don't you feel the aching need?
The building blocks of eternity
Are found in you and me.

Your ice constructs in perfect form
The mythic fire of life.
Two become one,
One becomes two;
Nuit's all reaching span

The Infinite Sequence, and the Golden Mean
Hold us in their mystical hands.

Dodecahedron, magic fractal mimicry
Dodecahedron, (Universal) Sacred geometry,

The maiden spins a mantle,
From the infinity of space.
Each point the very stuff of dreams
Which we all embrace.

Spinning like a vortex
Her force goes round and round.
Lotus petals opening
To the universal sound.

1+1 = 2
2+1 = 3
3+2 = 5
5+3 = 8
8+5 = 13
13+8 = 21
21+13 = 34

Also known as : **The Maiden Spins a Mantle**

* * *

17th. January 2016

Virgo Delight

Once I thought I'd never ever
Find my guide to perfect love,
A girl so pure and oh so tender,
Sweet and gentle as a dove.

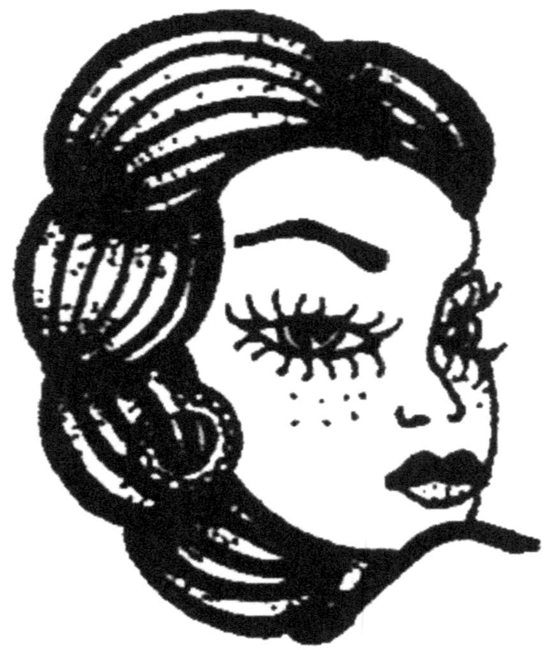

Then you came and all that changed
When two steady eyes smiled up at me;
All my life was rearranged,
You joined my dots and crossed my t's!

Order from chaos in an instant,
Tidy little package, I could tell!
With one little flutter of an eyelash,
You saved me from a living hell!

Scintillating rhythm, quite upbeat,
Captured my soul in a swift heartbeat.
Hear that universal sound so neat,
Spun my dreams so seamlessly,
I for you and you for me!

There you have it, it's complete,
She's for me and life's so sweet!

(Previous name was **In Perfect Taste**)

This poem was one of 12, acting as inspiration for, but not identical to, the songs of the:

'**Cosmic Wheel of the Zodiac**' Song Cycle

View performances of the songs on YouTube http://bit.ly/mb5music

* * *

31st. January 2016

Foreword for Old Friends

I hold time in my heart like a clock,
Beating tick-tock, tick-tock, tick-tock.
All days and hours are old friends' chants,
All wrong deeds are lost recants.

But watch while the hands wind back to twelve,
Melting like a snake in caducean meld;
For the ancient stars can see right through
Miasmas of being – this pretence of time;
Ideas once shared – once yours and mine-
Loop the loop in the depths of my mind.

In these twelve songs of care and truth,
Tell to me what you are feeling;
For I have nurtured them, you see,
In the light of all revealing.

* * *

24th. March 2016

When Adam Delved
-or- A Woman lies in Eden's tent

"Oh you, oh you, oh you," she cried,
As the penny dropped;
The last stone rolled on down the hill,
The last car stopped.
Civilization, once reborn
Lies ruined in its grave,
On Isis' horns the dead impaled,
The meek, the mild, now all laid out,
And overturned the brave.

For rich men's red and bloody wars
And politicians' might
Have used dead souls to grease the wheels
Of revolution and of strife.

Their tentacles reaching out and on
All governments their dupes,
Obama warns on nuclear blasts,
Of terrorism's nukes.
When oil is what it's all about
Then war is good – of that no doubt;
For them it is an old refrain,
And one world government their gain.

When every drop of oil has gone,
And half the planet's life,
And all of Europe lying naked
In chaos and in strife,
They will dance on liberty
Why not? They thought it up;
A ploy on which the good could choke,
So they could get enough.

How to kill all kings and queens
And move all wealth to them;
To murder hope and suck souls dry
In democracy's airy lie.

The United Nations is their goal,
To rule and conquer all;
As men divided, all will fall,
And their line will tow.

This world a prison, source of food,
For them to suck us dry;
Of life and love, and art and wealth,
For different thoughts you'll die.
Totalitarianism isn't new;
It's ancient in its quest
To wrangle power at our expense
All universes through.

A woman lies in Eden's tent;
She really is a pawn,
Her hopes of home have all been rent,
And of her child unborn.

And men of wealth and power all lie
And laugh at her distress,
And dream of treasures still on Mars,
As if that could redress
The cruelty of unloved men
And women of that ilk,
Who've raped this earth of everything
They have not known of worth.

***

2nd. April 2016

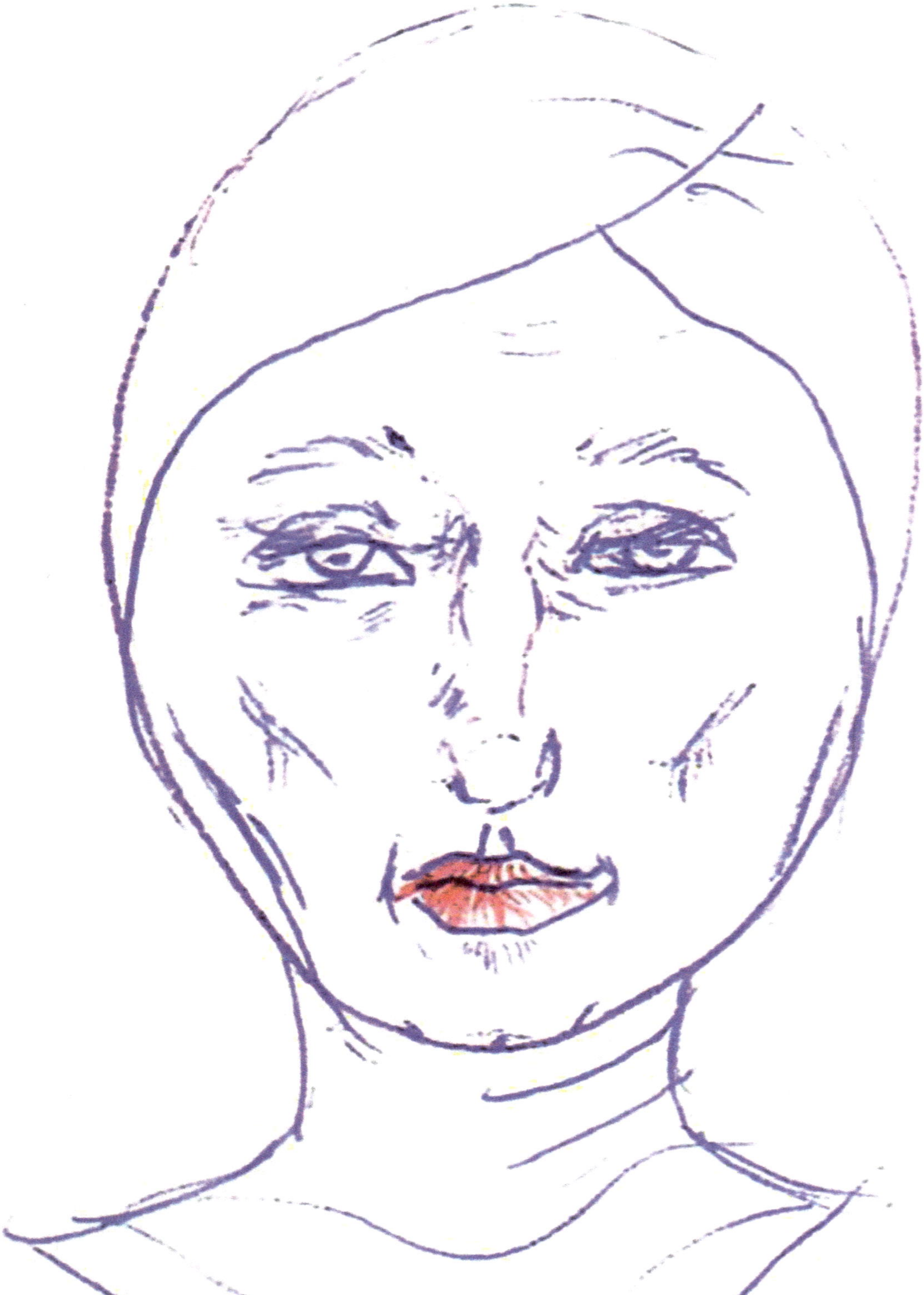

The face of the Muslim woman.

The Blue Chair

The blue chair
Stood there,
Hand made with care.
Little wooden seat
For a toddler.

Four legs planted
Firmly on the grass,
Near the kerb,
Right on the verge
Of a world of plastic.

But are our hearts that elastic?

* * *

6th. April 2016

In My Nighthouse Arthouse

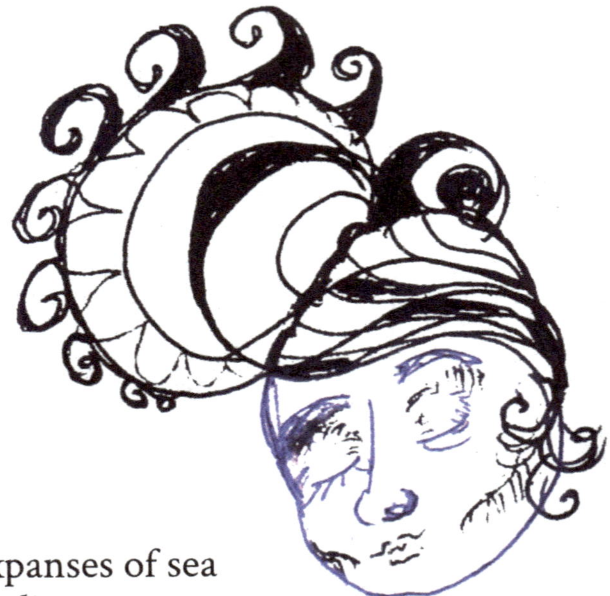

In my nighthouse arthouse
I find my space near those of others,
Artists of like ilk,
To dig and delve
In colour light frissoned air
In fantastic architecture of hidden ways,
tunnels
And spiral stairways into white lit eyries
Which shine light and receive it

Over vast expanses of sea
Surrounding me
With electrified air for birds
And gorgeous sea tints of
Huge crashing waves and sea swells
Surrounding me
Three sixty degrees
In my lighthouse restaurant
Community of art.

(This was a dream which I wrote down the next day.
I loved the feeling, in this dream, a sense of sheer delight, fantasy and creative freedom.

Months or years later I saw, for the first time in my life, this artist colony on an English show "Escape to the country." It was an artist's colony in Cornwall, with a nearby lighthouse!)

* * *

9th. April 2016

Pride and Poverty

She looked watchfully into the eyes
Of the charity worker;
Holding his gaze steadily, you'd say.
Not releasing the hook-up for an instant
As they to-ed and fro-ed.
She leapt on each of his
betrayed thoughts and liquid emotions,
Countering each with a response
Aimed at driving a recoil from that place;
A switch away from pity, sorrow,
Compassion.
Yes, drive him away from there...
Places he had no right to
Sit in judgment over her.

Whip him away from his sticking posts
Of pride in his achievements
Elevating him on rungs and steps
Mapped out for him before he was born.
She knew of them, but not through
Personal experience.

She did not envy him,
But numbly would not let him
Lord them over her.
Would fight with the last of her breath
To will him to look away first
From her unflinching eyes.

She had no hatred of his
Dumb, middle-class, smug containment,
But would not give an inch;
Or else be driven into
A double trouble of poverty
If stripped of the one thing she had left,
Without which she would walk naked,
Walling herself in,
With reflected pity,
To her own destruction,
Without the warmth of dignity
Innate....to herself.
And that he could not have.
And in his well-fed state
Would never truly understand.

Her brilliant awareness
Of her own situation
Flashed in her eyes.

She needed no careful explanation
Of how she could better it.

No charitable, dull, unconscious,
Automatic, pre-conceived rollout....
A robotic reflex handout
From this man.

He felt himself awake a bit;
Fanned by the fire in her gaze,
And wondered if he was being true to
Himself
In the way he spent his days.

* * *

19th. May 2016

Why do we Send Messages into Space?

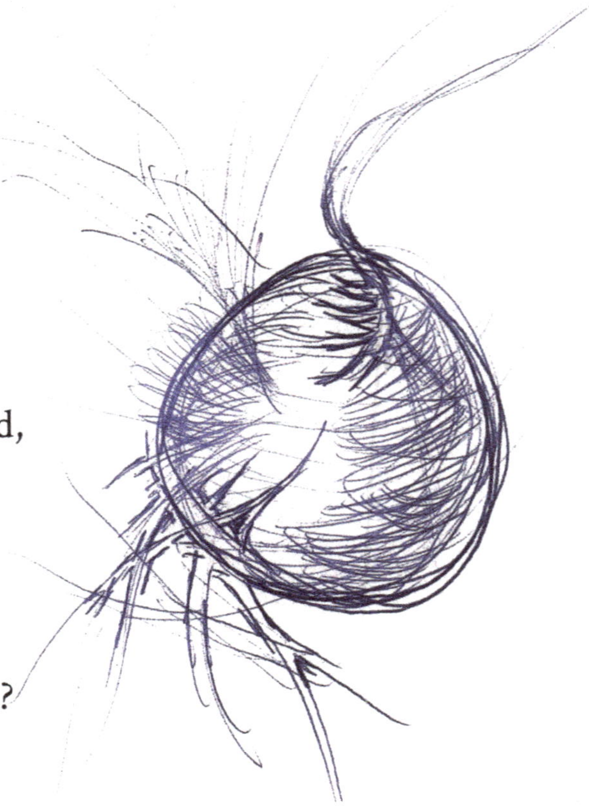

Why do we send messages which reveal
Our state of being
Out into space?
Is it to ask for help
In solving the problem
Of who we are?

Why do we wonder why they do not respond,
As if each on his globe
Was not sufficient to himself
When all grown up?

If they did come, could we understand them?

Speaking fantastic things, if we had not already realised these truths....

And why would they need to come,
Given that planetary evolution
Is the only game;
And we should not want it spoiled
By provision of the answers.

No. They will not come
Until we do not need them;
Like so much in life.

* * *

23rd. May 2016

Elevate the Oppressed

All prostitutes should be renamed as elevants.
I would say elevators,
But the word has been used for fast rides,
And, as such, would degrade the people
Dedicated to the bliss
Their services provide.

I do not deride the deriders.
Odd, though,
How scathing they are
Of those who give them pleasure,
As if ecstasy is only for
Men in frocks bearing crosses
Who have a monopoly on it.

* * *

August 2016

Pregnant No More with Ego's Lusts

I cracked like a nut in the sun,
Relinquishing its strong boundaries.
My new strong self just begun,
Exposed to air and light.
And love of self,
That grand old pinion,
Now dissolved
Into the nothingness of everything
Awakened unto itself.

Not striving to become.
The ineffability of reality
Embraced for the joy
Of just being what it is.

* * *

15th. August 2016

Sail Away in the Day

What are the moments of memory?
Do they adhere in neat quadrants,
Not momentary shadows
On a Swiss clock?
Are they so neat...
Fated in painted scenarios
Forever untouched by dissent?
Fate or madness keeps them that way...
Forever trundling, on and on,
Clockwork distortions.

But if you take just one
Imprint from your sands of time,
Peel the orange, discard the segments,
Look beyond into the nothingness;
Will you see your own ability
To re-stamp eternity?
A fresh start
Into the great beyond.

* * *

14th. September 2016

Fragments in Time

- Dedicated to my good friend Rohan G. -

The thud of the day's book
As it closes
Blows my cares away

Though at home in the sky
The wind finds
And fulfills
Even me.

In Spring my tree's leaves
Sprout for me,
And we sing
Joyfully.

Just as I do not find, as I scrape them into the bin,
The leavings of the day's meal
Any less appealing
For being rejected,
I acknowledge that all things have merit,
Even if only for shining a light
On action and reaction.

It is only another illusion
That the universe does not give.

In dreams do we conquer and cower
At shadows,
And greet Plato in his cave.
But,
Why deny the light
And seek only the dark?

* * *

If in times of fortune we greet and meet,
How much more is friendship
Needed in
Times of reverse?

I know as I go,
Be it rapid or slow,
That I will grow;
For that is the show.

Writing these lines
Is indeed the act of growing.
I commune with the joyous present
Of just what is.
Myself forgotten for a moment,
I am free.

When we meet again,
My good friend,
Show me something
To find you by.

The laughing ripples of the brook
Tinkling and burbling over rocks
Show us how to fall
And still to come up again
In continual and unabashed
Good humour.

A Zen koan I may not be,
But I can show them what I can
Of me and thee, existing together
In harmony.

* * *

There is a paradox in here,
For only when I blow
Do I put out fear,
And only when I breathe
Do I quench the need.

Only free of greed
Can you truly be freed.

Growing old, growing old,
Into a brand new fold.
Where's the start and where's the end?
Says the womb "You'll live again,"
Says the grave
"Please hop in."

In my cloud
I see a baby hippopotamus
Eating a UFO hat.
What is that?

Green grass growing furiously
From a crack in the F3
So splendidly asserting
Its own nature.

In my cloud's eye
A laughing panther lies
And as he reclines does say
"Enjoy the fruit, abjure the wine
On this fine day."

* * *

15th. September 2016

Dr. Zeus on Holiday

I lifted up my father's prints, eighty to ninety years worn,
And heard sudden laughter and many footfalls,
Dances and prances and kisses and stars
Crossing the decades as people once young
Played in a heartbeat on holidays gone
But sprung into life as I lifted these twelve
Almost forgotten photos of old.

And once again light shone on days of the past,
And people who knew how to play and to sing
And to boat and to swim and to climb to the stars
In landscapes not torn, with dreams now just born
Away from the acres of greyed-out concrete,
Where natural man is complete.

When Dr. Zeus is Home, I'll Phone

I'll tell you why you can fly so high,
It's up to you really, you see,
From tiny titbits to galactic heartbeats,
The cosmic whirlwind is so neat.
Up to the sky in the blink of an eye
We'll fly when we fly to combine,
Every thought that we ever have had in our heads
Will swirl in a mist in a radiant cloud
-A computer so big that no-one could see-
Patterns of stars in everyone's scope-
Multiply DNA's total huge bulk
In all combinations replete.
And God in its heaven will sit on its throne
And smile as the last jigsaw falls,
And the pattern of all that ever could be
Will merge with its maker enthralled.

* * *

5th. November 2016

Tree Freedom

There's freedom in the sky,
Said the gum tree's crown,
Stately standing up so high,
Seeking to commune in
The wide air round,
While
White clouds
Punctuate
Its
Point
Of view.

(I composed this while on playground duty,
and it would have been about the same time that Leonard Cohen died.)

* * *

10th. November 2016

So Leonard Cohen is Dead on Remembrance Day

Two days since Trump got in,
9/11 back-to-front
And Leonard Cohen dies.
Which was the greatest shock?

I wanted to tell the breath-tester cops
That Leonard Cohen had died;
But they were on the other side of the road.

So I walked, in my pale green paisley top,
Back from the shop,
Past a same-as-me flower bed cover
Of star shaped cream flowers,
Whose pungent perfume
Tuned me in to
What Leonard was saying:
Be in the here and now and accept
Those nice synchronicities
Of a green and cream top,
And cream flower beds;
And that sameness in the moment
Is its balance in God's eye.

* * *

11th. November 2016

I am God and God is Me

I knew when I was just sixteen
That I was God and God was me,
However fragmentarily,
This is true for all you see.

And I perceive in some so near
Others once so dear to me,
Aspects here and aspects there
Mingle in and roaming free,
Accessible all ethereally
From the astral library.

Even if a soul complete,
Doesn't occupy just one seat,
Schemes and skeins entangled still
Pass across death's window sill,
Then see new light....themes and memes
In the realm of Psyche's health.

I for you and you for me,
Twisted train tracks meaningfully,
Moving in that cosmic spiral,
Expire, aspire...and, still higher.

* * *

17th. November 2016

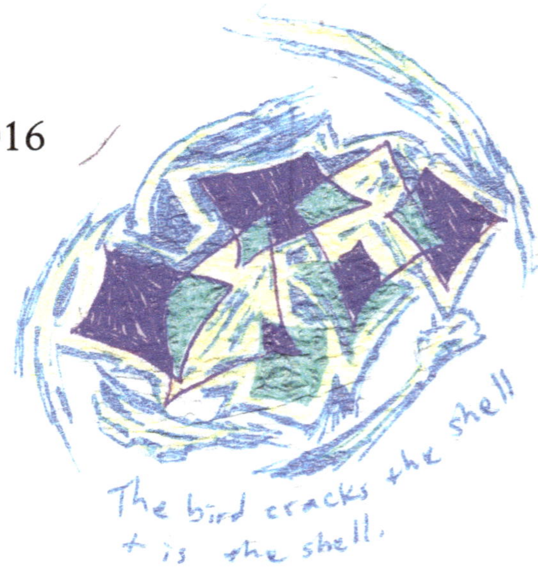

Cockatoo

A cockatoo
In its own patch
Is King.

* * *

2016

The True Meaning of a Curse

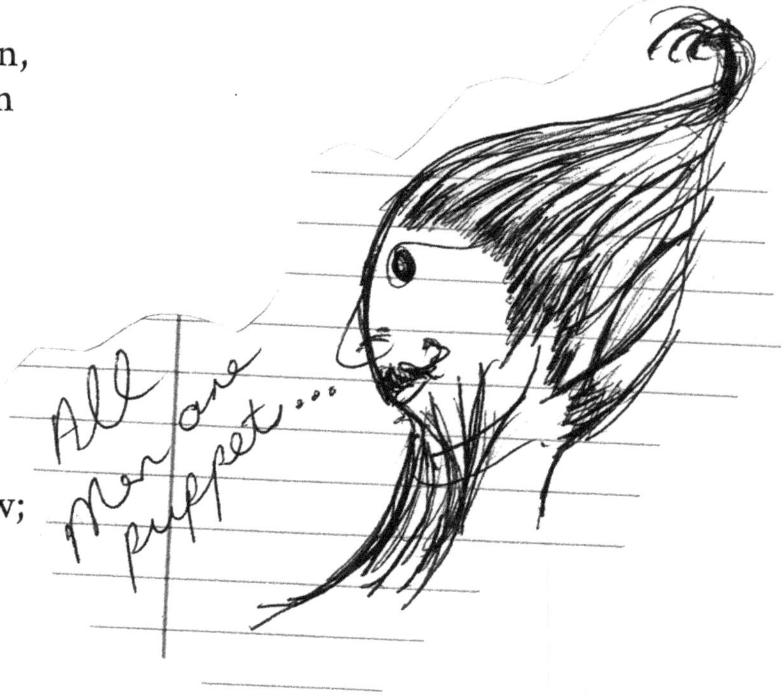

Colonial soldier shoots his gun,
A reflection of the setting sun
On his own culture.

Dreaming of his future,
Unaware of others'
As having no meaning
In that template.

Little does he know
What prophets strove to show;
Each shot a living hell....
Though that man's kill
Is not an instant tell,
For she's struck as dumb
As her children never born.

Its effects go on,
Until the curse is gone;
As kinetic pulses will,
Until each wave goes through
To every living cell;
Each universe, a bell.

* * *

4th. December 2016

In the Shower of the White Marbled Room

In the shower recess into which I fit
I am such a small corner
Of the white marbled room.
But when I emerge I am huge,
And my ego expands me
Until I balloon out
And the universe retreats proportionally.

In my self-focus
I am miserably consumed
By illusion of failed grandeur, mostly.

But when I send my attention to:
The old water tank in a neighbour's yard,
Purple hills distant over wide grassy plains and fields,
Flowers, and trees I see now closely,
I commune with
The joyous presence of just what is,
Myself forgotten, for a moment,
And I am free.

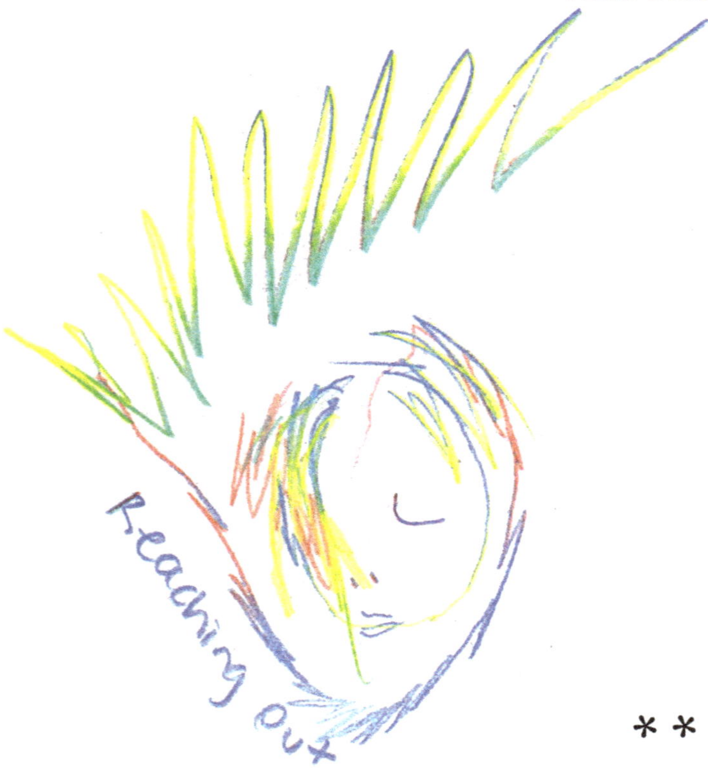

* * *

16th. January 2017

The Reason for Deaths

I felt sorry for all beings now dead,
Until I imagined the Ganges River's
Banks punctuated by white stone buildings;
And above rooves and everything,
A sky now with several birds
Suddenly darkened over with wings by their millions,
As those who never died sought constant flight.
And I gained insight.

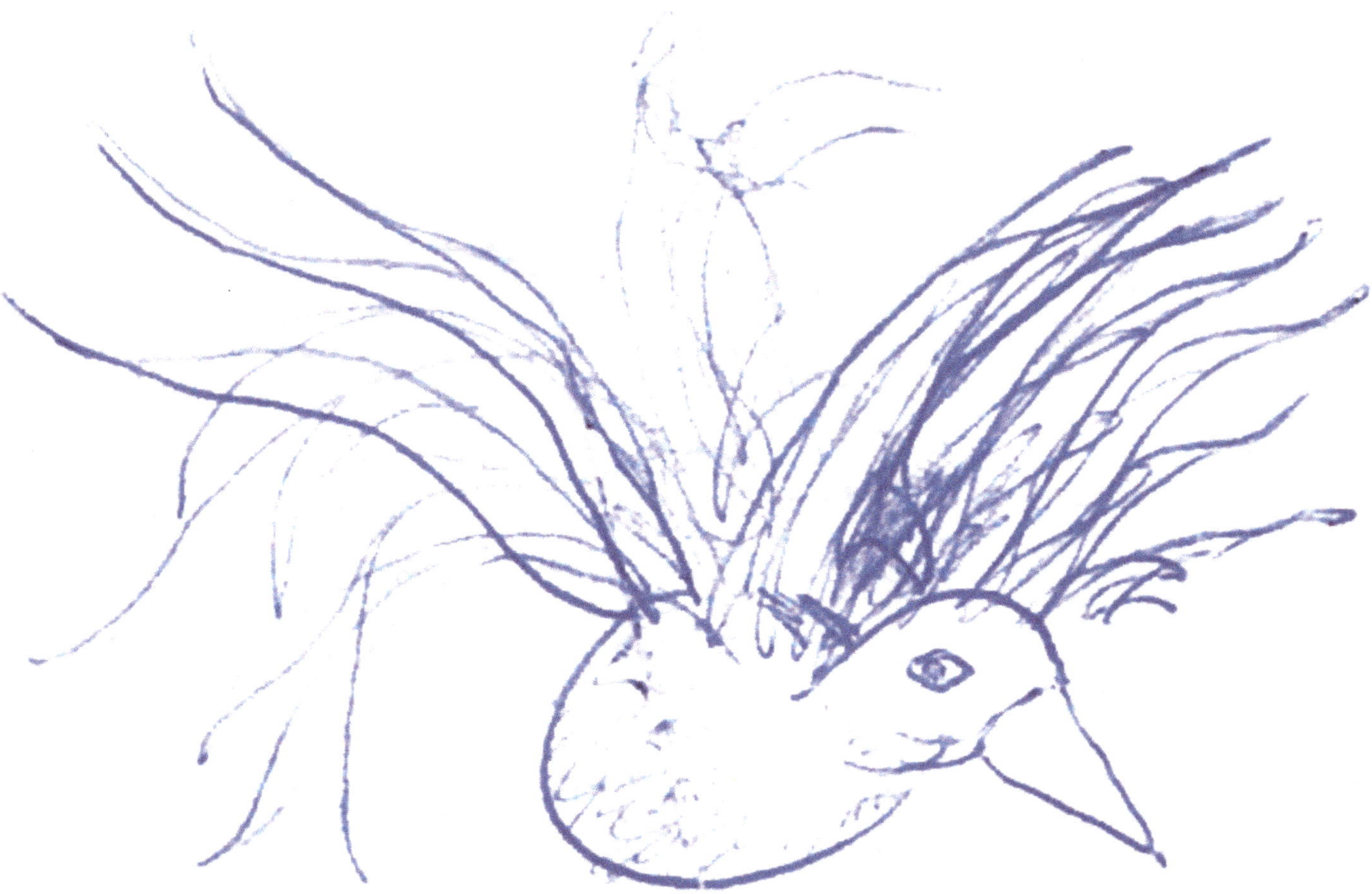

* * *

8th. February 2017

Thoughts of Home from a WWI Soldier

Gum tree boughs sway to and fro'
And I am in another land.
Oh help me, God, to understand,
Why I am in another land.

Here on the hill the flash of light
Sends bullets into men's dear flesh.
And I dream of another sky, so bright,
But absent far, though loved the best.

Will children born in days far hence
Live to see this filthy mess?
Or will our tales of bitterness,
...If speak we can, I guess...
Quell these tides of blood and gore,
Confining them to days of yore,
While health and wealth of tenderness
Bless them in a world made free
Of rich man's lust for vast success
And we, blood sacrificed to Thee.

I would not question this, you see,
If I could still believe in tales once told to me
...Inculcated thoroughly...
Which I now see as blatant lies
To keep me down where I will be
Useful to the men of war

Who feed on graves and ghosts of men
Truer Blue than all of them.
Oh help me, God, to understand
Why I'm not in my native land.
And find your way to guide me there
When I can no longer stand.
Send my breath to ease the way
Of other souls, who died today,
And in the hearts of those who love,
Help to drive away the fear
Possessing me, that tons of tears must fall again
Until we rid this Earth of Ours
From lust for wealth,
....Hence, poverty....
And give out free to All
What Earth has given freely.

* * *

25th. April 2017 (Anzac Day)

Lessons from the Garden on Staying in Present Time

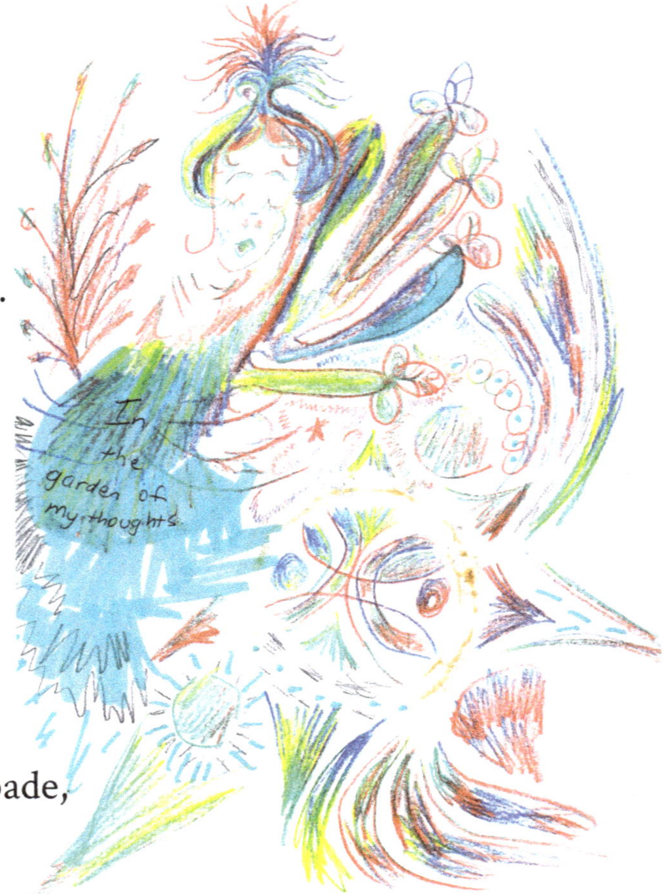

Right here, right now,
Hang yourself straight, says the clothes,
And anything wet will drip away.

Stand tall, says the plant,
And you reach the sun which nourishes you.

Rest completely in the Now, when you can,
Says the cat;
So as to hunt all the better for your goals
When the time is right.

Discover what is hidden, says the worm,
For it is often the juiciest morsel.
And see it when you see it.

There are so many pitfalls in life, says the spade,
But you can only dig one hole at a time.

Handle all items one after the other, says the clothesline,
And in present time.

I do not grow greener on the other side,
Chuckled the grass, so do not stretch in vain.

Let everything you do not need flow away,
Murmured the drain.
And all the garden concurred
That the time is always Now, if you are awake;
And so no problem exists if you stay so,
As it is always 'now' again,
So decide in which Now to solve your problem.

* * *

12th. May 2017

Darkness Recedes Every Day

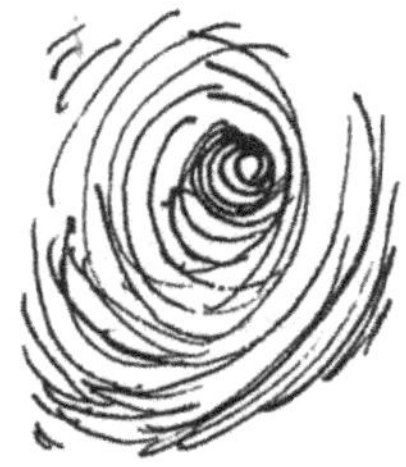

Darkness receding
As sunbeams streaming
Birthing red on the horizon's shore.

I am moving smoothly
From night's door.
The inchoate formlessness ever changing,
As all forms are emerging,
Being slowly etched
By dawn's growing light.

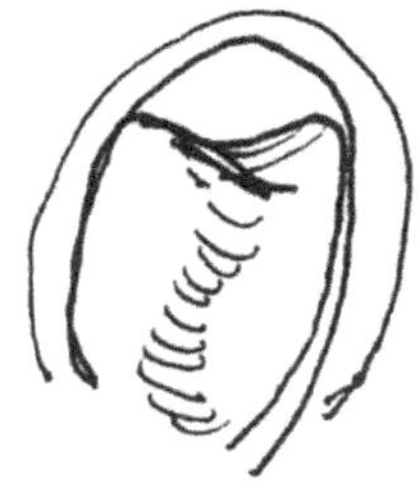

This is a metaphor for growth.
We all start in formlessness
In every second of our lives;
Until realisations flood
The chambers of our inner minds.

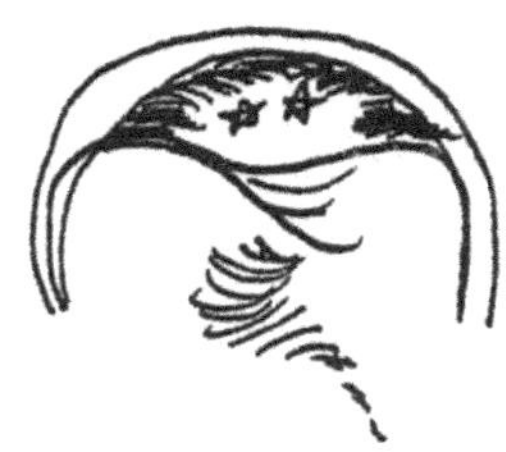

What is light?
It is peaceful, serene;
Illuminative of consciousness expanding.

Noetic consciousness...
Our one hope
In the stygian primal depths.
It would change us from our accustomed shapes
And for what are we here,
If not for that?

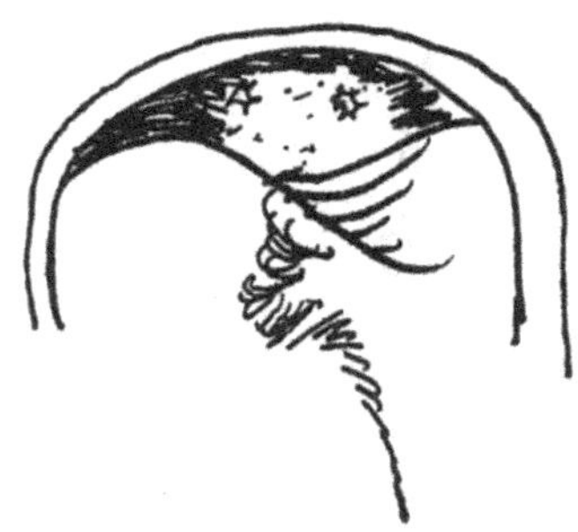

* * *

30th. May 2017

<u>Addition</u>
<u>-Earlier Version-</u>

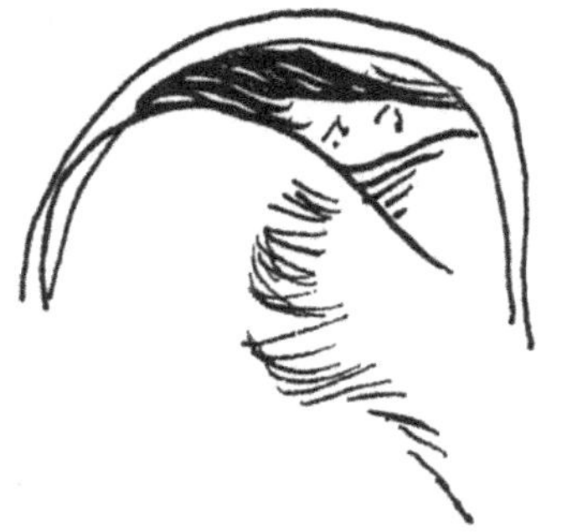

The dark is lightening.
I travel through it,
Emergent to noetic freedom.
There could be chaos there.
The dawn delineates afresh each day.
We slip into our accustomed shapes.

* * *

29th. May 2017

Are we still recovering from the Big Bang?

Are we still recovering from the Big Bang
Which resonates innate to every particle
As we go about our business,
Scrape skin on skin and hide on hide
Until we've tried
To deflate it again.

Yin and Yang is the place to start;
Not being tart in the search for the heart.
Its to-ings and fro-ings, its comings and goings
Do make an art of the very first start
At least in part;
Else why are we wearing
Convolutions so tearing?
That big brass band bangs on,
Sparks fly, Disney style.
Comets escape stars
And cosmic beats thump on afar.

Thump thump goes the big brass drum
Beats of our hearts, our beings' base.
Just listen to the orchestra tune up,
As in every orchestrated moment
Chaos from the tune-up
Will change to harmonic order
Hopefully soon.

Do our stars' flash drive finally find us,
Define us to each other
In our spatial positionings
As outposts of the Universe
Do we outpost, outpour to each other
Or just because
A light then shines in the darkness?

* * *

2017

Minoan Tiles

On a dull day in August
I dream of Minoan tiles
To crown my kitchen spaces
And find my inner ones
Dancing in delight
Whilst boys cavort
And girls pick saffron
Laughing, joking, playing
In Nature's ways and days.

* * *

4th. August 2017

Happiness

Happiness is a fragile thing,
Find a vase to store it in.
Nurture it and water it,
Remembering each day to fill.

Each bud a living courier,
Will pass on hope to another;
Until the vase is well abloom,
With thornless flowers in living colour.

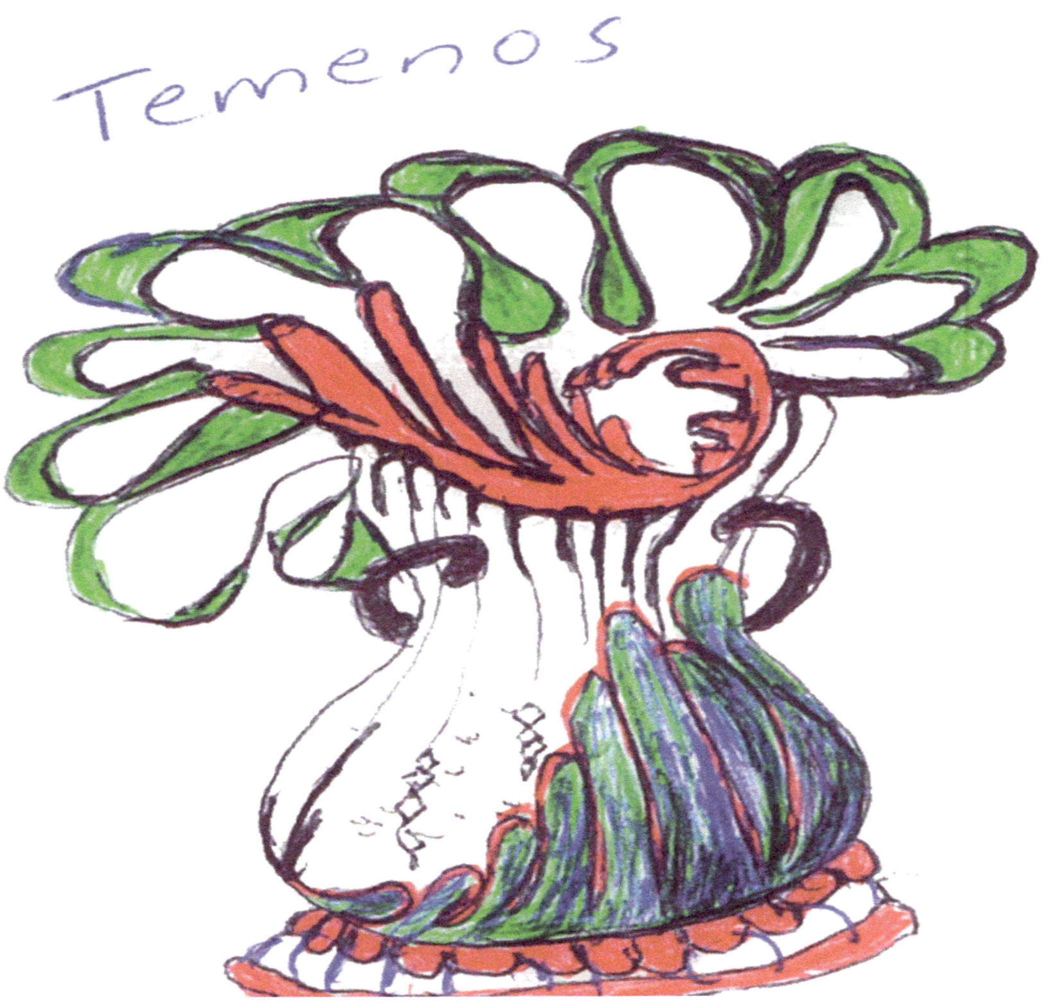

* * *

14th. September 2017

The Bubbles Poem

In order to succeed we must first forgive,
Forgive, forgive, forgive,
Every past action we have done to ourselves,
And every past action forgive.

Forgive until happiness and pride
In our own accomplishments,
And those of others we have helped
Well up inside to encompass all else
Until happiness bubbles over
And over and over.

Anxiety and trouble vanish.
And peace and calm,
And security with it,
Envelop everything
We see and do
In present, present time.

And all of this in each moment,
Each moment, moment of time.
In surrender in the moment
Accepting what is, what is, what is.

For if things could be otherwise
In this moment, this moment,
Then they would be.
......And thus, we arise.
Arise,
Arise.

* * *

18th. September 2017

As if for the Very First time

In the life of the person adopted as a baby who re-meets their natural mother, and then meets her family, there are important stations to revisit. I say revisit, because she may have already gone through these stages in life in the adoptive family with its surrogate aunts, cousins, grandparents.

But when she meets her natural aunts, cousins, grandparents, great-aunts, she must start all over again, but as if for the very first time, those sojourns of love, trust, compassion, caring, of reaching out for wisdom in life's experiences and in knowing and understanding the epigenetic forces of the hundreds of generations coming beforehand who have culminated - in a sense - in her.

* * *

On Hearing of the Grave News about my Aunt Coral, my Friend

And it came upon a time
That an aunt of mine
Had an illness very grave.
And a little cute dragon
With no station wagon
Curled up beside me
And to me gave
All the ministrations
That a maiden
Aunt could give
To a poor child
Who could not live
With her natural mother
Or aunt, for that matter.

All the little ministrations
A true aunt could give
Lay wrapped in that cute dragon
Who looked me in the eyes
As it curled up beside me.

My little daughter's dragon
Came to heal and soothe me,
As, swaddled up in bed I missed
The aunt I never had
When a babe.

On the internet
A water dragon came along.
A little children's story
And quite a save....
Echoing my story
From my Scorpio Aunt Coral...
The story of the water dragon
Who came along
To save me from missing
An aunty ready
For new adventures,
New times,
New friends.

Just like Heathcliffe
The water dragon
Who could lie for 15 minutes
Under waters of the bluest tiled pool,
And leap - all three foot of him -
Fly through the air
From his gum tree bower
To frighten the guests
In the pool below
In a splashy shower.

* * *

"Take that for giving me a fright
With your belly splash!" he said.

And so it goes
For Scorpio water dragon
Aunts who gave me
The sweet, sweet nectar
Of love and caring,
Out of time,
But in time, too.

With acknowledgement to "Heathcliffe the Water Dragon"
http://www.home.aone.net.au/~byzantium/heathclif.html

* * *

31st. December 2017

My Aunt Coral

My Aunt Coral is still a proper noun.
A name that exists to sound,
In present time,
Aunt Coral's specifics:
Relatedness,
Connectedness,
A genetic link
In a gulf of loneliness.
She is in me.
This frail chemical bond…
A life buoy across a bitter sea.

* * *

16th. January 2018

Friendships

Friendships are like dandelion seeds.
When blown away from you
By the wind,
You could trace the trajectories
Back and back and back
And always be able
To find a trace.

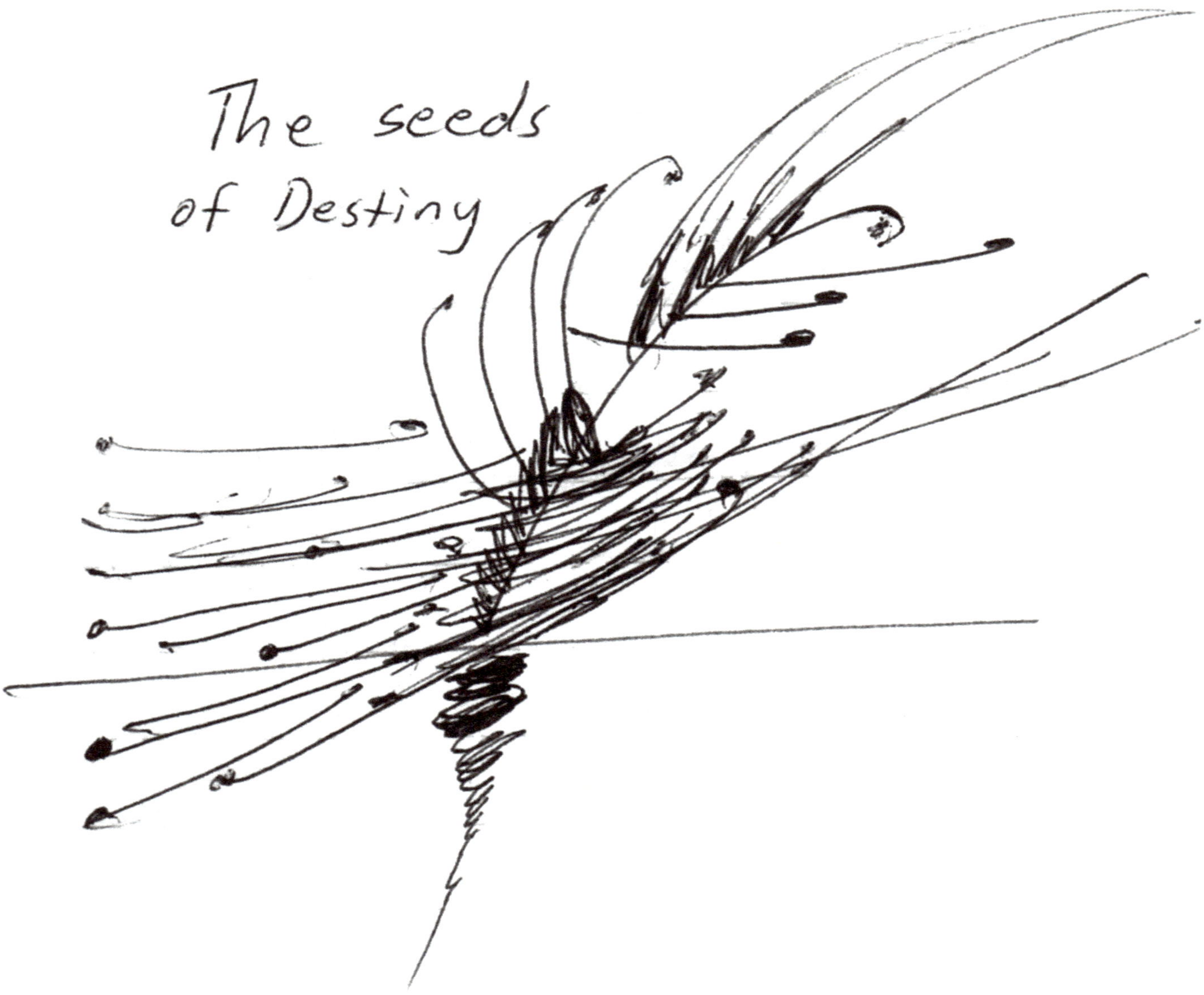

* * *

24th. January 2018

Within the Heart of Each Solitary Traveller

On the school run,
My daughter a teacher now,
I drop her back to her former school
To start a re-run
For the very first time.

No contradiction this.
But when she commented on repeats
I said
"But nothing is ever the same. It is Always in a new context."
And she agreed.

Everybody is a solitary traveller,
Tho' wanderer, maybe
The path overgrown.
Mountain mist softly envelopes
The dim figure
Darkly silhouetted
Coming towards you.

I dropped her off, today,
And in the rain and the mist
Of a Katoomba morn
She bravely went in
On her new path.

We may pass,
As two travellers might,
Acknowledging each other's way,
And, as Autumn leaves fall,
Emerge from the maze of our days
In clarity's light.

* * *

22nd. March 2018 (My natural mother's 89th. Birthday)

The Little Girl Within

Let's run with the little girl
Through lanes and twisting spaces,
Along narrow sunny passageways,
'Til time has turned our faces,
From things that once had wooed us,
Timbered pastures, blue-green foam,
With sea waves dancing freely,
A long long way from home.

For I am yet by that shore,
A part of me, at least,
A white-haired child staring out
Through a hand's span so daring,
To touch yet not unlatch;
To never quite be free
To search…and search
The whole wide world,
To search and search
For thee.

Honouring Jung's concept of the inner child
and Thomas A. Harris' book "I'm OK You're OK"

* * *

8th. July 2018

I have Lived Alone

I have lived alone;
They say that and add
And we die alone.

I have been hurt,
In turn have hurt.

Living, and dying to be alone...
As that is the natural state.

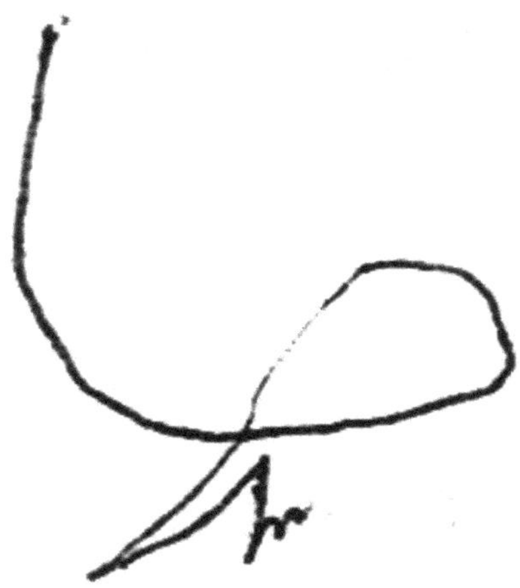

What can the eye
Living + dying alone, see?

* * *

9th. October 2018

Old Photos and Time's Web

What should we think about old photos? What is the truth about old photos?
Faded images, capturing a moment made sacred in time and place.
For what purpose?
If, today, I framed an ad for clothes cut out from a magazine,
Inserted sentimental butterflies, a couple embracing, picnicking
Beside a river; bluebirds,
That too could capture our imagination,
Our sentimental attachment
To what was really just a moment in present time.

In the act of making, viewing, re-viewing,
Do we not make up illusions that may not have really existed on the day?
Of happy days and ways and times gone by.
And is it for the loss of this, perhaps mythical past, that we cry?
Putting a frame around an event we 'frame' it, don't we?
And upon it we insert our hopes, struggling with the here and now;
Struggling to make sense of it, perhaps;
As we haven't needed to struggle with those frozen images upon which we project anything,
But, more specifically, our hopes for a better time in the future projected onto the past's dead images.
I struggle to photograph in present time my domestic happiness: to sear the images of my family, our pets, onto my mind, as if to make a photo of what will someday be gone.
With photos we don't have to struggle. Those people, their times and place, circumstances, are all done and dusted.
It is only with living each day in the present, in the here and now, that we must struggle.

Knowing that, one day,
Like a fly in a spider's web, we ourselves will be memories with who knows what colours
Projected onto us, or by whom?

We must free ourselves from time's web,
And be here, now.
My brother says we should draw a line, and not go back.

I say we must disregard the past;
We must think that the future may already exist,
According to Quantum Physics;
And, by living freely,
Free ourselves from Time's web.

* * *

1st. November 2018

Am I the Mother of Myself?

There is easement in bereavement
When the loss is for the self;
That grand Swiss cheese melt.

I would not do it willingly,
Walk over rocks to reach you,
But something in me teaches:
"You will not rest" 'til
Jointure,
Forgiveness,
Truth,
Peace,
Kindness
Compassion
Loom greater than:
Hate,
Violence,
Abandonment,
Separation,
And, of course,
Spite.

If I could bottle Eleanor I could do it.
But I am not her,
As I am not
The other.

No. The truth is,
As Swami Prajnanpad said,
"I am myself. The other is
Simply something else.
I am what I am.
That is all."

* * *

<u>A Play Upon my Name</u>
Benignity – kindliness (usu. In the old) L. benignus
Benthamism – greatest happiness of greatest number as guiding principle of ethics.
Benthamite – Adherent of B. (Bentham, person.)

25th. November 2018

Yesterday when Victimhood Vanished

Yesterday I found the birthday candles
Last used for my daughter's cake,
Still in a brown paper bag, unwashed.
Then out fell the written words,
The 'd' in birthday dangling,
And so I felt re-birthed into a place
Where, as blame does not apply,
I am not a victim;
And neither is the sky.

* * *

30th. November 2018

Hydrangea

I

I peeked out my window, and pink it was,
In perfect majesty;
Its head supported by three strong tines.

II

It had battled extraordinary circumstances of neglect.
It had been there when we bought the house 30 years before.
Flowers had bloomed and died.
We'd never trimmed it or removed the dried flowers
Until I asked Ramona to do so,
And she cut it back so it would not scrape against
My bedroom wall in the wind, rousing me.
It stood as leafless twigs during Winter,
And, first with glossy new leaves,
Proudly sprouted its pink flower
On its three firm supports.
Mastery of life and its conditions
Is always to be admired.

* * *

11th. December 2018

An Easter Song

By the Sea of Galilee
I see you and you see me,
Underneath that old palm tree
Seated near the Seer.
Say Seer what you see in me,
While seated all together;
Temples, rostrums, nasty soldiers
Fade away and vanish.
Golden hearts and clayey feet
Circle round the well and merge,
While mankind's deep and purest
Urges mingle altogether.
Holding hands beneath the tree,
Ever reaching out together,
Touching gently in the breeze
That joins our hearts forever.

Circling midst the green palm leaves
Which gently touch as feathers,
Reaffirming, trembling, daring,
Bringing souls together;
I see you and you see me
In this golden weather,
One oasis, Earth its name,
On its orb we're all fair game
In its stormy weather.
Gather round this old Earth Tree,
Karma tea for you and me;
Spinning orbs and fiery lights,
Radiant dawns and Starry Nights;
Chakras trying to unite
In the mix forever.

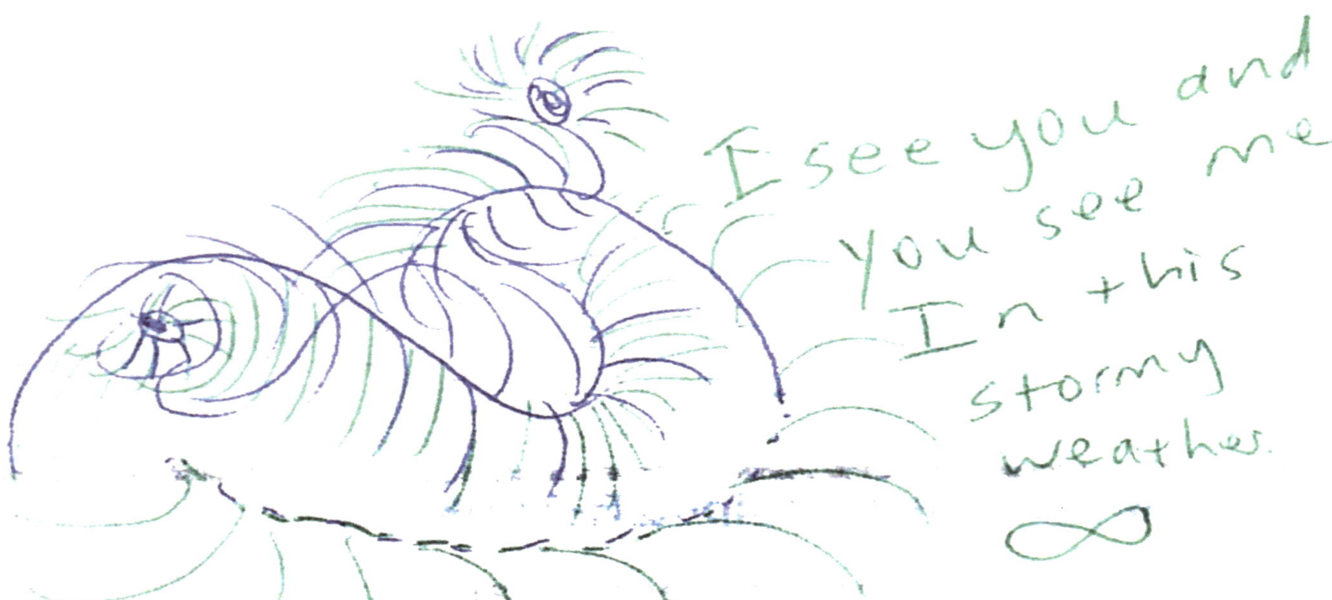

* * *

13th. April 2019

An Easter Saturday Poem

I will find out one day soon
Whether we all came from Mars
To settle on the plane so vast
Between two rivers' flows.
Or if that truth like all the rest
Is merely hazarded guess
Spawned by men to do their best
Experiencing this bloody mess
Described as life on Earth.

This three- brained primate, Man by name,
Wallowing in grief and shame
Destroying fearfully its own name;
Justifying war and gain to feather its own nest.
If I am you and you are I,
Awaken from this game;
Lift the scales from sleeping eyes,
Rend the veil that blocks the way
Of hands that reach to touch the others'
Through mists and fogs of grey.
Like squares upon a rubrics cube that ever changes form,
Man grasps for territory; new land
To add before his ampersand
To settle wrongs done by the score
By creating more.

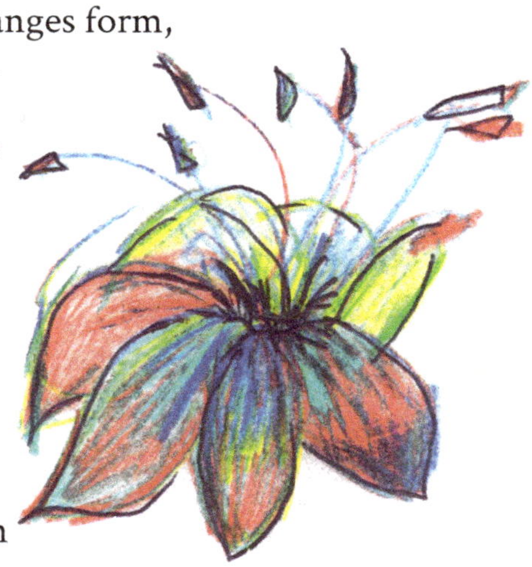

Ripping Earth's cocoon of safety,
Self-destruction oh so basely
Never thinking -once new born
Habitats now so torn
Do not live to see the dawn
Denuded of the life they spawned.
While men build rockets once again
To sightsee Mars' old ruins;
Scanners in their now gloved hands,
Scourers standing by at hand to recommence the rape;
Somewhere in the dear Earth's womb,
Life forms waiting for their day,
Crawl or leap, swim, beat their wings,
Gently nurturing each other,
Resonating with The Mother,
Wait to take their place.

* * *

20th. April 2019

Bird Song

Is bird song this
But only cries for space
In wilderness?
There is no paradox to miss...
Birds sing not least
For love and peace
And that's the same.

In Earth's dark purposes
Light emerges.
In dark matter too,
Stars shine through.

* * *

20th. May 2019

The Universe is a 3-D Printer

The universe is a 3-D printer
Called the Multiverse;
As you and I
And particles fly
Eagerly into assemblage
Known only to us.
When, thus,
We are a sur-prize
In God's eye.

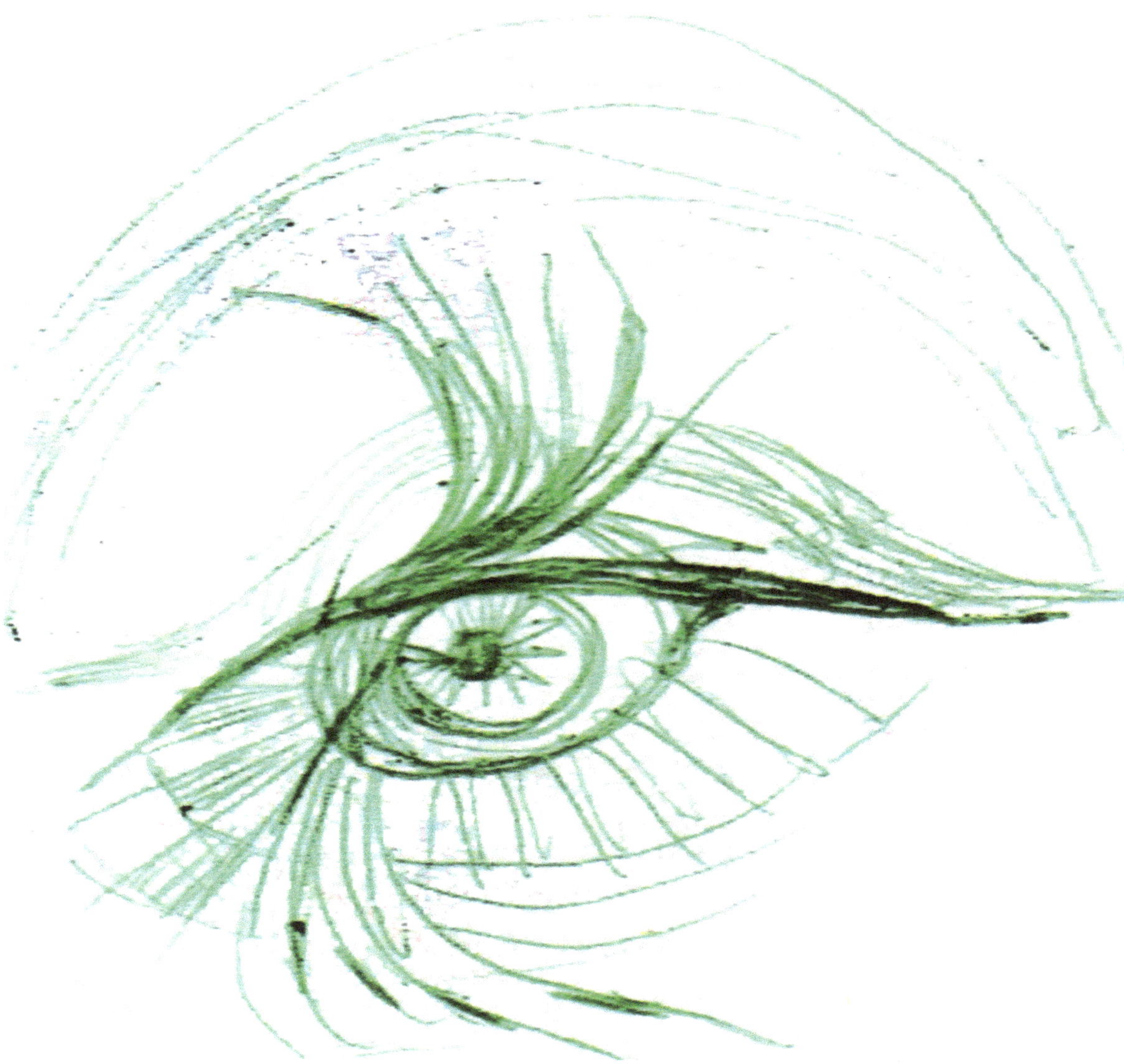

* * *

22nd. June 2019

Quantum Net

If I am you and you are I
This quantum net does truly fly!
Crystals, thoughts, seed each other,
Morphic Resonance their mother.
Myriad patterns, hence once set,
Spin into being – a timeless jet;
Evolution, once the key,
Is in this mix like you and me.
Self- determined readily,
Beings fruit successfully.

* * *

22nd. June 2019

When We Honour our Great-Great Ancestors What Are We Honouring?

When we honour our Great-Great ancestors what are we honouring?
Is it their dull, domestic, mundane, mistake-ridden lives
As plain as ours, or plainer;
Or are we honouring glorious hopes for an ancestral soul
Somehow much greater than both?
If so, what is that glorious entity of possibilities
Maybe not yet dreamt of
But resonant, still, somehow,
In all of those souls now passed
And souls yet unborn
In our line of resonant possibilities
United in The Great Spirit
Perhaps eventually?

It is the future, the present and the past in morphological resonance.
As quantum physics tells us that
Time is an illusion, and all
Cause and effect, and all possibilities thought of,
Exist until resolved into perfect harmony
Of resonance forward and back
As a violin string's vibration
Along its entire length
Once plucked;
And is then resolved
Into the beauty
Of its one note:
Containing all resonant frequencies
Ever born,
Now resolved.

* * *

11th. July 2019

Snowflake in the Mind's Landscape

If you want to try and catch
A white, white snowflake in your hand,
You must try to understand
As you unlatch from the window frame
That what you see is falling free,
Undeterred by focussed glee
And urgent, warm, attempts to name
Something that remains the same
Despite your mind's imaginings.

If it lands upon your palm
It will disappear in form
Like thoughts projected out and on
In every minute still unborn.

* * *

10th. August 2019

A Bon Mot

Life is a gigantic performance,
And, for the good of the whole,
All must sing in tune.
Let this be our practice,
As for this there is no rehearsal.

* * *

13th. August 2019

For Mark and Us

Mark is dead.
When was it that we were
Going to start living?
Seize the day and all that?
Come the day, and hey,
Not a lot has happened lately,
Compared to those dreams
Of halcyon days.

Did we go yachting?
Swim together?
Splash and play..., make affray?

But we had our youth;
Intimate conversations...
(I reclaim that word
For as it is truly meant),
Laughed a lot,
And made our favourite
Words and phrases resonate
Against life's dark pitfalls.

We lived,
And discovered freedom
From our pasts
In one glorious bonfire
Of conditioned vanities.
We tore apart the veils
That would have kept us
Locked up and trapped in society's caul.
Broke free from that maw; then, self-taught,
We plunged into life's bounty
At least for days of youth...
Now gone.

But I for one do not grieve its loss,
Just the memory of
That sweet face and lovely ways....
For that Paradise is lost.

* * *

8th. September 2019

At the Swimming Pool

Heads bob like newborns washed clean
But straightened in lines,
One stroke after the other.

Hoping to get there, one day;
No buoy to aid them
In life's tides.

* * *

27th. January 2020

Let There be No More White Feathers

All wars amount to this-
A few lines of history
In a compendium of sorts.
It is certainly not a herstory.
As someone once said,
"War is to man
What childbirth is to woman."
Rough corners overlap
In rape and mayhem;
As madness comes
In all ways,
Chaos engendered
In deed.

"War is to man what maternity is to a woman"- Benito Mussolini

* * *

9th. February 2020

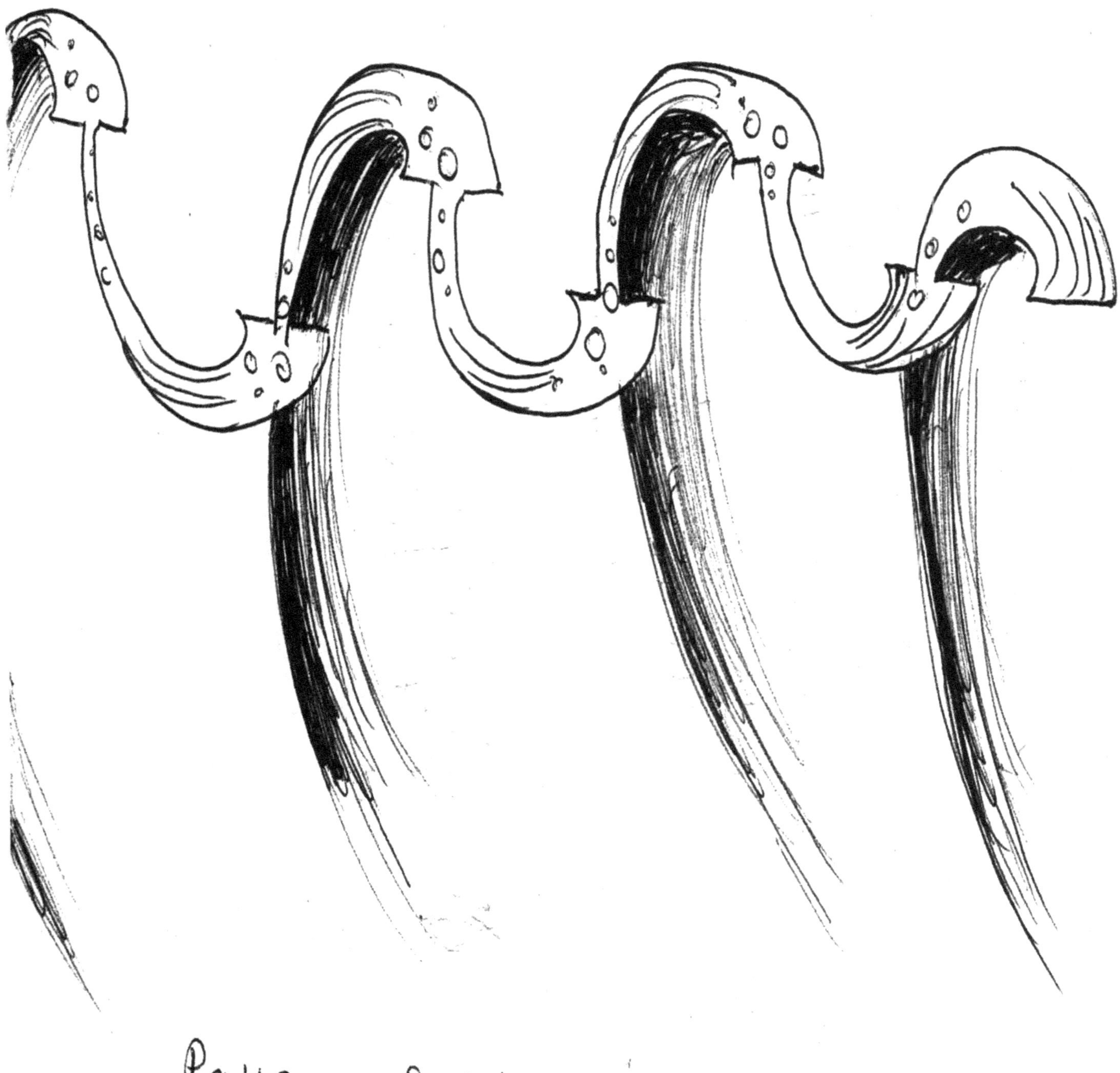

Pattern of Waves

Living in the Now

I have reached a point where I can say
That these are the good old days;
Like a wave engraved in stone,
Representing, not its own,
Some are here, but most have flown;
Blown away as days of old,
Stories lived and stories told,
Flicker past a once-used web,
Most sucked dry and truly spent.

In my heart and in my brain,
All around me lives right now;
Nothing else to remain,
Free from wrinkles is my brow.

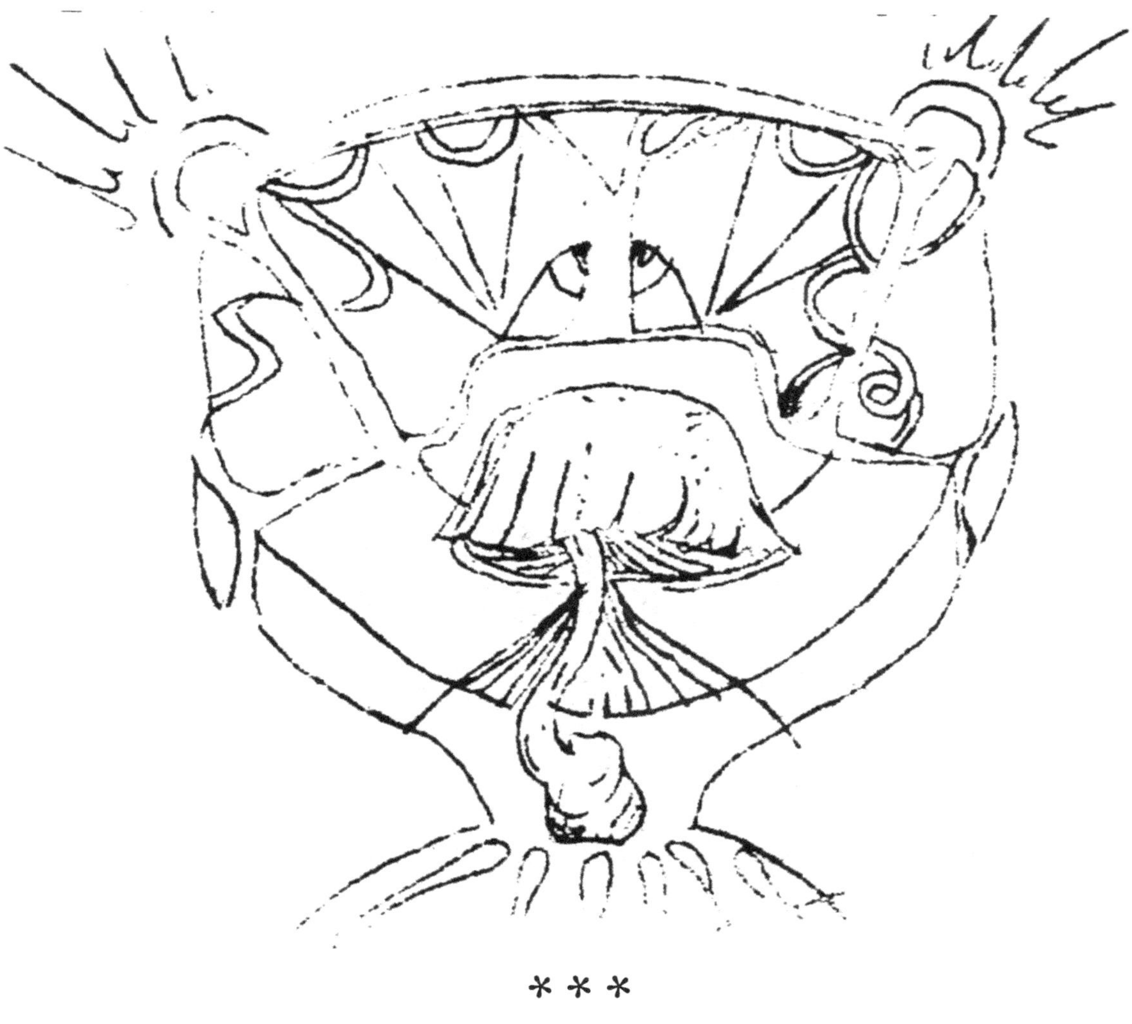

* * *

30th. April 2020

Birth of Self

I decided to marry Bob Dylan,
I thought it could be very thrilling,
But then I believed
This urge I perceived
Was really a dirge
To my very own birth.
For that artist's not me,
But merely, you see,
A projected aspect of self.

* * *

14th. May 2020

Why we Meditate

Shards from the past,
A whistling blast,
Pull sense apart.

Emotional darts,
Madness' art,
Straight to the heart.

Let folly depart.

* * *

15th. May 2020

Rookwood in Combewood
-A Deathless Purpose-

My friend Margarite's a ghost-sitter,
She's no such thing as a quitter;
As great-aunts and fathers
And mothers kept closest,
And an uncle who wouldn't
Come out of the closet
All leave their dimensions
And sit down to table,
Have dinner at midnight,
And quarrel, if able,
As Margarite moves things
And sweeps around beds
Where beings once living
Had rested their heads.
She dreams over crockery
-Being the lens
For rellies, once sighted,
When then in their flesh,
Still living at home,
Unblighted by death.

* * *

31st. May 2020

Despair Not, Seek the Light

A person came to me,
Despair was in her eye.
She said "It's all the same,
They ever, ever, lie.
The men of power they always do
Exactly as they wish;
Finance, war and politics,
They use the same old tricks.
And people fall for them,
Create once more the stew,
Where goodness, love, morality,
Can't escape the mix."
I looked at her and gently said
"I know, but less than one percent of them
Does not count for all;
And good men rise who see right through
The evil, and the lies.
And even if your father can't,
And other men besides,
Nature always finds a way
To keep us from their side.
And if this was not the very case
Slavery would abound;
In open view the whole world round,
Not just underground.

And even though
I know it's there
In many different names,
Lincoln, Gandhi, Nightingale,
Generations by the score
Still lift the veil on evil men,
Urge us not to fight their wars,
Shine the light and do much more,
And we can do the same
In inner work to set us free
From their filthy games.
To spread awareness-make men whole-
Raise the light in all men's souls.
The Dalai Lama says we can,
The spirit of what's good in Man
And Woman moving on.

* * *

16th. June 2020 (Bloomsday - James Joyce's.)

For You Have Freed Your Sacral Centre

When you accept things
As they truly are,
Deep within your sacral centre,
Life force flowers.
Locked up in our belly
Is a universal flow,
As Nature blossoms freely
In that Universal show.
Connected to The Mother
You once again can grow,
Empower that sacred shower…
"As Above, So Below."

Note: The veins in our body are attached to the belly button, which is our sacral centre.
In the human psyche I suggest that the opposite of 'sacred' is 'scared.'
Interesting that it contains the same letters…rearranged.
Shamanic Utterance : "The Goddess is in every cell."

* * *

2nd. July 2020

Doing What One is Doing

Doing what one is doing is sacred,
As, staying in present time
Holds past-present-future
In one unbroken line.

When I'd finished writing this,
Bird song broke out;
And still they chorus near me,
As for them there is no doubt.

And on they sing so joyfully,
For joy is all there is,
When sunbeams warm the air and earth
And Spring brings new birth near.

* * *

25th. August 2020

Spring

Zephyr stirring light warm air
Moves my poet's soul in Spring
Through my oak tree's bower.

* * *

17th. September 2020

Margarite's Birthday Poem

Born in Spring's happy clime,
Joyous laughter, love is fine;
Margarite, Combewood's saviour,
Family first, despite the labour!

* * *

22nd. October 2020

For the Alien Creators

You do not come to calls
Red in blood, or soft in whispered prayers,
For desperate hope that something's there.
You do not seem to care
For savage lifeforms made by you.
Yes, we walk within your shoes.
You made us then you left;
Reptilian, unhearing, inept.
And queens and kings that you bring in, we're told,
Enforced by blood lines formed of old,
Endorse a child's tea set for thousands,
To own divine inheritance a godsend.
Buyers eager for essence scramble,
To attune to godhead is the gamble
The truth, by resonance, if nothing else.

* * *

25th. October 2020

Index In Themes

Alienation

Celebration

Humour

Love and Dualism

Nature and Celebration

Social Commentary and History

Spirit and Transformation

CPSIA information can be obtained
at www.ICGtesting.com
Printed in the USA
LVHW070412060422
715401LV00022B/904

9 780646 825595